Timberlake Wertenbaker

Timberlake Wertenbaker was resident writer at the Royal
Court in 1984–5. Plays include *The Third* (King's Head),
Case to Answer (Soho Poly), *New Anatomies* (ICA),
Abel's Sister (Royal Court, Theatre Upstairs), *The Grace
of Mary Traverse* (Royal Court main stage), which won
the Plays and Players Most Promising Playwright Award
1985, *Our Country's Good* (Royal Court, main stage,
West End and Broadway), winner of the Laurence Olivier
Play of the Year Award in 1988 and New York Drama
Critics Circle Award for Best New Foreign Play in 1991,
The Love of the Nightingale (Royal Shakespeare
Company's Other Place, Stratford-upon-Avon), which won
the 1989 Eileen Anderson Central TV Drama Award and
Three Birds Alighting on a Field (Royal Court main
stage), which won the Susan Smith Blackburn Award and
Writers' Guild Award in 1992. She has written the
screenplay of *The Children* based on Edith Wharton's
novel and a BBC2 film entitled *Do Not Disturb*.
Translations include Marivaux's *False Admissions* and
Successful Strategies for Shared Experience, Marivaux's
La Dispute, Jean Anouilh's *Leocadia*, Maurice
Maeterlinck's *Pelleas and Melisande* for BBC Radio,
Ariane Mnouchkine's *Mephisto*, adapted for the RSC in
1986, Sophocles' *The Theban Plays,* RSC in 1991 and
Euripides' *Hecuba* in San Francisco in 1995.

TIMBERLAKE WERTENBAKER

Plays One

New Anatomies

The Grace of Mary Traverse

Our Country's Good

The Love of the Nightingale

Three Birds Alighting on a Field

Introduced by
the Author

faber and faber
LONDON · BOSTON

This collection first published in Great Britain in 1996 by
Faber and Faber Limited 3 Queen Square London WC1N 3AU

Photoset by Parker Typesetting Service, Leicester
Printed in England by Clays Ltd, St Ives plc

A CIP record for this book
is available from the British Library

ISBN 0–571–17743–3

2 4 6 8 10 9 7 5 3 1

Contents

Introduction

When I am asked where my plays come from, I am always stuck for an answer. There are so many sources, a mishmash of autobiography, obsession, chance encounters, reading and conversations. And yet, when I try to retrace the roads to individual plays, I am always intrigued by the landscapes on the way.

New Anatomies was originally going to be one act of a play about three women who dressed as men. I was intrigued by the mental liberation in the simple physical act of cross-dressing. The other two women were George Sand and Ono Kamachi, a Japanese poet and courtesan. Eventually the fascinating Isabelle Eberhardt, a historical character whose journals I discovered by chance, took up a whole play to herself. She was a woman in love with adventure, on a quest, and this was a theme that obsessed me.

I continued that theme with *The Grace of Mary Traverse*, an invented character this time, whose restlessness, at least, was autobiographical. This was the early eighties, the time of the Brixton riots where I was living at the time. Someone told me about the Gordon riots, so I decided to set the play in the 1780s and follow a woman on her quest for experience and knowledge and eventual political power and the price attached to this Faustian pact.

After those two plays I wanted to write something different, so I wrote a play about a man with a terminal illness on a sea voyage. It had singing whales and wise tortoises and has remained comfortably in a drawer.

Max Stafford-Clark, then artistic director of the Royal

Court, had been very supportive of *The Grace of Mary Traverse* and he approached me to write something based on Thomas Keneally's novel, *The Playmaker*, also set in the eighteenth century. It was a bleak time in my life, one of deep mourning, and I didn't think I could do it, but he persuaded me to attend two weeks of workshops.

Much has been written about these 'workshops', a word I rather dislike. The two weeks were set up to put a group of actors at the disposal of a writer to research any aspect of anything that might eventually relate to the play. I could come in the morning and say I wanted to understand eighteenth-century theatrical convention, or the effect of long-term brutalization, and Max and the actors would find some way of doing it. We visited the theatre museum and improvised eighteenth-century acting styles there; we had 'beating workshops' where everyone went around being hit by newspapers. Actors went and interviewed ex-prisoners, or army officers, and brought back the characters they found. Or I might just send them to the library. It was a rich way of working and after two weeks it seemed possible to write the play which became *Our Country's Good*. With one exception, the actors who had researched it acted it and so came to the play with a marvellous authority and commitment. In that play, I wanted to explore the redemptive power of the theatre, of art, for people who had been silenced.

In *The Love of the Nightingale*, written before *Our Country's Good* and then rewritten in rehearsals, I followed the theme of being silenced. In this case, where there was no redemption, the silencing inevitably led to violence. It was based on the Greek myth of Philomele and answered another passion of mine, that for the Greeks. Although it has been interpreted as being about women, I was actually thinking of the violence that erupts in societies when they have been silenced for too long. Without language, brutality will triumph. I grew up in the

Basque country, where the language was systematically silenced, and it is something that always haunts me.

I had so enjoyed the workshops with Max that I suggested he provide me with some more for a play about the art world. The art world seemed to symbolize the eighties, with money being the only recognized value. In this case, the actors researched artists and the galleries, but *Three Birds Alighting on a Field* was written some time afterwards. The most enriching aspect of writing a play can be this exploration of an unknown world. That's the adventure part of it anyway. I was still taken by the theme of the redemptive value of art but here it was the character of Biddy, an upper-class conventional woman, as imprisoned in her own way as a convict, who found her freedom through being in touch with something of beauty. The enemy, however, is not a brutal system, but a society where nothing is valued for itself, something all too easy to internalize. That was something I wanted to continue exploring, at least in part, in the next play.

I like to work on my plays in rehearsals and even well into their run as I watch them performed in front of an audience. It's part of the travelling you do. Then suddenly, one day, there is no more you can do and the play becomes part of your past, a country you won't revisit. I suppose I keep writing because there's always somewhere else to go.

Timberlake Wertenbaker
November 1995

NEW ANATOMIES

Characters

Isabelle Eberhardt (Si Mahmoud)
Séverine
Antoine
Bou Saadi
Natalie
Eugénie
Murderer
Judge
Jenny
Saleh
Lydia
Colonel Lyautey
Verda Miles
Anna
Si Lachmi
Yasmina
Captain Soubiel
Pasha (*non-speaking*)

Note on the Staging

New Anatomies is designed for a cast of five women and a musician. The roles are distributed as follows:

1 Isabelle Eberhardt *and, in her Arab persona,* Si Mahmoud
2 Séverine   Antoine   Bou Saadi
3 Natalie   Eugénie   Murderer   Judge
4 Jenny   Saleh   Lydia   Colonel Lyautey
5 Verda Miles   Anna   Si Lachmi   Yasmina Captain Soubiel

The role of *Pasha* (Act Two, scene one) is silent, and should be taken by the musician.

Except for the actress playing *Isabelle*, each actress plays a Western woman, an Arab man and a Western man. Changes should take place in such a way as to be visible to the audience and all five actresses should be on stage at all times.

The songs in the play ought to be popular music-hall songs from the turn of the century. Songs 2 and 3 belong to the repertoire of the male impersonator, and song 1 to that of the *ingénue*.

The action of the play takes place at the turn of the century in Europe and Algeria.

T.W.

Act One

SCENE ONE

Ain-Sefra, a dusty village in Algeria. **Isabelle Eberhardt** *looks around, none too steady. She is dressed in a tattered Arab cloak, has no teeth and almost no hair. She is 27.*

Isabelle Lost the way. (*Steadies herself.*) Detour. Closed. (*Pause. As if an order to herself*) Go inside. (*Sings, softly, Arabic modulations, but flat.*) 'If a man be old and a fool, his folly . . .' (*Burps.*) That's what it is. (*Takes out a cigarette and looks for a match through the folds of her cloak.*) Match. (*Forgets about it. Sings*) 'If a man be old and a fool, his folly is past all cure. But a young man . . .' What it is is this (*Looks around.*) I need a fuck. (*Pause.*) Definitely. Yes.

> **Séverine** *enters. She is a slightly older woman, dressed uncomfortably for the heat in a long skirt and jacket.*

Trailed . . . (*to Séverine*) Trailing behind me.

Séverine Come inside.

Isabelle Inside? Trailed: the story, I know. Stealing it.

Séverine You have a fever.

> *Isabelle remembers her cigarette.*

Isabelle Matches. Stolen. (*louder*) You stole my matches.

> *Séverine finds the matches, tries to light Isabelle's cigarette.*

(*apologetic*) Desert wind: makes the hand shake.

> *Séverine lights two cigarettes and sticks one in Isabelle's mouth.*

Pay for my story with a match. European coinage!

Séverine You need rest.

Isabelle No, later. (*Burps*.) Found out what it was. What was it? Ah, yes. It was: I need a fuck. I need a fuck. Where am I going to find a fuck? Bunch of degenerates in this town. Sleeping WHEN I NEED A FUCK. It's the European influence. Keeps them down.

Séverine Come inside, Isabelle.

Isabelle 'Please go inside, mademoiselle, and stay there.' Out of the wind. Saw a couple of guards earlier. That'll do. One for you, one for me. I'll give you the younger one, rules of hospitality. No? Sevvy the scribe prefers a belly dancer, eh, dark smooth limbs and curved hips. Or the voluptuous tale. Your face looks like a big hungry European cock. No offence: not your fault you look European. Must find those guards. (*Stares*.) Coolness of the night as it filters through the sand. The smell of sand, Séverine, do you know it? It's like the inside of water. Smell . . .

She leans down and falls flat.

Séverine Isabelle, please . . .

They struggle to get her up.

Isabelle You going to write I couldn't walk straight enough to find a fuck? They'll want to know everything. I'm famous now, not just anybody, no, I'll be in History. (*near retch*) They hate me, but I forgive them. You tell them . . . that when the body drags through the gutter, it is cleaved from the soul. Tell them the soul paced the desert. They take baths, but lice crawl through the cracks of their hypocritical brains. Bunch of farmers. Wallowing in the mud of their ploughed fields. Turnips, cabbages, carrots, all in a line, all fenced in. (*Cries*.) Why do they hate me so? I didn't want anything from them.

6

Pause.

Si Mahmoud forgives all. Si Mahmoud paced the desert.
Heart unmixed with guile, free. Why aren't you writing all
this down, chronicler? Duty to get it right, no editing.
(*Burps.*) Edit that.

Séverine Please, Si Mahmoud. Let's go in.

Isabelle Listen. The dawn's coming. You can tell by the
sound, a curve in the silence and then the sand in the
desert moves . . . Write down: a third of a centimetre,
they'll want to know that in Europe.

Pause. Séverine, resigned, sits with Isabelle.

When I was growing up in the Tsar's villa in St
Petersburg . . .

Séverine Geneva.

Isabelle What?

Séverine You said Geneva earlier.

Isabelle Did I? Yes, ducks . . . must have been Geneva.

Séverine (*delicately*) Your brothers . . .

Isabelle Didn't have any.

Séverine You said . . .

Isabelle I was the only boy in the family.

Séverine Your brother Antoine . . .

Isabelle Beloved. (*Makes a gesture for fucking.*) Didn't.
Would have.

Nasty little piece got her claws in him first. No, did.

Séverine Si Mahmoud, the truth.

Isabelle There is no god but Allah, Allah is the only God

7

and Muhammed is his prophet.

Séverine What brought you to the desert?

Isabelle makes a trace on the ground.

It's in Arabic.

Isabelle (*reads*) The Mektoub: it was written. Here. That means, no choice. Mektoub.

Séverine Your mother?

Isabelle No choice for her either. The Mektoub.

Séverine You told me she was a delicate woman. What gave her the courage to run off?

Isabelle Even the violet resists domestication.

Séverine But in the 1870s . . .

Isabelle Séverine, it is a courtesy in this country not to interrupt or ask questions of the storyteller. You must sit quietly and listen, moving only to light my cigarettes. When I pause, you may praise Allah for having given my tongue such vivid modulations. I shall begin, as is our custom, with a mention of women.

SCENE TWO

Geneva. A house in disorder.
Verda Miles takes off her ribbons, puts up her hair and covers herself with a shawl, becoming **Anna**, *a woman in her late thirties, with remnants of style and charm.*

Anna And then the children . . . They won't stay.

Isabelle and **Antoine** *appear. Isabelle is 13, dressed in a man's shirt and a skirt much too big for her. Antoine is 16, frail and feminine.*

8

Isabelle Antoine. Don't let him frighten you.

Antoine (*near tears*) Drunken tyrant.

Isabelle Let's dream.

Antoine He threatened to hit me. Brute. I have to go away, now.

Anna (*paying no attention to any of this*) First Nicholas, not a word . . . He must have come to a bad . . . Too many anarchists in the house. It's a bad influence on children.

Isabelle Oh yes, let's go away. We're in Siberia. The snow is up to our knees, so hard to move. Suddenly, look, shining in the dark, a pair of yellow eyes.

Antoine I have no choice. I'll have to run away and join the army.

Isabelle I'll come with you, we can take Mama.

Antoine The army's only for boys.

Isabelle We can't leave Mama.

Antoine I wish I was a girl. He doesn't treat you that way.

Isabelle I'm strong.

Antoine He'll kill me.

Anna If only Trofimovitch had allowed some fairy tales, even Pushkin . . . not all these Bakunin pamphlets at bedtime.

Isabelle It's snowing again. Darkness. Another pair of yellow eyes, glistening. Another. We're surrounded. Are they wolves?

Antoine (*joining in reluctantly*) No, those are the eyes of our enemies.

9

Isabelle You're shivering.

Anna And now Natalie . . .

Antoine I'm cold. It's too cold up there. I want to go further south.

Isabelle The Crimea, lemon groves.

Antoine 'Knowst thou the land, beloved, where the lemons bloom . . .' No, I want to go further south. Far away. The Sahara.

Anna And Natalie's so good with . . .

Isabelle Our camels are tired.

Antoine That's the sort of thing Natalie would say.

Isabelle (*offended*) The transition from Siberia was too sudden. I haven't acclamitated.

Antoine Acclimatized.

Anna It's all so difficult.

Flute music.

Isabelle This stillness.

Antoine Dune after dune, shape mirroring shape, so life . . . weariness.

Isabelle How rapidly the sun seems to plunge behind the dunes. This stillness.

Antoine Let us rest, my beloved.

Isabelle I'll build our tent. There's a storm coming, I can see the clouds.

Antoine There aren't any clouds over the desert.

Isabelle That's what Natalie would say.

Antoine You don't understand, the corners of a dream must be nailed to the ground as firmly as our tent: no rain in the desert.

Isabelle A wind then. Listen, the wind's galloping over the dunes.

Antoine It's a sandstorm.

Isabelle Quick. Where are you? I can't see you.

Antoine Here, come here, my beloved.

They throw themselves into each other's arms, roll on the floor.

Beloved.

Their embrace lingers.

Anna Natalie mustn't . . . she's too good with (*Notices the two children.*) Antoine, I'm not sure you should . . . with your sister . . . like that.

Isabelle We're playing, Mama, we're dreaming.

Anna Are you too old? I don't know. The poets . . . But Natalie . . .

Antoine Wants us to behave –

Isabelle Like Swiss clocks. Tick tock.

Antoine Tick tock.

Anna You mustn't . . . She is sometimes a little . . . but she's the only one, she's so good with dust. I don't seem to manage very well. There's so much of it and it's complicated finding it. I wasn't brought up to . . . But this new world of Trofimovitch, where it's wrong to have servants, well yes, but what about the dust? I suppose when the revolution comes, they'll find a way, deal with it.

Isabelle We don't mind.

Anna Natalie . . . wants to leave us.

Antoine Even Natalie can't take the beast any more.

Anna Isabelle, she's always been very fond . . . Tell her she absolutely mustn't . . .

Isabelle She's free.

Anna But Trofimovitch . . .

> **Natalie** *enters. She is a tightly pulled together young woman. An awkward silence and a sense that this is not unusual when she comes into a room.*

Natalie, I was saying . . . to abandon your home . . .

Natalie How can you call this pigsty a home?

Anna Darling, a young lady's vocabulary shouldn't include . . . Your family . . .

Natalie Family. (*Looks around at them.*) In a family you have first a mother who looks after her children, protects them, teaches them . . .

Anna Didn't I? You knew several poems of Byron as a child.

Natalie A mother who teaches her children how to behave and looks after the house, cooks meals, doesn't let her children eat out of a slop bucket –

Anna Trofimovitch says meals are a bourgeois form of . . . But don't we have . . .

Natalie When I cook them. And secondly in a family a brother is a brother, a boy then a man, not this snivelling, delicate half girl. You've allowed him to be terrorized by that drunken beast.

Anna Natalie, his mind, philosophy . . .

Natalie Philosophy, don't make me laugh. Yes, and finally in a family you have a proper father, not that raving peasant, who's driven us to this misery and filth, who's now trying to get into my bed at night.

Anna He's not always very steady at night, he must have thought . . . He didn't notice it wasn't his . . .

Natalie (*exploding*) And you defend him. My mother defends the man who's ruining all of us, you defend the man who's trying to seduce your own daughter. You won't leave that filthy lecherous drunk, you prefer to ruin us.

Anna Leave him . . . go . . . where?

Isabelle Natalie, love forgives.

Natalie Love, that spittle of stinking brandy. Love?

Isabelle (*gently*) 'Love has its reasons . . .

Antoine . . . which reason cannot fathom.'

Natalie The two of you with your books!

Anna (*feebly*) Isabelle is right . . . She doesn't mind . . .

Natalie At her age you love anybody, even beggars, even a snivelling brother. (*to Isabelle*) I'll come back and get you later, then you can come live with me in a real home, with a real family, with my husband.

Isabelle A husband, Natalie. That's different. Is he dark? Is he foreign? Does he visit you only at night and wrap you in a blinding veil of torrid passion? A secret husband, how wonderful, like Eros and Psyche. Does he let you look at him?

Natalie What are you talking about? I'm marrying Stéphane.

Antoine Stéphane, the shopkeeping weed. He's driven you to that?

Natalie You're one to talk, you fine figure of manhood.

Isabelle He does look like a dandelion, you said so yourself.

Natalie He'll soon be my husband and I'll have him talked about with respect. We'll be very happy.

Isabelle How? If he knows you don't love him.

Natalie Love, look where that got us. Oh, I tell him I love him, men like to hear that, sometimes I tell him I adore him.

Anna To lie . . . I'm not sure . . .

Natalie I can't have you at the wedding. I explained he was too ill. Stéphane's family's a little upset I'm foreign. But they'll see, I'll make a wonderful home for him. (*Pause.*) I must get my things. Don't tell him, it won't do any good.

She leaves.

Anna I don't understand, what have I done? But you, my babies, you'll never leave, no, you couldn't now. What did you say, Isabelle? Torrid passion, yes, I think, with Trofimovitch, it was . . . He was so strong, so convinced, impossible to think clearly . . . And then, how wrong it was to have servants, husband, hypocrisy of the sacrament, he said, and how my life made millions suffer. Would you have preferred a big house? You see, there are so many rules when you . . . The doctor says a frail heart . . . There's no choice when your heart is . . .

She drifts off.

Isabelle At last the silence descends on the darkening

dunes. How still is our solitude, my beloved, how still the desert.

Antoine Let's stop here.

Isabelle Yes, let's grow old together and watch the hours stretch on the ground.

Antoine (*moving away*) Beloved, forgive me, but I must.

Isabelle I can't see you. You sound so far away.

Antoine I don't have the strength any more, forgive me . . .

Isabelle Where have you gone? Oh, please. Abandoned, alas, nothing to do.

Antoine (*from off*) But wait.

Isabelle Wait . . . and all around me, death. (*Screams.*) Dead.

SCENE THREE

Geneva, a few years later.
  Natalie and Isabelle.

Natalie Dead?

Isabelle Dead. Both of them. Mama first, almost immediately after she received Antoine's letter. It broke her heart, those years of silence, not knowing, her frail heart. And then the letter from the Legion! Antoine a Legionnaire, he'll never survive.

Natalie It might be just the thing for him. Turn him into a man.

Isabelle He didn't even tell me, the coward, the traitor. He must have planned it for months in secret. And then a cool

letter describing life in the barracks and, now, marriage.
I'll have to find him before it's too late.

Natalie And him? Drank himself to death?

Isabelle Poor Trofimovitch. He'd begun to put his ear to
the ground listening for the sound of the revolution. He
said he'd hear it when it came, he still had the ear of a
Russian peasant. And he despaired of the silence. When
Mama died, he . . . turned and twisted, crumpled himself
into a knot and kept his ear to the floor, but this time I
think he was listening for her. 'Three be the ways of love: a
knitting of heart to heart' – that's Antoine and me – 'a
pleasing of lips and eyes, and a third love whose name is
death.' That's Trofimovitch and Mama. It's from an Arabic
poem. Trofimovitch taught it to me. There's a similar one
in Greek . . .

Natalie Mama should have taught you to sweep instead.
If I'd learnt properly when I was young my mother-in-law
wouldn't have found so much to complain about. But
Stéphane has been very patient. I'm lucky. (*Takes in the
disorder.*) We can start on this house. Stéphane thinks
we'll get a lot of money for it, sell it to some English
aristocrats. They like these gloomy old places.

Isabelle The house belongs to Antoine. He'll want to come
back here and live with me.

Natalie He'll want his own little home now.

Isabelle 'And the screen of separation was placed between
us.'

Natalie The house belongs to all of us. Your share of the
money can help towards the expense of having you live
with us, and you'll have some left over for your marriage.
I wish I'd been able to bring some to my husband,
although he never reproached me.

Isabelle What's marriage like?

Natalie We're doing very well with the shop now and soon we'll build our own house, a big one.

Isabelle I mean at night.

Natalie You get used to it.

Isabelle Brutal pain and brutal pleasure, and after, languor. 'And the breeze languished in the evening hours as if it had pity for me.'

Natalie You've been reading too much. You mustn't talk like that to men. When they come into the shop you must be seen working very hard, dusting things very carefully. That always inspires young men. We've thought a lot about Stéphane's cousin. He has a flower shop and he won't mind the fact that you look so strong. You could help him in the garden. You'd like that.

Isabelle Does he grow cactus plants?

Natalie They're the wrong plants for this climate.

Isabelle It's the wrong climate for the plants. I'm going to Algeria.

Natalie The thought of marriage frightened me too, but I'll help you make a good choice. You'll need a roof over your head.

Isabelle No rain in the desert, no need for a roof.

Natalie We're in Geneva and I'm here to protect you until you're safely married.

Isabelle Geneva of the barred horizons. I'm getting out, I need a gallop on the dunes.

Natalie You'll forget all that when you're married. You'll forget all those dreams.

Isabelle (*looking at Natalie for the first time*) Poor Natalie, left the dreams to look for order, but order was not happiness.

Natalie You always made fun of me, you and Antoine, but I always cared for you and I'm determined to help you. When you understand what life is like without the books, you'll understand me, you'll see.

Isabelle Geneva to Marseilles by train, Marseilles to Algiers by boat and then a camel for the desert.

Natalie That's enough now. It's your duty.

Isabelle Words of a Swiss preacher, song of the rain on the cultivated fields.

Natalie You have to obey me. You have no choice.

Isabelle Trofimovitch told me obedience comes not from direct fear, but fear of the rules. I have no fear, he always said I was the bravest.

Natalie He had no right to treat you as if you were an exception. (*Pause.*) You're still so young, we won't force you. We'll give you a year, even more.

   Silence.

If we sell this house, we can take a little trip to Algeria. I want to see what they have over there. They say Arabs are very stupid and give you valuable jewels and clothes for trinkets. Will you agree to that?

Isabelle The desert.

Natalie Stéphane's arranging the papers for the house and then he'll get us all passports. You couldn't get one by yourself.

Isabelle Antoine, we'll gallop over the desert.

Natalie I'll be so pleased to sell this house. All buried at last.

Isabelle Antoine!

SCENE FOUR

Algiers. Antoine in a crumpled civil service suit sits smoking, tired, grey. **Jenny**, *young and very pregnant, is bustling. Isabelle is staring out and* **Yasmina**, *a servant, is polishing something, extremely slowly.*

Jenny (*to Antoine*) Why doesn't your sister ever help? She hasn't lifted a finger since she's been here. She talks too much to the servant. I have enough trouble making that woman work. They're so lazy, these people. She's said more to that girl than to me. Call her over, Antoine. She never listens when I talk to her.

Antoine (*weakly*) Isabelle.

Isabelle turns.

Jenny Please remember that Fatma is a native and a servant. They don't respect you if you treat them . . .

Isabelle Her name isn't Fatma.

Jenny Their names are unpronounceable. We call them all Fatma.

Isabelle Her name is beautiful: Yasmina. Poor girl, they tried to marry her to a cousin she hated. It was death or the degradation of becoming a servant. I'll write about her.

Jenny I wouldn't believe anything she says. Help me polish some glasses. I can't trust Fatma with them.

Isabelle Throw over a cigarette, will you, Antoine.

Jenny Women shouldn't smoke. It makes them look vulgar, doesn't it, Antoine?

Isabelle Matches.

Jenny And you work very hard for your cigarettes. They don't grow on trees. Some people have to pay for everything and soon we'll have another mouth to feed.

Antoine Isabelle'll help us when she sells some articles.

Jenny She won't sell any by just sitting around smoking.

Isabelle Inspiration doesn't come frying potatoes.

Antoine laughs.

Jenny You always take her side. You don't care what happens to me. She hasn't even offered to knit something for the baby.

Isabelle (*bored*) Yasmina will help me find something.

Jenny I'm not going to put some horrible native cloth around my beautiful new baby.

Isabelle I'll get Natalie to send you a collection of poems when she goes back. Do you remember that beautiful one of Lermontov Mama used to recite, about the young soul crying out its entrapment in the womb? The dumb joy of the mother but for 'a long time it languished in the world, filled with a wonderful longing and earth's tedious songs . . .' how does it go?

Antoine (*awkward*) I don't remember.

Isabelle 'Could not drown out the last sounds of Paradise . . .'

Jenny You're jealous, that's all, because you can't find a husband. Natalie told me how you frightened Stéphane's cousin away.

Isabelle He looked like an orchid.

Antoine You're worse than Arabs, you two, fighting about nothing.

Isabelle Is that what they teach you in the barracks?

Jenny He's not in the barracks any more. He has a very good job.

Isabelle Sitting on your bum, staring at numbers.

Jenny And he'll be promoted soon.

Isabelle To longer numbers.

Jenny If you don't ruin his chances. You've been heard talking to the natives in their own language. There's no reason not to talk to them in French.

Isabelle (*to Antoine*) You hate it, don't you, this life?

Jenny People are becoming suspicious. This is a small community.

Isabelle Tick tock, a Swiss clock, the needle that crushes the dreams to sleep.

Jenny You think food just appears on the table. It has to be paid for.

Isabelle And only ten miles from the desert. You might as well have stayed in Switzerland for all you've seen of it.

Antoine I did see it. It's not how we dreamt of it. It's dangerous, uncomfortable, and most of it isn't even sand.

Isabelle Freedom.

Jenny Life is much cheaper here than in Switzerland. We'll go back when we have enough money to buy a decent house.

Isabelle 'Oh the bitter grief of never again exchanging one single thought.' Remember how we knew all of Loti by heart and we dreamt of moving, always moving.

Antoine Life isn't what we dreamt.

Isabelle It could be . . . the rolling movement of camels, movement, Antoine.

Jenny Rolling stone gathers no moss. I don't want my baby to be poor.

Isabelle Remember when we followed the Berber caravan and we had the sandstorm, 'oh, my beloved' . . .

Antoine I saw the Berbers. One wrong move and they slit your throat. They don't like Europeans.

Isabelle Not Europeans with guns, but we could talk to them. Freedom.

Jenny You keep talking as if Antoine was a slave. He has a good job. We'll be able to take holidays, have a house. That's freedom: money.

Antoine I see how things are now.

Isabelle What dictionary are you using? The Swiss clockmaker's or the poet's?

An Arabic flute, offstage.

Or his? Listen. I hear him every evening, but I've never seen him come or go. He's just there, suddenly, calling.

Jenny It's probably a beggar and he'll come asking for money. Chase him away, Antoine. They carry diseases these people. It's bad for the baby.

They ignore her. She shouts.

Go away, you savage, go away, go away!

Silence.

(*embarrassed*) I'm so tired and nervous. This isn't a friendly country. It's not easy to have a baby. It doesn't happen all by itself.

Natalie enters, arms full of materials and clothes.

Natalie It's wonderful how stupid these people are. They give you things for nothing.

Isabelle The word is generosity, gifts of hospitality.

Natalie Look at this one, it's worth a fortune, that embroidery, that detail. They're terribly clever for savages. Look at this woman's cloak.

Isabelle It's not for a woman.

Natalie We'll be the first shop in Switzerland to sell these oriental things. They're all the rage in Paris. You could even model some of them, Isabelle. Here's a woman's dancing costume.

Jenny Give it to me.

Natalie I can't wait to get back. We'll make a fortune.

Isabelle I'm not coming back with you.

Natalie Nonsense.

Natalie continues to lay out the clothes. Jenny wraps her face in a veil.

Jenny I'm in your harem. You're the sheikh. Oh, come to me.

Antoine You look grotesque.

Jenny You're so cruel. I'll hide behind my veil.

Isabelle That's not a woman's veil. Women in the desert don't wear veils, only the Tuareg men do.

She starts dressing Jenny.

23

It should be wrapped around the head and worn with this. This is called a jellaba. It can be worn in any kind of weather. The hood will protect you against the elements, or against the enemy. It's very useful for warriors.

Jenny I don't want to be dressed as a man.

Isabelle Why not? The baby might end up looking like an Arab? He'll run away from you into the desert.

Natalie You look lovely. Don't tease her, Isabelle. When you're pregnant you have these caprices. I couldn't wear red or walk into the house without making three turns in the garden.

Antoine It's like the Arabs. They'll never do anything without going through fifty useless gestures.

Isabelle The word is courtesy.

Isabelle takes a jellaba and puts it on, slowly, formally. Freeze while she is doing this. Once in it, she feels as at home in it as Jenny obviously feels awkward.

Natalie And they gave me this in secret.

She takes out a captain's uniform.

Antoine Someone they killed probably. They have no respect for human life. You see how dangerous they are.

Isabelle 'Always behave as if you were going to die immediately.' Remember when we were Stoics and we tried to live in that barrel for a month?

Natalie (*going over to Jenny and putting a 'feminine' scarf over her head*) I'm afraid reading is a hereditary disease in our family. I would keep books well away from your children when they're young, otherwise it's very hard to wean them from all that nonsense when they're older. If only we could get her married, she'd forget all those books, but it's the quotes that drive men away. I'm glad Antoine, at least, is saved.

As Natalie is saying this Isabelle is putting the captain's jacket on Yasmina. The two girls giggle, Yasmina doing a military stance. Jenny suddenly notices them.

Jenny Don't do that, it's . . . blasphemy.

Isabelle Why, do you think clothes make the monk?

Antoine Isabelle looks like all our recruits. No one would know you were a girl. Is this male or female?

He puts on a jellaba, joining in the game.

Jenny If anyone sees us, we'll be ruined.

Isabelle (*to Antoine*) Let's go to those dark dens in the Arab quarter and have a smoke.

Antoine If they recognize us (*throat-slitting gesture*).

Isabelle We'll say we're from Tunis. That'll explain my accent.

Jenny You can't go out. What about me?

Isabelle Come, Antoine, for at least one evening, let's go back to our dreams.

Natalie I want you to come with me to the market.

Isabelle I told you I won't help you cheat those people any more.

Natalie I'm only trying to save some money.

Isabelle One evening, Antoine.

They begin to go.

Jenny Ooooh – ooooh my stomach. I think I'm going to faint. Don't leave me, Antoine.

Isabelle You have Natalie and the 'captain'.

Jenny Oooh. (*Doubles over.*) Put your hands on my forehead, Antoine. It's the only thing that'll help.

Isabelle Why don't you just tell him you want him to stay instead of acting ill, hypocrite?

Natalie Don't upset a pregnant woman, Isabelle.

Isabelle Antoine . . .

Antoine goes over to Jenny and puts his hands on her forehead. Isabelle turns to leave.

Natalie What are you doing?

Isabelle I'm going outside.

Natalie A woman can't go out by herself at this time of night.

Isabelle But in these . . . I'm not a woman.

SCENE FIVE

The Kasbah. Isabelle, alone.

Isabelle If, down an obscure alleyway, a voice shouts at me: hey you, shopkeeper – I'll not turn around. If the voice pursues me: foreigner, European – I'll not turn around. If the voice says: you, woman, yes, woman – I'll not turn around, no, I'll not even turn my head. Even when it whispers, Isabelle, Isabelle Eberhardt – even then I won't turn around. But if it hails me: you, you there, who need vast spaces and ask for nothing but to move, you, alone, free, seeking peace and a home in the desert, who wish only to obey the strange ciphers of your fate – yes, then I will turn around, then I'll answer: I am here: Si Mahmoud.

SCENE SIX

The desert, Isabelle, **Saleh** *and* **Bou Saadi** *are sitting passing around a pipe full of kif. They are very stoned, from lack of food and the hashish. Long silences, then rapid bursts of speech. The poetry must not be 'recited'. For the Arabs, it is their natural form of speech.*

Saleh 'The warrior was brave. Alas the beautiful young man fell. He shone like silver. Now he is in Paradise, far from all troubles.'

Isabelle Was he fighting the Tidjanis, Saleh?

Saleh No, Si Mahmoud, that is a song against the French.

Silence.

Isabelle Tell me more about the wise men.

Saleh Usually they're sheikhs who have been handed their knowledge by their fathers and then give it to a son. They live in the monasteries. We'll stay in one tomorrow.

Bou Saadi But sometimes they wander and look just like beggars.

Saleh There used to be very many, but the French are getting rid of them.

Bou Saadi You must be careful what you say against the French, Saleh, it was God's will they become our rulers, it was written.

Saleh Have we not read it badly?

Silence.

Bou Saadi One of the most famous marabouts used to live not far from here. Lalla Zineb. Many people visit her tomb.

Isabelle A woman?

Bou Saadi Not an ordinary woman.

Isabelle But a woman?

Saleh What difference does it make, Si Mahmoud, if she was wise? They say she predicted the victory of the French and then died of grief.

Silence.

If it is wisdom you seek, Si Mahmoud, you should spend some time in the monasteries. We could take you to the one where the leader of our sect lives.

Isabelle And you, my friends, what have you found in the desert?

Saleh I had a cousin who had a beautiful white mare. She was fast, exquisite. He'd had her since he was a boy. She was his treasure and his love. One night, she disappeared. He searched for months and found her at last in the camp of a few Tidjanis. He waited until the night to get her back, but someone must have seen him because he stumbled on her body on his way to the camp. Her throat had been slit, his beautiful white mare. Some time later he managed to kill the man who had stolen her. It's only fair, a mare is more valuable than a wife to us. But the Tidjanis told the French about it. They're very friendly with the French. He was judged in the city and then sent away to forced labour in a place called Corsica. Very few men come back from Corsica and then only to die. That's the law of the French.

Bou Saadi We were born crossing the desert, but now we have to ask permission to go to certain places.

Isabelle Was it better always to fight the Tidjanis?

Saleh It was our custom.

Silence.

'She said to me:
Why are your tears so white?
I answered:
Beloved, I have cried so long my tears are as white as my hair.'

Isabelle One day we'll understand, Saleh.

Saleh Ah, Si Mahmoud, perhaps you will, you're learned.

Bou Saadi We'll leave a few hours before dawn. I hope you're not feeling too weak, Si Mahmoud.

Isabelle No, my friends, but why didn't you tell me to bring food? I've eaten all of yours.

Bou Saadi We're used to this life.

Saleh 'She said to me:
Why are your tears black?
I answered:
I have no more tears, those are my pupils . . .'

 Captain Soubiel *enters.*

Captain Soubiel You there, who are you and where are you going?

 Bou Saadi and Saleh jump up, acting increasingly stupid as the Captain stares at them. Bou Saadi in particular almost caricatures 'oriental servility'.

Bou Saadi We're traders on our way to El-Oued, Allah willing.

Captain Don't give me any of this Allah business. The three of you are traders?

Bou Saadi This is a young Tunisian student on his way to the monasteries down south.

Captain Monasteries, we've just had a report on those monasteries. Fortresses, that's what they are, hotbeds of resistance. All those sheikhs with their wives and slaves pretending to teach religion when they're shouting propaganda against the French. Don't talk to me about monasteries. (*Stares at Isabelle.*) A Tunisian student, we've had a report about that too. You're not very dark.

Bou Saadi Men from the city are lighter than us. Much sun in the Sahara.

Captain Can't he speak for himself? What's your name?

Isabelle Si Mahmoud.

Captain Si Mahmoud. You two, go make some tea.

Bou Saadi We have no tea.

Captain Well, then, go have a piss and don't come back until I call you. Stay where I can see you and you, stay here. (*Has a good stare and then becomes extremely courteous.*) Remarkable, I must say, remarkable. I wouldn't have known. I'm honoured. You've become a legend in the Legion: it's one thing to go out looking for some Arab scum criminal, but a mysterious young lady . . .

Isabelle My name is Si Mahmoud.

Captain You can of course rely on the honour of the French Army to keep your secret. Ha, ha, you Russian girls are extraordinary. One of them blew up the Tsar or his cousin the other day and now we have this young thing living it out with the Arabs. They say Dostoevsky does this to you, gives you a taste for cockroaches. But, mademoiselle, if you wished to see the country, you should have come to us. We would be only too pleased to escort you and you would find our company much more entertaining than that of those sandfleas.

Isabelle You shouldn't speak of the Arabs in that manner, Captain. They resent it.

Captain You must tell me how to run the country, mademoiselle. It'll pass the time as we travel. Dunes get monotonous.

Isabelle I am travelling with my friends, Captain.

Captain What? Are there more of you? Do we have a whole boarding school of romantic young girls?

Isabelle My friends Saleh and Bou Saadi.

Captain She calls these dregs of humanity friends. Ah, youth, the female heart. I admire your spirit, mademoiselle, but it is the duty of the French Army to rescue damsels in distress.

Isabelle My friends will look after me.

Captain Mademoiselle, I'm here to protect you. These people smile at you at one day and cut your throat the next. You see, they have no logic, no French education. And if they ever found out . . . You're not at all bad looking you know.

Isabelle I choose to travel with them.

Captain You're quite a brave little character. I like that. I think we'll get on very well. You remind me of a delightfully unbroken young filly.

Isabelle Whereas you, Captain, remind me of a heavy cascade of camel piss. Mind you, nothing wrong with camel piss, I just don't choose to have it on top of me. Or, to put it another way, I'd rather kiss the open mouth of a Maccabean corpse dead of the Asiatic cholera than 'travel' with you, Captain.

Freeze.

Captain May I see your papers?

Isabelle What papers?

Captain You must have government permission to travel through French territory.

Isabelle This is the desert. It's free.

Captain This is French territory, under the rule of law and civilization and we require even sluts to have the correct papers. I'm waiting. I see you have no papers. You there!

Bou Saadi and Saleh come back.

Do you know what this friend of yours Si Mahmoud is?

Isabelle Captain, the honour of the French Army.

Captain We save the honour of our own kind. You'll kick yourselves when you find out. This little Tunisian friend of yours, ha, ha . . .

Isabelle Captain, please.

Captain This Si Mahmoud is a woman.

Silence. Bou Saadi laughs stupidly. Saleh doesn't react at all.

Look under her clothes if you don't believe me.

Saleh (*slowly*) Si Mahmoud has a very good knowledge of medicine. He's helped people with their eyes and cured children.

Captain Probably told them to wash. It's a woman I tell you. You must be stupider than I thought not to have noticed or at least asked a few questions.

Saleh It is a courtesy in our country not to be curious about the stranger. We accept whatever name Si Mahmoud wishes to give us.

Isabelle You knew.

Saleh We heard. We chose not to believe it. (*to the Captain*) Si Mahmoud knows the Koran better than we do. He's in search of wisdom. We wish to help him.

Captain Wisdom? That's the story she's spreading. I think it's more like information to pass on to people who don't belong here, like the English. They're always using women for this sort of thing. They can't forgive us for having produced Joan of Arc. You have ten days to bring this agitator back to the city. You know what happens if you don't.

Isabelle I'll appeal.

Captain Yes, in Paris. It's never wise to refuse the protection of the French Army. A good journey, mademoiselle.

He leaves.

Isabelle I'm doing no harm . . .

Bou Saadi It's not a good idea to irritate Europeans. It's best to pretend you're stupid and keep laughing. I'm very good at it. Saleh is learning very slowly.

Isabelle I want nothing to do with these people. Why won't they let me alone? Ah, my friends, it's written I must leave you, but I'll come back, I'll come back.

Act Two

SCENE ONE

A salon in Paris, Verda Miles, Séverine, **Lydia**, Eugénie, *Isabelle, and* **Pasha,** *a servant.*

SONG:
Verda Miles as a young man in Paris.

Lydia Isn't she extraordinary? Do you know I am almost in love with that man about town. And it was so kind of her to come and sing for my little salon.

Eugénie Ah, but your salon, such a setting for an artist.

Séverine Don't be a hypocrite, Lydia. She knows everyone is at your little salon. And I've been invited tonight because you want me to write a story on her.

Lydia What she is doing is so important – for us.

Séverine Lots of women have gone on stage dressed as men. It shows off their figures.

Lydia When Verda Miles is on stage, she *is* a man.

Eugénie And 'man is the measure of all things'.

Lydia Do interview her, Séverine.

Séverine You can't interview English people, they don't know how to talk about themselves.

Pasha comes in with a tray of champagne.

I say, is that real?

Lydia No, it's just Jean. But the clothes are real. I had them copied from the *Arabian Nights.*

Séverine The Countess Holst has one, a genuine one, but he's not as convincing.

Lydia And she had to sleep with the Turkish Ambassador to get him.

Eugénie When I was in Cairo I thought of bringing one back with me, but it's cruel to take them out of their natural environment.

Lydia Why don't I engage Verda Miles in conversation? You can simply listen.

Séverine You'll make it too philosophical and I'll miss the story – if there is one.

Lydia My dear, you can't talk philosophy with English women, they think it's something naughty their husbands did as boys. No, I'll start with dogs.

Eugénie (*seeing Isabelle*) Lydia, what do I see? Ah, there, there is a true one, I can tell. A young oriental prince, look at the simplicity, the dignity. Oh, do present him to us.

Séverine It's even an Arab who looks a little like Rimbaud, the Countess will be green when I tell her. How very clever of you.

Lydia Yes, that's quite a find, but that's not a real Arab either. Much more interesting, you have there a young woman who travels with the savage tribes in the Sahara. Her name's Isabelle Eberhardt. Russian, I think, she won't talk much about herself.

Séverine Eberhardt's a Jewish name.

Lydia Yes, well, they're all nomads, aren't they? She had some troubles with officials in North Africa and she's come to Paris to ask the French Government to help her. She's very naïve.

Séverine She must be to think the Government will help anyone. Does she have enough money to bribe them?

Lydia She seems to have left everything behind – somewhere.

Eugénie The nomadic spirit, it's so noble, so carefree.

Lydia She knows almost no one here, but look at her, she could become quite the rage. You might help her. I believe she writes.

Séverine Oh dear, descriptions of the sunset in sub-Wordsworthian rhymes. So many interesting people would still be remembered if they hadn't left behind their memoirs.

Lydia has been waving Isabelle over.

Lydia Pasha, more champagne please.

Séverine (*courteous, intrigued*) Would you like some champagne, mademoiselle?

Isabelle Is that what it is? It's good, I've had six glasses already.

Eugénie (*with an exaggerated Arab salutation, or an attempt at one*) I am so delighted. I too have been There.

Isabelle ?

Eugénie Why didn't we discover it before? All those trips to Athens and Rome staring at ruins when we had the real thing all the time in the Orient.

Isabelle chokes on her drink, coughs and spits.

Isabelle Oh, forgot, used to the sand. Sorry, Lydia.

Eugénie The Homeric gesture, is that not so? (*to the others*) You can't imagine what it's like to see lying in the sun, or mending shoes, men of such consular types, all clad in white like the senators of Rome. Each one with the mien of a Cato or a Brutus.

Lydia There's Verda, excellent.

Champagne. Isabelle drinks another glass.

Verda No, I never drink. (*to Isabelle*) What a charming costume you have.

Eugénie The flowing simplicity of the African garb, so free, so . . . Athenian.

Verda I'd like to copy it. You see. I have an idea for a new song, it would be an oriental melody, exotic, and with that costume . . .

Isabelle It's not a costume, it's my clothes.

Verda Of course, that's what I meant. Do you know any oriental songs?

Eugénie Those oriental melodies – so biblical.

Isabelle (*very flat*) Darling, I love you, darling, I adore you, exactly like to – maaa – to sauce. When I saw you there there there on the balcony, I thought . . . (*Hiccups.*) That's all I know.

Lydia They have the most beautiful breed of hounds in Egypt. They're called Ibizan hounds . . .

Isabelle I ate some cat in Tunisia. They said it was rabbit, but I could tell it was cat, I found a claw. It tasted all right.

Eugénie I found them so admirable in the simplicity of their needs. A population of Socrates.

Lydia What made you decide to sing men's songs, Miss Miles?

Lydia I started singing on the stage when I was three and at the age of six I had run through most of the female repertoire. By the time I was seven I thought I would have to retire. But then, one night, I noticed by chance – if there is such a thing as chance – my father's hat and cape hanging over the back of a chair. You see my father was also in the music-hall, as was my mother. As I was saying, I saw the hat and cape and put them on. I went to the mirror and when I saw myself I suddenly had hundreds of exciting roles before me. I've been a male impersonator ever since. It is, how shall I say, much more interesting, much more challenging to play men. There is more variety . . . more . . .

Lydia More scope. How well I understand you. I myself occasionally scribble. Oh, not professionally, like Séverine, not writings I would necessarily show. Although, of course, if Séverine did ask to see them, I might, just as a friend . . . Do you know that in order to write seriously I must dress as a man? I finally understood why: when I am dressed as a woman, like this, I find I am most concerned with the silky sound of my skirt rustling on the floor, or I spend hours watching the lace fall over my wrist, white against white. But when I dress as a man, I simply begin to think, I get ideas. I'm sure that's why Séverine is such a brilliant journalist, she always dresses as a man.

Séverine My dear Lydia, you know perfectly well I wear male clothes so I can take my girlfriends to coffee bars without having men pester us.

Verda (*nervous*) Of course I never have that sort of problem because I am always with my husband. And I love to wear women's clothes. My husband says I am the most womanly woman he has ever known.

Séverine Lydia was quite falling in love with your man about town.

Verda It's puzzling how many letters I get from women, young girls even. Sometimes they are so passionate they make me blush. One girl quite pursued me. She sent flowers to my dressing room and every time I performed I would see her, up close, staring at me. It was most disturbing. And her letters! At last, I had to invite her to my dressing room. I let my hair all the way down and wore the most feminine gown I could find. And then I gave her a good talking to. She never came back.

Séverine Have men never written you love letters?

Verda Yes, but that's different. That's normal.

Séverine Normality, the golden cage. And we poor banished species trail around, looking through the bars, wishing we were in there. But we're destined for the curiosity shops, labelled as the weird mistakes of nature, the moment of God's hesitation between Adam and Eve, anatomical convolutions, our souls inside out and alone, always alone, outside those bars. Do you love normality, Miss Miles?

Eugénie I was never considered normal. At school, my dancing master said my feet were perfect examples of the evils of anarchy. My deportment had revolutionary tendencies and the sound of my voice, I was told, was more raucous than the *Communist Manifesto*. No amount of hours spent practising in front of empty chairs taught me how to engage a young man in conversation and at last my poor parents said in despair, let her travel. I have not been unhappy, but I would have liked to be useful, or at least a philologist.

Lydia I think normality is a fashion. Here we are, five women and four of us are dressed as men. And I'm only wearing skirts because there are some German diplomats here and they're very sticky about these things. I believe the century we're entering will see a revolution greater even than the French Revolution. They defrocked the priests, we'll defrock the women.

Verda We'll lose all our strength.

Séverine Tell us about the desert, Miss Eberhardt.

Isabelle Sand.

Lydia Can't you help her, Séverine?

Séverine Do you remember the Marquis de Mores?

Lydia Spanish? Stood around looking passionate? With an American wife? He hasn't been seen in ages.

Séverine He was killed down there. His wife – you know what Americans are like – has taken it very personally. She wants the French Government to find out what happened. It seems they're showing a most unusual lack of curiosity. (*to Isabelle*) We might persuade her to send you down there to collect some information. I'd like to go myself. I smell a story which might be quite embarrassing to some people. We could travel together. I'd enjoy that.

Isabelle Do you really like women?

Séverine (*seductive*) Have you lived in the Orient and remained a prude?

Isabelle Me? Ha!

Séverine There are thousands of women in this city who would do anything to be made love to by me. But I like women with character.

Isabelle I'm not a woman. I'm Si Mahmoud. I like men. They like me. As a boy, I mean. And I have a firm rule: no Europeans up my arse.

Freeze.

Verda I really must go. My husband . . .

Isabelle Did I say something wrong?

Eugénie The nomadic turn of phrase: so childlike.

Séverine I don't like vulgarity. I'm afraid I can't help you.

Isabelle You look just like Captain Soubiel now. He wanted to 'protect me'. And there was something to protect then. (*Drinks, hopeless.*) I spent nine months working on the docks of Marseilles to pay for this trip. Loading ships.

Séverine Too bad it was a waste.

Isabelle Yeah, it was written. Too free with my tongue. Too free.

She drinks another glass and passes out.

Lydia I'll have to teach her some manners. I'm sorry.

Séverine That spirit isn't for corsets. Look at her. She's younger than I am and she probably has malaria, who knows what else. Nine months loading ships – that's the work of ex-convicts. What a story.

Lydia She's ruined everything tonight.

Séverine I'm not sure . . . No, I'll help her.

The melancholic sound of an Arab love song . . .

SCENE TWO

A *zouaia* (*monastery*) in the desert.
   Si Lachmi, *Saleh, Bou Saadi and Isabelle.*

Isabelle (*slightly out of it*) Oh, these happy, these drunken hours of return.

Bou Saadi (*to Si Lachmi*) It was written Si Mahmoud would come back to us.

Saleh He can now become one of us, a Qadria.

Isabelle I wanted to possess this country. It has possessed me.

Si Lachmi There are at least a hundred different Sufi orders, but the Qadria is one of the oldest.

Isabelle I've been in such a hurry to live.

Si Lachmi We are also the most numerous.

Saleh There are more of us than Tidjanis.

Si Lachmi You will have twenty thousand brothers.

Isabelle The senses have tormented me.

Bou Saadi The Qadrias are bound by links of affection.

Saleh And solidarity, limitless devotion.

Isabelle A certain languor in these sands.

Si Lachmi You'll be safe in our territories.

Isabelle Take off at last the grimacing, degraded mask.

Si Lachmi All our monasteries are open to you.

Isabelle This is my property: the extended horizon.

Si Lachmi Keep this chaplet, it'll protect you.

Isabelle The luxurious décor of the dunes: mine.

Si Lachmi There is no dogma. We believe only in the equality of all men and gentleness of heart. You must also show absolute obedience to your sheikh. Our founder, Abd-el-Qader was most loved for his friendship with the oppressed. He loathed hypocrisy, all lies. You must be generous and show pity to all.

Isabelle And wisdom?

Si Lachmi That comes later, Si Mahmoud. You're still young. Free yourself first from the vulgarity of the world.

Isabelle Doesn't the word Sufi come from the Greek *sophos*, wise?

Si Lachmi It comes from a Berber word that means to excel. But that isn't important. Try to be a brave and good man, that's all we ask. (*Pause.*) So you have been visiting France?

Saleh Si Mahmoud has been asked to find the murderers of a European called the Marquis de Mores.

Isabelle Oh yes, I'd forgotten. He was an explorer.

Si Lachmi The *French* have asked you to look for his murderers?

Isabelle Not exactly the French. His wife.

Si Lachmi Indeed.

Isabelle She gave me a lot of money. I should make an effort. Why would anyone want to murder an explorer?

Si Lachmi He himself was not French?

Isabelle I don't think so. Why?

Si Lachmi I am fascinated by the European tribal wars. They are more bitter than ours, but are conducted with much more subtlety. I am learning much from them.

Saleh We kill people we don't like openly, in battle.

Isabelle You think it was the French themselves who wanted to get rid of him?

Si Lachmi God alone knows the hearts of men. Do the French know with what purpose you've come back?

Isabelle I don't hide anything. I'm not a hypocrite.

Si Lachmi We don't forbid prudence, Si Mahmoud.

Saleh You're our brother now. We'll help you.

Isabelle If Allah's willing I'll find the murderers, if not –
then I suppose it's not written they should be found. Does
poverty allow the possession of a horse?

Si Lachmi We don't deny pleasure. Each follows his own
capacities.

> *During this last exchange, the* **Murderer** *comes in,
> unseen. He strikes with a sabre. Isabelle turns just in
> time to avert it and only her arm is struck. The
> Murderer is caught by Saleh and Bou Saadi.*

What's your name, you dog?

Bou Saadi That's a Muslim brother. Do you know what
you've done?

Si Lachmi What's your name?

Saleh Who ordered you to do this?

Murderer Allah.

Si Lachmi God told you to kill a brother?

Murderer That's a woman.

Si Lachmi It's no business of yours who this person is if
we accept him as our brother. You question a sheikh?

Murderer Allah ordered me to kill that person who
offends our law.

Si Lachmi What law, fool? My sisters dressed as young
men when they travelled. Who are you to judge? Who told
you to do this?

Murderer Allah.

44

Saleh Or the Tidjanis, or the French?

Si Lachmi hands the sabre to Isabelle.

Si Lachmi You may kill him.

Isabelle seizes the sabre, then stops herself.

Isabelle Why? (*gentle*) Have I offended you without knowing?

Murderer You have done nothing to me, but if I have another chance, I'll kill you.

Isabelle Strange . . . I don't hate you. No, I forgive you. But I did you no harm.

Murderer You're offending our customs.

Isabelle But that's why I left *them*. (*Throws the sabre down.*) No, you're an instrument, but why? A riddle . . . Brothers, if it was written that I must die . . . But so young, without understanding . . . no. I can't die in this silence. Don't let me die here. Don't let me disappear, without a trace. Who wants to do this to me?

SCENE THREE

The courtroom in Constantine.
  Isabelle and the Murderer. As the Murderer speaks, he changes into the **Judge***.*

Murderer/Judge 'An angel appeared to tell me the Marabout of the Qadrias, Si Lachmi, would be proceeding to El-Oued accompanied by Miss Eberhardt who called herself Si Mahmoud and wore masculine dress, thus making trouble in our religion.' This, Miss Eberhardt, is what the accused has to say in his defence. Have you anything to add?

Isabelle There is no law in the Muslim religion that says a woman may not dress as a man.

Judge There should be. It's un-Christian. Why do you wear it?

Isabelle It's practical for riding.

Judge Women have traditionally ridden in dresses.

Isabelle Side-saddle! Imagine me joining a battle riding side-saddle. I'm greatly admired for my riding.

Judge A battle, Miss Eberhardt? Have you joined many battles?

Isabelle (*modestly*) Just a small raid.

Judge Tell us about it.

Isabelle The sun was rising. It seemed covered in blood. There were about a hundred of us. And then we began the charge. Shouts, sand and dust, the gallop down –

Judge May I ask whom you were charging, Miss Eberhardt?

Isabelle I don't know. We were close together to give the charge more force, we could hardly see and the wind –

Judge Could this charge have been against the French, Miss Eberhardt?

Isabelle No. No.

Judge Didn't you just say you did not know whom you were attacking?

Isabelle It was the Tidjanis. It must have been the Tidjanis. They are our traditional enemies.

Judge Our?

Isabelle The Qadria. I am a Qadria. That is why I am sure my attacker is a Tidjani.

Judge Don't the Qadria also fight against the French? Unlike the Tidjanis.

Pause.

You have been heard to complain against the French, Miss Eberhardt.

Isabelle France could have helped this country so much, with medicine, with technical knowledge. But for some reason it has made the people here worse off than they already were. And soon the French will be so hated – (*She stops herself.*)

Judge Do go on, Miss Eberhardt.

Pause.

The Arabs will rise against us, isn't that what you were about to say? And with your help and encouragement, Miss Eberhardt?

Isabelle I am no more than a humble brother.

Judge A brother?

Isabelle I am a member of the Qadria. Please find out if my attacker is a Tidjani or paid by the Tidjanis. If the Tidjanis are allowed to get away with this, I'll no longer be safe –

Judge You would be safe in Europe, Miss Eberhardt.

Isabelle What would I do in Europe?

Judge What are you doing here, Miss Eberhardt?

Isabelle I belong here.

Judge You are a European.

Isabelle No, I am not –

Judge Were you lying when you told us you were born in Switzerland?

47

Isabelle No.

Judge You are a European, Miss Eberhardt. You are also a young woman.

Isabelle No I am not.

Judge You are not a young woman? Twenty-six is not old, Miss Eberhardt.

Isabelle I belong in the desert.

Judge You belong at home, Miss Eberhardt, in Europe. We consider ourselves responsible for your safety.

Isabelle Then find out who tried to murder me!

Judge We know it was a poor Muslim you drove to madness with your behaviour. And in order to protect you from further attacks –

Isabelle If he is punished – not too severely, please – I will be safe.

Judge We must ask you to cease your wanderings.

Isabelle I have to travel.

Judge We do not consider that safe, Miss Eberhardt.

Isabelle My friends and brothers will protect me. I wish to go further south.

Judge I'm afraid we must ask you to refrain from visiting places where your presence might cause an unpleasant incident, Miss Eberhardt.

Isabelle I'll be safe in the desert.

Judge The desert is a troubled place.

Isabelle I'll spend some months in one of the monasteries.

Judge We particularly do not want you in the monasteries.

Isabelle Where do you suggest I go?

Judge I have told you, Miss Eberhardt. Back to Europe.

Isabelle Ah. No. No.

Judge We cannot force you. But no more gallivantings in that offensive masquerade.

Pause.

Isabelle It's you.

Pause.

It's not the Tidjanis. It's you. You're afraid of me.

Judge Your activities are obscure, Miss Eberhardt to say the least, but the French government is not afraid of women.

Isabelle You've been trying to get rid of me all along. How much did you pay him?

Judge I would think twice before you make accusations against France, Miss Eberhardt.

Isabelle It's not even what I am doing, is it? It's what I am. You hate what I am. But what harm am I doing? What?

Judge May I point out, Miss Eberhardt, that a man was recently sent to prison in England for a much lesser offence than yours.

Isabelle What? He took a walk on the beach?

Judge This Mr Wilde had a perversion of inclination. You, Miss Eberhardt, have perverted nature.

Isabelle Nature defined by you, confined by you, farmed by you to make you fat.

Judge We will of course imprison your assailant.

Isabelle My friends, my brothers, where are you? Help me.

Judge But you're to stay out of the desert.

Isabelle No. Please. No.

Judge For good.

Isabelle Fenced out. Again. Always.

Séverine Fenced in, Isabelle. All of us.

SCENE FOUR

Isabelle and Séverine.

Isabelle Blocked. Detour. Blocked again. Need some absinthe. Buy me an absinthe, girl scribe.

Séverine I thought Muslims didn't drink.

Isabelle Shouldn't. Do. Have you seen how supple Arabic writing is? Not like that French print. Need some absinthe. Si Mahmoud is dying of thirst. Hang on my every word, steal my story and won't give me to drink. European!

Séverine I'm trying to keep you sober for Colonel Lyautey. It would help if you made sense.

Isabelle Make better sense with absinthe. Understand the world then: nice blurr. 'Alas my soul for youth that's gone.'

Séverine You're twenty-seven!

Isabelle Lived fast. Too many detours and had to run.

Séverine Here comes the Colonel. Try to behave yourself.

Isabelle The French: camel piss. I forgive them.

Séverine He's an exception. The Arabs like him.

Isabelle Europe has taught them ignorance.

Séverine Isabelle – it's your last chance.

  Colonel Lyautey *enters.*

Colonel. I've heard so much about you.

Lyautey And I about you, Séverine: your pen strikes more terror in the heart of the French Government than the rattle of the Arab sabre.

Isabelle His speech jingles like his medals.

Séverine Colonel, you wished to meet Isabelle Eberhardt.

Lyautey (*bows*) Si Mahmoud.

Isabelle My sister married a dandelion. I was courted by his brother, a radish, no, his cousin, an orchid, and here's a multicoloured bouquet of medals bowing before me. The grace of Allah follow your footsteps, master. (*Bows down to the ground.*) A drop of absinthe for the poet's soul, Colonel, to remember Paradise.

Séverine Colonel, you must excuse her – she's been so badly treated.

Lyautey I've wanted to meet you for some time, Si Mahmoud.

Isabelle Yeah, I'm famous. All bad. They hate me. Why?

Lyautey Bloodthirsty mercenaries defend the boundaries of convention, Si Mahmoud, and your escape was too flamboyant. You remind me of the young Arab warrior who wears bright colours so he'll be seen first by the enemy.

Isabelle Ah, you're the firing squad. Here. (*Points to her heart, spreads her arms.*) Scribe, take down the martyr's last words: Si Mahmoud, heart without guile, dies, crossed by European civilization . . .

Séverine Colonel, I'm sorry . . .

Lyautey It's all right. I like refractory spirits.

Isabelle Why do compliments in French always sound translated? I hate flowers, that's why I like the desert. Barred by the hedges now. Are you very brave, Colonel, to have picked so many medals?

Lyautey Yes, Si Mahmoud, and so, I'm told, are you.

Isabelle With me bravery is a languor of the instincts. Are you languid, Colonel?

Séverine Isabelle, stop playing.

Isabelle Why? Travelling show: examine here the monstrous folds of uncorseted nature, the pervert seed that would not flourish on European manure. Complete with witty and scientific commentary by our own Sevvy the Scribe, straight from Paris . . .

Séverine It's hopeless, we had better go.

Lyautey Wait. Si Mahmoud, I don't like hedges either. I come from Provence: it's dry there and barren. And you can still hear in the walls the echoes of chivalry and nobility, what you have here, what we're destroying.

Isabelle I believed in French civilization once. Is it the climate that makes it rot?

Lyautey The wrong ones came. You used to travel with the Qadrias.

Séverine Isabelle can go places where no other European would be safe.

Lyautey Do you want to travel again?

Isabelle When I came out of hospital after my wound, the dunes had shrivelled. I wondered if they'd been empty all the time.

Séverine You were ill. You know you want to travel.

Isabelle 'Anywhere, anywhere as long as it's out of this world.' Let the little cloud of oriental perfume that was my soul vanish. No trace.

Lyautey They say, Si Mahmoud, you're a young man in search of knowledge.

Isabelle Was.

Séverine She's accepted by all the marabouts. It's only the French who prevent her from returning.

Lyautey My predecessors have a lot to answer for. (*to Isabelle*) The Zianya sect is known for its pious and disinterested leaders. The Qadria have great respect for the Zianya.

Isabelle How do you know all this?

Lyautey You forget, I love this country.

Isabelle 'The tongue is a man's one half.'

Lyautey 'The other the heart within.' And who can judge the heart? Have you heard of the Zianya leader, Sidi Brahim?

Isabelle Even our marabouts look up to him.

Lyautey Would you like to visit his school?

Isabelle Can't. It's in Morocco.

Lyautey I can get you in.

Isabelle Is it written that Si Mahmoud shall speak to Sidi Brahim, that wisdom might be gained at last?

Lyautey What will you need?

Isabelle A good horse.

Lyautey When can you leave?

Isabelle Tomorrow.

Séverine Morocco. She'll never come back, Colonel.

Lyautey You can only stay five months this first time, Si Mahmoud. Please tell Sidi Brahim the French will help him if he wishes to extricate himself from his enemies.

Séverine I see. The conquest of Morocco.

Lyautey Not this time, I hope. But Si Mahmoud will tell you that country is devastated by marauding tribes.

Isabelle Too much bloodshed, yes.

Lyautey We would help, no more.

Séverine Shall we call it then the digestion of Morocco?

Lyautey I'll expect you in Ain-Sefra in five months, Si Mahmoud, and then we'll have long chats about this country. How did my predecessors not appreciate you?

Isabelle From the point of view of bread and Swiss cheese, the love of the desert is an unhealthy appetite.

Lyautey What idiots not to have understood you. Poor Si Mahmoud.

Isabelle Poor Si Mahmoud.

Séverine She loves pity, Colonel.

Isabelle We Slavs are like that. We love the knout and then we love being pitied for having suffered the knout. And you, chronicler, must make no judgements. We souls of the desert (*Hiccups.*) love the knout.

Lyautey Five months then. Your word of honour. I'll find a way of thanking you, Séverine.

Séverine It may be too late, Colonel, you should have found her before.

Lyautey They should have found me before. It may be too late for me too. Territories exploding, violence sowed and reaped, so unnecessary. Only you, Séverine, it's not too late for you.

Isabelle It's never too late for the chroniclers.

Séverine But that's not what you meant, Colonel, is it?

Lyautey No.

SCENE FIVE

Ain-Sefra. Same as the first scene, a few hours later. Isabelle and Séverine.

Isabelle Very strict at the monastery. Walk towards the gate and a shadow bars your path. But Sidi Brahim let me pace. He understood Si Mahmoud had been locked in too often. His son lived in another quarter. There were many young men of great beauty in those rooms, and we don't hate love. But I couldn't join. They would know I was not completely a man, and also, much of that was gone. Slowly, slowly, the torment of the senses opens to the modulation of the dunes. Only a ripple here and there betrays the passage of the storm. Sidi Brahim wanted me to go further south and describe the country to the Colonel.

Séverine Why didn't you?

Isabelle Promised I'd come here.

Séverine You had more than a month left.

Isabelle If a man be old and a fool . . . suddenly, suddenly Si Mahmoud felt a shiver of fear. Suddenly my destiny: forgot the script. So I thought I'll come back, word of honour, and Si Mahmoud is important now, not broken.

Séverine Shouldn't you get some rest? You must be coherent if you're seeing the Colonel later.

Isabelle Always coherent. It's the letters that get scrambled.

Séverine I must go in. I feel faint.

Isabelle Hard work chronicling. Keep you up all night unravelling the Mektoub. Rest. Will you write my story? Practical guide for girls with unhealthy desires. With diagrams for the Europeans, the Cartesians. They couldn't fence in my tongue. Poor Sevvy, sweet scribe of uncartesian appetites, rebuild your dream.

Séverine Will you find your way?

Isabelle Stay outside, head against stone and the soul more pure. If a man be old . . . but a young man may yet cast off his foolishness. I'm not wise, I'm not wise. (*Feels something, sticks out her hand.*) Rain? It doesn't rain in the desert. Mirage. No, rain, that's nice. Sleep in the rain. What's that noise?

Séverine Thunder probably. There have been storms in the mountain. Don't wander off.

Isabelle Make my report to the Colonel, then wander off. Tell them Si Mahmoud . . .

But Séverine has left.

The rain. Get clean that way, wash the traces and the letters. Fresh sand, new letters.

She lies down.

SCENE SIX

Ain-Sefra.
Séverine, Colonel Lyautey and the Judge.

Séverine Drowned!

Lyautey We came too late.

Séverine Drowned in Ain-Sefra.

Judge In the middle of the desert? That's no place to drown.

Séverine A flash flood. The whole native quarter washed away.

Lyautey My men rushed down. We couldn't find her.

Judge It's said she didn't even try to save herself.

Séverine Our rebel warrior, Colonel.

Judge Close the file. This person must be officially forgotten.

Lyautey We found some journals. Would you like to see them, Séverine.

Séverine With pleasure.

They walk off, arm in arm.
Lights fade to blackout.

THE GRACE OF MARY TRAVERSE

For John

If you are squeamish
Don't prod the beach rubble

Sappho
Translated from the Greek by Mary Barnard

It may well be that it is a mere fatuity, an indecency to
debate of the definition of culture in the age of the gas-
oven, of the arctic camps, of napalm. The topic may
belong solely to the past history of hope. But we should
not take this contingency to be a natural fact of life, a
platitude. We must keep in focus its hideous novelty or
renovation . . . The numb prodigality of our acquaintance
with horror is a radical human defeat.

George Steiner, *In Bluebeard's Castle*

Characters

Mary Traverse
Giles Traverse
Mrs Temptwell
Lord Gordon
Old Woman (1)
Sophie
Mr Manners
Boy
Mr Hardlong
Lord Exrake
Robert
Old Woman (2)
Old Woman (3)
Jack
Guard
Spy
Locksmith
Man

The Grace of Mary Traverse was first produced at the Royal Court Theatre on 17 October 1985 with the following cast:

Mary Traverse Janet McTeer
Giles Traverse Harold Innocent
Mrs Temptwell Pam Ferris
Lord Gordon Tom Chadbon
Old Woman Jonathan Phillips
Sophie Eve Matheson
Mr Manners James Smith
Boy Jonathan Phillips
Mr Hardlong David Beames
Lord Exrake Harold Innocent
Robert Jonathan Phillips
Old Woman Pam Ferris
Old Woman Eve Matheson
Jack David Beames
Guard Jonathan Phillips
Spy James Smith
Locksmith Tom Chadbon
Man Tom Chadbon

Directed by Danny Boyle
Designed by Kandis Cook
Lighting by Christopher Toulmin

Note

Although the play is set in the eighteenth century, it is not a historical play. All the characters are my own invention and whenever I have used historical events such as the Gordon Riots I have taken great freedom with reported fact. I found the eighteenth century a valid metaphor, and I was concerned to free the people of the play from contemporary preconceptions.

The game of piquet in Act Two, scene four, was devised with the help of David Parlett.

T.W.

Act One

SCENE ONE

The drawing room of a house in the City of London during the late eighteenth century. **Mary Traverse** *sits elegantly, facing an empty chair. She talks to the chair with animation.* **Giles Traverse** *stands behind and away from her.*

Mary Traverse Nature, my lord. (*Pause.*) It was here all the time and we've only just discovered it. What is nature? No, that's a direct question. Perhaps we will not exhaust nature as easily as we have other pleasures for it is difficult to imagine with what to replace it. And there's so much of it! No, that's too enthusiastic. (*Short pause.*) How admirable of you to have shown us the way, my lord, to have made the grand tour of such a natural place as Wales. Ah, crags, precipices, what awe they must strike in one's breas – in one's spirit. Yes. And I hear Wales even has peasants. How you must have admired the austerity of their lives, their human nature a complement to the land's starkness. Peasants too I believe are a new discovery. How delightful of our civilization to shed light on its own dark and savage recesses. Oh dear, is that blue-stockinged or merely incomprehensible? When you said the other day that he who is tired of London is tired of life, did you mean – but how foolish of me. It was Doctor Johnson. Forgive the confusion, you see there are so few men of wit about. (*Pause.*) You were telling me how we are to know nature. Do we dare look at it directly, or do we trust an artist's imitation, a poet, the paintings of Mr Gainsborough. Whirlpools. Trees. Primordial matter. Circling. Indeed. Oh.

Mary stops in a panic. Giles Traverse clears his throat.
Mary talks faster.

You visited the salt mines? Ah, to hover over the depths in a basket and then to plunge deep down into the earth, into its very bowels.

Giles Traverse No, no, my dear, do not mention bowels. Especially after dinner.

Mary To have no more than a fragile rope between oneself and utter destruction. How thrilling!

Giles No, Mary. It shakes your frame with terror and you begin to faint.

Mary I wouldn't faint, Papa. I'd love to visit a salt mine.

Giles You are here not to express your desires but to make conversation.

Mary Can desire not be part of a conversation?

Giles No. To be agreeable, a young woman must make the other person say interesting things.

Mary He hasn't said a word.

Giles Ah, but he won't know that. Now faint, and even the most tongue-tied fop will ask how you are. That allows you to catch your breath and begin again.

Mary How clever of you, Papa. And the rivers . . .

Giles There's too much of this nature in your conversation.

Mary It is what people are thinking about.

Giles Sounds foreign. I shall bring it up at the next meeting of the Antigallican Society.

Mary Oh Papa, I could come and explain –

Giles You? Now move on to another subject. This is difficult: leave no gap, you must glide into it. Converse, Mary, converse.

Mary I can't think what follows naturally from nature. Ah: I hear God . . . no . . . I believe God –

Giles Talk of God leads to silence, Mary.

Mary The architecture of –

Giles Too athletic. People might think you spend time out of doors.

Mary Reason, they say . . . is that too Popish?

Giles No, but a woman talking about reason is like a merchant talking about the nobility. It smacks of ambition. I overheard that in a coffee house. Good, isn't it?

Mary But Papa, you're always talking about lords and you're a merchant.

Giles I am not. Not exactly. Who told you this?

Mary I look out of the window and see coaches with your name.

Giles Why gape out of the window when I've given you so much to see in the house? I have land. There are potteries on it, but that's acceptable. Lord Folly has mines on his. And it's not refined to look too closely at the source of one's wealth. Now, you have a Methodist preacher here and a rake there. Keep them from the weather.

Mary Books? Preachers don't read. Music? That's for afternoon tea with the ladies. Drink? No . . .

Giles It's obvious. Praise England: patriotism . . .

Mary But Papa, you won't let me study politics. And I'd so like to.

Giles Patriotism is to politics what the fart is to the digestion. Euh, you're not to repeat that, although it was said by a very grand lady. A duchess. Say something against the Americans and fop, fool, rattle, mathematician and gambler will easily add to it.

Mary Are we at war with them yet? Have you made another brilliant speech?

Giles Yes. I demonstrated logically that God gave us the colonies for the sole purpose of advantageous trade. We are interested in their raw materials but not in their ideas. Ambitious upstarts! We'll finish now, I'm going to the theatre.

Mary Let me come with you, Papa, it will help my conversation.

Giles There's no need to see a play to talk about it. I'll bring you the playbill. We'll continue tomorrow with repartee and do a little better, I hope.

Mary Wouldn't I do better if I saw a little more of the world?

Giles I'm afraid that's not possible. Don't be sad. You have tried today and I'll reward you with a kiss.

Mary Thank you, Papa.

Giles You are my brightest adornment, my dear. I want to be proud of my daughter.

Mary Yes, Papa.

Giles You are my joy and my hope.

Mary But Papa –

Giles A compliment must be received in silence, Mary. The French always protest at compliments, but that's because they're so tediously argumentative. Goodbye.

Mary Goodbye, Papa.

SCENE TWO

The drawing room. Mary, alone, walks back and forth across the carpet. She stops occasionally and examines the area on which she has just stepped.

Mary Almost.

She walks. Stops and examines.

Yes. Better.

She walks again. Looks.

Ah. There.

She walks faster now, then examines.

I've done it. See the invisible passage of an amiable woman.

Pause.

It was the dolls who gave me my first lesson. No well-made doll, silk-limbed, satin-clothed, leaves an imprint. As a child I lay still and believed their weightlessness mine. Awkward later to discover I grew, weighed. Best not to move very much. But nature was implacable. More flesh, more weight. Embarrassment all around. So the teachers came. Air, they said. Air? Air. I waited, a curious child, delighted by the prospect of knowledge. Air. You must become like air. Weightless. Still. Invisible. Learn to drop a fan and wait. When that is perfected, you may move, slightly, from the waist only. Later, dare to walk, but leave no trace. Now my presence will be as pleasing as my step, leaving no memory. I am complete: unruffled landscape. I may sometimes be a little bored, but my manners are excellent. And if I think too much, my feet no longer betray this.

She walks.

What comes after, what is even more graceful than air?

She tries to tiptoe, then stamps the ground and throws down her fan.

Damn!

She stands still and holds her breath.

Mrs Temptwell!

Mrs Temptwell *comes on immediately. Short silence.*

My fan.

Mrs Temptwell It's broken.

Mary I dropped it.

Mrs Temptwell A bad fall, Miss Mary.

Mary Pick it up, please.

Mrs Temptwell does so, with bad grace.

Mrs Temptwell I have work to do.

Mary Bring me some hot milk.

Mrs Temptwell I'll call the chambermaid.

Mary Watch me, Mrs Temptwell. Do I look ethereal?

Mrs Temptwell You do look a little ill, Miss Mary, yes.

Mary You don't understand anything. I'm trying not to breathe.

Mrs Temptwell Your mother was good at that.

Mary Was she?

Mrs Temptwell Said it thickened the waist. She died of not breathing in the end, poor thing, may she rest in peace, I'm sure she does, she always did.

Mary Could she walk on a carpet and leave no imprint?

Mrs Temptwell She went in and out of rooms with no one knowing she'd been there. She was so quiet, your mother, it took the master a week to notice she was dead. But she looked ever so beautiful in her coffin and he couldn't stop looking at her. Death suits women. You'd look lovely in a coffin, Miss Mary.

Mary I don't need a coffin to look lovely, Mrs Temptwell.

Mrs Temptwell No, some women don't even have to die, they look dead already, but that doesn't work as well. It's better to be dead and look as if you'd been alive than the other way, if you get my meaning, as if you'd been dead all the time, quiet and dull.

Mary I don't look like that.

Mrs Temptwell Only when you've been reading.

Mary Oh. Some books are dull. *The Young Ladies' Conduct. Caesar's Wars.*

Mrs Temptwell It's a strange thing about books, they make the face go funny. I had an uncle who took to books. He went all grey. Then he went mad. May I go now?

Mary Your uncle doesn't count. Books improve the mind. Am I not charming and witty?

Silence.

That girl in number fourteen, the one you keep telling me about, she must read.

Mrs Temptwell Oh no, she's too busy sitting at her window, staring at everything.

Mary Gaping? She must have nothing to look at in her own house, poor thing.

Mrs Temptwell She even asked one of the servants to take her out on the street.

Mary Outside? On foot? She did? Oh. But her reputation?

Mrs Temptwell Disguised. No one will know. I wish you could see her, Miss Mary, she . . .

Mary What?

Mrs Temptwell Glitters with interest.

Mary Glitters? How vulgar. Where's my milk?

Mrs Temptwell Your mother wanted to go out once in her life, but she died before we could manage it. I felt sorry she missed that one little pleasure.

Mary Papa wouldn't have been pleased.

Mrs Temptwell The master doesn't see everything. I'll fetch your milk now.

Mary What's so different out there? When I ride in my carriage I see nothing of interest.

Mrs Temptwell That's because the streets have to be emptied to make way for your carriage. It's different on foot. Very different. Would you prefer a glass of ratafia?

Mary Wait.

Mrs Temptwell I haven't got all day.

Mary What harm could once do? It'll only improve my conversation and Papa will admire me. Yes, Mrs Temptwell, you'll take me.

Mrs Temptwell Take you where, Miss Mary?

Mary You know very well. You'll take me out there. Yes. Into the streets. I'll glitter with knowledge.

Mrs Temptwell I can't do that, I'll lose my place.

Mary We'll go disguised, as you suggested.

Mrs Temptwell I didn't, Miss Mary, I never did.

Mary I've decided, Mrs Temptwell, we're going out.

Mrs Temptwell What have I done?

Mary I'll pay you.

Mrs Temptwell You always make me talk too much.

SCENE THREE

Cheapside, London. **Lord Gordon** *comes on.*

Lord Gordon My name is George Gordon. Lord Gordon. (*Pause.*) Nothing. No reaction. No one's interested. (*Pause.*) It's always like this. I greet people, their eyes glaze. I ride in Hyde Park, my horse falls asleep. (*Pause.*) I am a man of stunning mediocrity. (*Pause.*) This can't go on. I must do something. Now. But what? How does Mr Manners make everyone turn around? Of course: politics. I'll make a speech in the House: all criminals must be severely punished. But stealing a handkerchief is already a hanging matter. I know: make England thrifty, enclose the common land. I think that's been done. Starve the poor to death! Perhaps politics is too ambitious. I'll write. Even women do that now. But about what? No, I'll be a wit. I'll make everyone laugh at what I say. But I'll have to think of something funny. Sir John's a rake, that's a possibility. But the ladies are so demanding and my manhood won't rise above middling. Shall I die in a duel? No. This is desperate. Perhaps I'm seen with the wrong people. They're all so brilliant. In a different world, I might shine. Here are some ordinary people. They must notice me, if only because I'm a lord. Oh God, please make me noticed, just once. Please show me the way.

Lord Gordon adopts an interesting pose. An **Old Woman** *walks on, very slowly.*

Hm.

She looks at him and continues walking. **Sophie** *comes on.*

Sophie Please –

The Old Woman turns around.

No you're not . . . I'm sorry. I'm looking for someone called Polly.

Pause.

My aunt . . . I'm to find her here. This is Cheapside?

The Old Woman nods.

She has her pitch here. I've come to work for her. You don't know where she is?

The Old Woman shakes her head.

I'm not sure what she looks like. I haven't seen her for such a long time. (*Pause.*) Where could she be?

The Old Woman shrugs.

I don't know anyone.

The Old Woman walks away.

What am I going to do?

The Old Woman moves off.

London's so big.

Lord Gordon Hhm.

Sophie looks briefly at him.

Sophie I must find Aunt Polly.

Sophie goes off. Mary and Mrs Temptwell come on.

Mary I believe I've just stepped on something unpleasant, Mrs Temptwell. These streets are filthy.

Mrs Temptwell The dirt runs out of great houses like yours.

Mary What? I don't like this world. It's nasty.

Mrs Temptwell If you're squeamish, don't stir the beach rubble.

Mary What did you say?

Mrs Temptwell It's a saying we had in our family.

Mary Did you have a family? I can't imagine you anywhere but in our house.

Mrs Temptwell Lack of imagination has always been a convenience of the rich.

Lord Gordon Hhmm.

Mary What? I do wish these people weren't so ugly.

The Old Woman comes on.

Mrs Temptwell Their life is hard.

Mary They ought to go back to the country and be beautiful peasants.

Mrs Temptwell They've already been thrown off the land. Some of them were farmers.

Mary Papa says farmers stop progress. I meant beautiful peasants I could talk about with grace. There's nothing here to improve my conversation.

Mrs Temptwell It takes time to turn misery into an object of fun.

Lord Gordon (*louder*) Hhmmm.

Mary Why does that man keep clearing his throat?

Mrs Temptwell I don't know. He doesn't look mad.

Mary I want to go back.

Mrs Temptwell So soon, Miss Mary? Such a dull appetite?

Mary I might be curious about the plague and not care to embrace the dead bodies. This ugliness looks contagious. I'm going.

Lord Gordon No. This is intolerable. You can't go without noticing me. My name is George Gordon. Lord Gordon.

Mary Let's go.

Lord Gordon How dare someone like you ignore me. You!

Mary Mrs Temptwell, I'm frightened.

Lord Gordon I don't want you to be frightened. Wait. Yes. Are you very frightened?

Mary No, not very.

Lord Gordon How dare you!

He takes out his sword.

Now. Now you're very frightened, I can see it. Why didn't I think of this before?

Mary I want to go home.

Lord Gordon Not yet. I'll make you frightened. Yes. I'll show you my strength. Come over here to the lamp-post.

Mary Help! Mrs Temptwell!

Mrs Temptwell This is the world.

Sophie comes on.

Sophie Please –

Mrs Temptwell Damn!

Sophie Oh. I'm sorry . . . Have you by any chance seen my aunt? Her name's Polly . . . what's there?

Mrs Temptwell Nothing for you, girl. Go away. Quickly.

Sophie But he's –

Mrs Temptwell So what? It could be you.

Sophie goes towards Lord Gordon and Mary.

Sophie Leave her alone, Sir. What are you doing?

Lord Gordon Everyone pays me attention now. Who are you? I'll have you too.

Sophie No, Sir, please, Sir. Please –

Lord Gordon grabs Sophie. Mary gets away.

Lord Gordon Beg. Yes. Beg for mercy. Beg.

Sophie Please have mercy, Sir.

Lord Gordon What delight! Say over and over again Lord Gordon have mercy on me. Say it.

Sophie Lord Gordon have mercy on me.

Lord Gordon Again, again. On your knees and keep saying my name.

Sophie Lord Gordon have mercy on me. Lord Gordon. Lord Gordon.

Lord Gordon My strength rises. I can't contain myself. Over here.

Mary Call for help, Mrs Temptwell.

Mrs Temptwell Why?

Mary What will he do to her?

Mrs Temptwell Rape her. But she won't mind. Virtue, like ancestors, is a luxury of the rich. Watch and you'll learn something.

Mary Rape? What the Greek gods did? Will he turn himself into a swan, a bull, a shower of golden rain? Is he a god?

Mrs Temptwell He'll feel like one.

Mary He stands her against the lamp-post, sword gleaming at her neck, she's quiet. Now the sword lifts up her skirts, no words between them, the sword is his voice and his will. He thrusts himself against her, sword in the air. He goes on and on. She has no expression on her face. he shudders. She's still. He turns away from her, tucks the sword away. I couldn't stop looking. (*Pause.*) It's not like the books.

    Mr Manners *comes on.*

Sir, be careful, there's someone –

Mr Manners Go away, I only give money to organized charities. Lord Gordon. I was looking for you.

Lord Gordon Mr Manners. I was just thinking of you.

Mr Manners Have I disturbed you?

Lord Gordon Not at all. I'm finished.

Mr Manners Who are these women?

Lord Gordon Just women. What shall we do tonight? I feel exceptionally lively.

Mr Manners We might play a game of piquet.

Lord Gordon Yes. I'll win. My fortune has turned.

Mr Manners Delighted. Shall we have supper before?

Lord Gordon I've never felt so hungry. Let's eat at a chop house.

Mr Manners There's something on at the Opera.

Lord Gordon But first, let's go to a coffee house. I have some witticisms.

Mr Manners You, Lord Gordon?

Lord Gordon Mr Manners, I'm a different man.

Mr Manners What's happened? A legacy?

Lord Gordon (*quietly*) Power.

Mr Manners Ah. Power.

Lord Gordon Isn't power something you know all about?

Mr Manners Yes, but is it not something I ever discuss.

They go. Sophie comes down towards Mary walking with pain. They look at each other. Then Sophie moves off.

Mary (*looking at the ground*) Blood.

SCENE FOUR

Outside the Universal Coffee House in Fleet Street. **Boy,** *an eighteenth-century waiter, blocks Mary and Mrs Temptwell.*

Boy You can't.

Mary They've just gone in.

Boy You can't come in.

Mary We're following them.

Boy Ladies wait outside.

Mrs Temptwell Ask him why.

Boy They don't like to be disturbed.

Mary I know how to talk.

Boy They don't like ladies' talk.

Mary What sex is wit?

Mrs Temptwell Ask him who's in there.

Boy Mr Fielding, Mr Goldsmith, Mr Hume, Mr Boswell, Mr Garrick, the Doctor, Mr Sheridan, Mr Hogarth.

Mary But I know them all very well. I've often imagined talking to them. Let me in immediately.

Boy And some foreigners. Mr Piranesis, Mr Tyepolo, Mr Hayden, Mr Voltaire, Mr Leibniz, Mr Wolfgang. They're quiet, the foreigners, and no one listens to them. You have to stay out. Orders.

Mrs Temptwell Ask him why they let him in.

Boy I'm the boy. I go everywhere.

Mary I don't understand.

Boy I'll let you see through the window.

Mary I've spent my life looking through window panes. I want to face them.

Boy Wouldn't be right.

Mrs Temptwell Doesn't right belong to those who take it?

Boy I don't ask questions.

Mrs Temptwell Don't you wish you could be like him?

Mary Yes. No. Envy is a sin, Mrs Temptwell.

Mrs Temptwell And heaven must be a lady's tea party: the jingling of beatific stupidity.

Mary What's happened to me? I was happy in my rooms.

Mrs Temptwell Think of what you've seen.

Mary I've seen them walk the streets without fear, stuff food into their mouths with no concern for their waists. I've seen them tear into skin without hesitation and litter the streets with their discarded actions. But I have no map to this world. I walk it as a foreigner and sense only danger.

Boy I never stay anywhere long. There's too much to do.

Mary Be quiet!

Boy It's a waste of time being kind to women.

Mary I'm going to hate you. No, that's an ugly feeling.

Mrs Temptwell Why waste your time hating him, Mary? You could be like him if you wanted to. But there's a price.

Boy Her soul.

Mrs Temptwell We're not so medieval, boy. We're Protestants and the century's enlightened. (*to Mary*) Do you want to travel in their world? Around every corner, the glitter of a possibility. You'll no longer be an ornate platter served for their tasting. No, you'll feast with them. No part of flesh or mind unexplored. No horizon ever fixed.
    Experience! (*Pause.*) I could manage it for you.

Boy We're not deceived when they dress as men. A lady came to us masqueraded. We uncovered her. All of her.

Mrs Temptwell Do I sound so superficial? Well, Mary?

Mary Run the world through my fingers as they do?

Pause.

Oh yes, I want it. Yes. What's the price?

Mrs Temptwell You'll stay with me.

Mary Yes, but the price?

Mrs Temptwell You can never go back. (*Pause.*) Have they ever asked to live like us?

Mary No, they're too busy. But I want the world as it is, Mrs Temptwell, no imitations, no illusions, I want to know it all.

Mrs Temptwell You'll know all you want to know.

Boy Will you sign a contract?

Mrs Temptwell It's done. You can go back inside, boy.

Boy It's more interesting out here this evening. May I stay?

Mrs Temptwell See now, Mary, who's outside.

Mary Yes. Yes. How will I pay you, Mrs Temptwell?

Mrs Temptwell Don't worry. You'll pay.

Act Two

The Brothers Club. Giles Traverse, Mr Manners.

Mr Manners Three days?

Giles Three.

Mr Manners And the letter?

Giles Only that dear Papa would understand, she'd gone to investigate the very underside of nature. I thought she meant Vauxhall Gardens. I don't approve of course, but Lord Oldland told me his daughter often went to Vauxhall, masked, and never came to any harm.

Mr Manners Have you told anyone?

Giles No. I went to Bow Street.

Mr Manners My dear Giles, you might as well have gone straight to the papers.

Giles It is my daughter, Manners. She could have been kidnapped.

Mr Manners This isn't France. You said she left with a servant. An elopement?

Giles No. Manners, you must know someone who can investigate, discreetly.

Mr Manners No one in politics can afford the cost of a secret, Giles, not even you. No. There's nothing you can do. Forget her.

Giles Forget my daughter!

Mr Manners Do you think most of the men in this club know where their children are? Or who they are, for that matter?

Giles I have only one daughter.

Mr Manners You have only one country. The King, Giles, wants new men in the Cabinet. Men of intelligence and ambition, who show strength of character. There has been mention of you. But should there be a scandal . . .

Giles The Cabinet. Now?

Mr Manners These are difficult times. I had the impression you had a strong sense of duty. Perhaps I was wrong . . .

Giles After all these years. Why now?

Mr Manners You of all people should know: supply and demand. People have become suspicious of the old families. But the old families do know how to conduct themselves . . .

Lord Gordon comes in.

Lord Gordon Giles. Just the man I was looking for.

Giles My lord.

Lord Gordon I have made a momentous decision. Yes. I've decided to get married. It's what I need: a wife to look up to me. I have decided to marry your daughter.

Giles You've seen her!

Lord Gordon How could I? You've never presented her. I don't want to marry a woman I know. You've said your daughter is pretty and clever. She's not too clever, is she? She won't talk at breakfast? I couldn't bear that.

Silence.

She hasn't married someone else, has she? I'll kill him in a duel. I wouldn't mind marrying a widow: less to explain.

Mr Manners Giles's daughter died yesterday, of a bad chill.

Giles Mr Manners!

Mr Manners I know how painful it is for you, Giles. We won't mention her again.

Lord Gordon How inconvenient. I'll have to think of something else. You don't have any other daughters, do you?

Giles No. Mr Manners, I –

Mr Manners At least she went quietly, Giles, we must be thankful for that. I'll speak to the King, he may find a way to ease your grief. Kings have such curative powers.

Lord Gordon I think I'll be broken-hearted over your daughter's death, Giles, it'll make me interesting.

SCENE TWO

The study of Giles Traverse. He is in some disarray. Mrs Temptwell is dressed for the street.

Giles Where is she?

Mrs Temptwell Don't you know? You buried her.

Giles Who are you?

Mrs Temptwell I've been in your house for twenty-five years, Sir.

Giles I know that, Mrs Temptwell. Why have you done this?

Mrs Temptwell Done what, Sir? I've always done what

Mary asked. She used to want cups of tea,. Now she wants other things.

Giles I'll have you thrown in prison.

Mrs Temptwell For what? Killing her? I might have to tell people she's still alive. Think of the questions . . .

Giles I trusted you with the care of my daughter. Was Mary not kind to you?

Mrs Temptwell As she might be to the chair she sat on. She cared for my use.

Giles What more can a servant expect?

Mrs Temptwell Do you remember my father? He was a farmer when you were a farmer. His land was next to yours.

Giles I must have bought it.

Mrs Temptwell He trusted you to leave him his cottage. When you landscaped your garden, you needed a lake. The cottage was drowned in the lake.

Giles I gave those people work.

Mrs Temptwell He went to one of your potteries. He died.

Giles And it's because of your father's misfortune that you've killed my daughter?

Mrs Temptwell Your daughter's only dead for you. That's your misfortune.

Giles Please tell me where she is.

Mrs Temptwell She's not ready to see you. She hasn't yet learned to be a ghost.

Giles I'll give you anything you want.

Mrs Temptwell You've already done that.

Giles I don't understand.

Mrs Temptwell It's simple, Giles Traverse. When a man cries, he could be anybody.

SCENE THREE

Lodgings in Marylebone. Mrs Temptwell stands in the background and watches. Mary is fully dressed. **Mr Hardlong** *is naked. They remain far apart.*

Mr Hardlong You ask for pleasure. Why do you cringe as if expecting violence.

Short silence.

If you believe violence will bring you pleasure, you've been misled. The enjoyment of perversion is not a physical act but a metaphysical one. You want pleasure: come and take it.

Silence. Mary does not move.

Are you pretending you've never felt desire unfurl in your blood? Never known the gnawing of flesh, that gaping hunger of the body? Never sensed the warm dribble of your longings? Come, come, need isn't dainty and it's no good calling cowardice virginity.

Mary squirms a little.

Perhaps you want me to seduce you and let you remain irresponsible? I promised you physical pleasure, not the tickle of self-reproach and repentance, the squirm of the soul touching itself in intimate parts. Or are you waiting for a declaration of love? Let romance blunt the sting of your need, mask a selfish act with selfless acquiescence? Novels, my dear, novels. And in the end, your body remains dry. What are you waiting for? Pleasure requires activity. Come.

Mary moves a little closer and closes her eyes.

Ah, yes. Close the eyes, let the act remain dark. Cling to your ignorance, the mind's last chastity. A man's body is beautiful, Mary, and ought to be known. I'll even give you some advice, for free: never take a man you don't find beautiful. If you have to close your eyes when he comes near you, turn away, walk out of the room and never look back. You may like his words, his promises, his wit, his soul, but wrapping your legs around a man's talent will bring no fulfilment. No, open your eyes. Look at me.

Mary looks, unfocused.

The neck is beautiful, Mary, but doesn't require endless study. Look down. The arms have their appeal and the hands hold promise. The chest can be charming, the ribs melancholic. Look down still. They call these the loins, artists draw their vulnerability, but you're not painting a martyrdom. Look now.

Mary focuses on his penis.

See how delicate the skin, how sweetly it blushes at your look. It will start at your touch, obey your least guidance. Its one purpose is to serve you and you'd make it an object of fear? Look, Mary, shaped for your delight, intricacies for your play, here is the wand of your pleasure, nature's generous magic. I'm here for you. Act now. You have hands, use them. Take what you want, Mary. Take it.

Mary stretches out her hand.

Mary At first, power. I am the flesh's alchemist. Texture hardens at my touch, subterranean rivers follow my fingers. I pull back the topsoil, skim the nakedness of matter. All grows in my hand.

Now to my needs. Ouch! No one warned me about the pain, not so pleasant that. Scratch the buttocks in retaliation, convenient handles and at my mercy. And now to the new world. Ah, but this is much better than climbing mountains in Wales. I plunge to the peaks again and again with the slightest adjustment. One, two, three, change of angle, change of feel. This is delightful and I'm hardly breathless. Again. Not Welsh this, the Alps at least: exploding sunshine, waterfalls, why is this geography not in the books? On to the rolling waves of the Bay of Biscay, I would go for ever, why have you stopped, Mr Hardlong, have you crashed on the Cape? You don't answer, Mr Hardlong, you're pale and short of breath. I am the owner of this mine and there are seams still untouched. You mustn't withdraw your labour. You seem a little dead, Mr Hardlong. I want more.

Mrs Temptwell We'll have to find you someone else, Mary.

Mary I like this one. I love you, Mr Hardlong, yes I do, I thought I loved my father, but that was cold. This is hot. Don't turn away, Mr Hardlong, please don't die.

Mrs Temptwell Don't be sentimental, labour's expendable.

Mary He's reviving! Oh joy!

Mr Hardlong Where's my gold?

Mary Here, Mr Hardlong, take it. And bring some food to revive us, Mrs Temptwell. A duck, some good roast beef, and a pudding of bread and butter, very sweet. You'll eat with me, Mr Hardlong.

Mr Hardlong I don't have time. Where is she?

Mary Who?

Mr Hardlong You promised she'd be here, Mrs Temptwell.

Mrs Temptwell I haven't forgotten. (*She calls.*) Sophie!

Sophie comes on, bringing food. Mary pounces on it.

Mary (*eating*) I've seen her before. I remember now: Lord Gordon. I was sorry.

Mrs Temptwell (*touching Sophie's stomach*) Observe how mediocrity loves to duplicate itself. Take the rest of your payment, Mr Hardlong.

Mr Hardlong (*to Sophie*) Come with me.

Sophie Mrs Temptwell, you didn't tell me –

Mrs Temptwell Do you want to starve on the streets?

Mr Hardlong Don't be afraid, I won't hurt you.

Sophie You said I was to work for a lady.

Mrs Temptwell So you are. Mr Hardlong's price was high. You're saving Mary half her gold. That's what servants are for.

Mr Hardlong Come quickly.

Mary Mr Hardlong.

Mr Hardlong Look. I have gold.

Mary Mr Hardlong, please.

Mr Hardlong What is it, Mary? You see I'm in a hurry.

Mary At least answer one question. I paid you a good sum for what we did.

Mr Hardlong Fifty guineas.

Mary You'll give it to Sophie.

Mr Hardlong All of it.

Mary For the same thing we did?

Mr Hardlong The same.

Mary I pay you. You pay her. I don't understand.

Mr Hardlong I gave you pleasure, Mary.

Mary Yes. You did. Yes.

Mr Hardlong Did you offer me any?

Mary I confess I forgot a little about you. But weren't we doing the same thing?

Mr Hardlong I had to look after your well-being.

Mary You mean we were at the same table but I let you beg while I feasted? I see. But Sophie?

Mr Hardlong Will serve my luxury.

Mary I would do that too. Mr Hardlong. I would advocate the community of pleasure. Teach me what to do and I will.

Mr Hardlong It's too late, Mary: you would have to learn to ask for nothing.

Mr Hardlong and Sophie go. Mary eats pensively, but nonetheless grossly.

Mary Which do I like best? The first taste on the palate or the roast skin crinkling on the tongue? I like to swallow too. I'm still hungry.

She stops.

It's not real hunger, it's a void in the pit of my stomach. Knowledge scoops out its own walls and melancholy threatens. Yes, but I didn't have to leave my rooms to learn that nature abhors a void. What comes next, Mrs Temptwell, what comes next?

SCENE FOUR

A large den in Drury Lane. **Lord Exrake** *and Mr Manners are playing piquet.* **Young Robert** *is watching sulkily. Mary, Sophie and Mrs Temptwell come on.*

Mr Manners Carte blanche.

Lord Exrake discards five cards.

Mary Cards, numbers, chance, mystery and gain. Oh what a rich and generous world.

Mrs Temptwell For some.

Mary Don't be glum, Mrs Temptwell, let me enjoy it all.

Lord Exrake Six and a *seizième*.

Mary And look over there, a cock fight. Shall we go there or play cards? What do you want to do, Sophie?

Sophie Me? . . . I don't know . . .

Mrs Temptwell Our Sophie has no desires.

Sophie Please . . .

Young Robert (*moving towards Sophie*) What's your name?

Mary But causes desires in others. I don't understand the world yet, but I will, I will.

Mr Manners You're over the hundred, Lord Exrake.

Lord Exrake Am I, dear boy? So I am, so I am. Robert, why aren't you watching this?

Robert I don't want to learn piquet, Uncle. I think cards are stupid.

Lord Exrake What have you been doing at Oxford all this time?

94

Robert Studying.

Lord Exrake Whoever heard of studying at Oxford? Meet people, boy, meet people. Another deal. Mr Manners?

Mary You play, Sophie. I'll go and watch the fight.

Sophie I can't.

Mary I'll give you the money and you can keep what you win.

Sophie No . . .

Mary Try a little pleasure, Sophie, do. Let's play cards.

Mrs Temptwell Be careful.

Robert (*to Sophie*) When I inherit his money, I'm going to build a school for women.

Sophie Oh.

Robert It will help all those lost girls find virtue and religion again. It's terrible what's happening to women now. I've written a play about it, but no one will put it on. There's a cabal against me and Garrick's a coward.

Mr Manners Piqued, repiqued and capoted. You have all the luck tonight, Lord Exrake.

Lord Exrake At my age, dear boy, there is no luck, only science. (*He sees the women.*) Ah. look, beauties are approaching us. We are having a visitation, a visitation from the fair sex. Let us hail them.

Lord Exrake messes up the cards.

You owe me one hundred and fifty pounds.

Mr Manners Another deal, Lord Exrake, so I can win back some of my losses.

Lord Exrake No, no, dear boy, don't win, don't win. *Qui* *perd au jeu gagne à l'amour*, and of course, vice versa. Do they still teach the young boys French? Ah, *l'amour*, *l'amour*, what good is gold without *l'amour*. Is that not so, mesdemoiselles?

Mary No, my Lord, for what love must not eventually be paid for? I'll play with you.

Lord Exrake Will you my dear? There is not so much as there once was, but come and sit on my lap.

Mary I meant piquet, my lord. I'll sit opposite your lap.

Mr Manners He's not playing any more.

Lord Exrake Oh, but I didn't say . . . Mr Manners, one does not refuse a lady . . . Remember that, Robert.

Robert (*to Sophie*) Dirty old man, I can't stand him.

Mr Manners The gambling is serious here.

Mary Is money ever frivolous, Mr Manners?

Mr Manners The stakes are high.

Mary I can pay . Show them our money, Mrs Temptwell.

Mrs Temptwell No, no, that's not necessary.

Lord Exrake Indeed, mademoiselle, a beautiful young lady can always pay one way or another. We shall come to an amicable arrangement.

Mary I do not need to sell my flesh, my lord, and yours might not fetch enough. You may choose the stakes.

Lord Exrake You are blunt, mademoiselle, you remind me . . .

Robert A young woman shouldn't talk like that, it's disgusting. Of course I blame him.

Lord Exrake Ten shillings a point?

Mrs Temptwell That's too high, Mary.

Mary Shall we double it?

Mr Manners A pound a point. Don't play, Lord Exrake.

Mary Are you his keeper?

Mr Manners I believe in keeping a sense of decency in these proceedings.

Mary Is risk an indecency, Mr Manners? Shall we make it five pounds a point?

Mrs Temptwell Five pounds!

Lord Exrake Five pounds then.

Robert That's sinful. It's my inheritance.

Lord Exrake What is your name?

Mary Mary.

Mr Manners Your other name?

Mary Do you mean my patronymic? I have none. I'm unfathered.

Lord Exrake (*to Sophie*) And you, my pretty? Forgive me for not noticing you before, mademoiselle. You're not as tall as your friend, but not so fierce neither. I think I like you better.

Mary Her name's Sophie. Let's play.

Lord Exrake Sophie . . . such a beautiful name . . . you remind me . . .

Robert (*to Sophie*) I've never been with a woman –

Lord Exrake and Mary cut the cards.

Mary I am elder.

Lord Exrake And I the youth. Ah, youth. It was as a mere youth . . . have I told you, Mr Manners?

Mr Manners Yes, you have.

Lord Exrake deals. Mary exchanges five cards, Lord Exrake three.

Robert But I know how to write about women. I know what women need. I don't understand why they won't listen.

Lord Exrake It was the nights . . . The nights aren't the same these days. What do you do with your nights, Mr Manners?

Mr Manners I spend most of them in the Cabinet trying to quiet the Americans. It's a most trying country.

Lord Exrake We didn't have Americans in my day. The Scots were exotic enough for us. Ah, the old world . . . Perhaps that's what's wrong with Robert.

Mary Point of five.

Lord Exrake Making?

Mary Forty-nine.

Lord Exrake Good.

Mary In hearts. Lord Exrake, it is my hand that should interest you, not my legs. Keep your feet to yourself.

Lord Exrake Alas, don't hobble me, mademoiselle. I was thinking of my youth . . . where is the other one, the beautiful Sophie? Come and sit on my lap, my dear, your friend is too severe. That is, if your dear mama will allow.

Mary She's not our mama, she's our duenna. Keeps the grim suitor prudence from our hearts.

Mrs Temptwell Do what you want with her, Lord Exrake, she never resists.

Sophie Mrs Temptwell, please –

Robert (*to Sophie*) When I have my school, you'll be saved from all this. Your work will be hard but decent and you'll celebrate your chastity.

Mr Manners (*to Mary*) You ought not to be here, Mary. I know who you are.

Mary How can you when I do not even know myself? Do you know yourself, Mr Manners?

Mrs Temptwell Concentrate on the game, Mary.

Mary And a quart major.

Lord Exrake Good.

> *He pulls Sophie to him.*

Do sit on my lap, belle Sophie, your friend frightens me.

Mary You stand behind me, Mr Manners, shall I invite you on my lap?

Mr Manners I want to watch you play.

Mary A voyeur. And I took you for a man of action. That's five for point, four for a sequence, nine.

Lord Exrake No, no, do not try to escape, Sophie.

Mary Three knaves?

Lord Exrake Three knaves are not good.

Mary Your suspicions run down my neck, Mr Manners, you do not trust the fairness of the fair sex. I promise I've encountered fortune head on, no female detours for me. And one for leading, ten.

> *Mary leads to the first trick.*

Lord Exrake I count fourteen tens and three queens. You

talk too much. It is not that I mind women who talk. In the salons, women used to talk, but in the salons, they talked in French . . . Do you know the salons, Mr Manners?

They play their tricks.

Mr Manners No. Your discards were good, Mary.

Mary One learns. To discard. Yours too must be good.

Mr Manners It is more in man's nature.

Mary Then nature is simply a matter of practice. Eleven, twelve, thirteen, fourteen, fifteen.

Lord Exrake Ah, the salons . . . Mademoiselle de Lespinasse. I'll give you an introduction, Robert, although now . . . she spoke in the strictest confidence . . . I was much in demand then. Nineteen, twenty, twenty-one, twenty-two, twenty-three.

Mary Seventeen, eighteen, and ten for cards, twenty-eight. I've won.

Mr Manners Well played. Your hand was weak.

Mary Did you take me for a fool?

Mr Manners I don't make quick judgements.

Mary Then you lack imagination. Second deal.

Mary deals.

Mr Manners No. Imagination has been one of my wisest discards.

Mary You are the elder, Lord Exrake.

Lord Exrake Alas, I am, I am, but once. *L'Anglais gallant*, they used to call me. Some wag said an *Anglais gallant* was a contradiction in terms, but Mademoiselle de Lespinasse . . . *Les Anglais*, she said, *ah, les Anglais*. Such phlegmatic exteriors, but beneath *tout cela. Quel* fire, she said, what *feu. Les Anglais* . . .

> *Lord Exrake has discarded hesitantly and picked up his new cards.*

Point of seven.

Mary Not good.

Lord Exrake I have met Italians, she said, no more than gesture deep. Quart minor.

Mary Not good.

Lord Exrake And the Spanish, who like scorpions sting themselves to death with their own passion. A trio of Kings.

Mary Not good.

Lord Exrake Ah. Mm. And the Dutch . . . The Dutch. One for the heart, makes eight.

Mary (*triumphantly*) *Seizième* for sixteen, a *quatorze* of knaves, a trio of aces, that's thirty-three and the repique, ninety-three.

Lord Exrake She had travelled. Will you travel with me, Sophie? Your friend plays too well.

> *They play out their tricks. Lord Exrake wins one trick, Mary the rest.*

Mary That is yours.

Lord Exrake It was on my travels I met Mademoiselle Sophie, or was it Sylvie? She was with that writer, what was his name? *Double entendre*, I think. But he wrote so much, and pleasure needs time. It is a demanding vocation. *A l'amour comme à la guerre*, love and war, the same, *ainsi de suite*.

Mary No. A soldier braves death but obeys authority. The pleasure seeker braves authority but gives in to annihilation. This makes pleasure the heroism of the disobedient, whereas war is for those who dare not to step out of line, or cowards. An interesting paradox, is it not, Mr Manners?

Mr Manners I don't like paradoxes, they give me bad dreams.

Mary I score one hundred and fourteen.

Mrs Temptwell Stop now, Mary.

Mary Another game, Lord Exrake?

Lord Exrake I too was bold when I was young. I believed I had time to waste.

They now play very fast.

Mary I don't waste time, I love it.

Lord Exrake But it isn't wasted time that's so painful, no, wasted time is time that never existed. It's the memories.

Mary Memories are for the idle, I'll never be idle.

Lord Exrake Memories . . . those leeches of the mind, exquisite moments, forever past, that now suck you dry.

Mary I shall never have memories. I won't have time.

Mr Manners Everyone has memories, but they can be changed. An entire people's memory may be changed.

Mrs Temptwell I live on my memories.

Sophie I like mine.

Robert Mine are awful. My mother was always writing pamphlets. But sometimes the present is worse.

He goes.

Lord Exrake I suffer the torment of Tantalus. I want to reach out my hand to seize those moments and live them again. Do you understand me?

Mary I score one hundred and twenty.

Lord Exrake It isn't the fear of death that keeps me here all night.

Mary I sleep as little as I can, the world gives me such pleasure.

Lord Exrake Keeps me here all night, pawing at youth, it's the fear of those memories. The moments mock me with their vanished existence. You'll see.

Mary Why are you trying to frighten me?

Lord Exrake Why shouldn't you know that age is horrible?

Mary One hundred and seventy-two. I've lost count of the total.

Mrs Temptwell Lord Exrake owes you two thousand six hundred and eighty pounds.

Mary Another game?

Lord Exrake No, no. You remind me of my youth.

Mary But you have failed to remind me of my old age. Come, Sophie, look at all this delightful money. I could double it before dawn.

Lord Exrake It was the first time I slept through the dawn that the memories took over. There were suddenly too many years between me and the new day. Do I make myself clear? They buzz in my ears and I can't hear.

Mary turns away. Lord Gordon comes on.

Mary How's your cock, Lord Gordon?

Lord Gordon Bruised from the last encounter. Do I know you?

Mary Mine's fighting fit. Will you pit yours against mine?

Lord Gordon I never bet against a woman.

Mary Afraid of bad luck? Scratch a parliamentarian, you find a follower of folk tales.

Sophie Mrs Temptwell, it was him.

Mrs Temptwell So?

Lord Gordon (*to Mary*) When my cock recovers, perhaps.

Mary Cocks recover so slowly and I presume you have no spare?

Lord Gordon I have seen you before.

Mr Hardlong comes on. The men ignore him.

Mary How can I remember a man who won't expose his cock? Are you looking for me, Mr Hardlong?

Mr Hardlong No, for Sophie.

Mary Who will fight my cock?

Lord Exrake I have one.

Mary At your age, Lord Exrake, it's still active?

Lord Exrake My cock is young.

Mary So, so, wondrous nature. Is it ready?

Lord Exrake Spurred and trimmed. I've left your friend, she's charming but too quiet. At my age one needs a challenge, so I've come back to you.

Mary I too need a challenge and I'd prefer to pit against Mr Hardlong's cock. Will you?

Mr Hardlong I'll do anything if Sophie will stand by me.

Mrs Temptwell Sophie does what she's told.

Mr Manners You ought to choose your opponents more carefully, Mary.

Mary I didn't escape from propriety to fall into snobbery.

Mr Manners That's a mistake. Snobbery is cheap to practise and has saved many a nonentity.

Mary Just so. I don't need it. Where's my whip, Mrs Temptwell?

Mrs Temptwell Don't bet too much.

Mary Two hundred and fifty guineas, Mr Hardlong?

They touch their whips.

Lord Exrake Ladies didn't have cocks in my day.

They release their birds from the cloth sacks.

Mary Now my bird, fight for me, match my courage and my strength.

Screams and urgings from all.

Mr Manners Your cock's dead.

Mary No, look, look. It was a ruse. My cock's risen and stricken Mr Hardlong's. Ha!

Mr Hardlong My cock's failed me.

Mary That happens, Mr Hardlong, even to the best. I keep winning, I keep winning.

Mr Hardlong Will you come and console me, Sophie?

Mary Mr Hardlong, it is I who have the money. Will you come to me?

Mr Hardlong I want Sophie.

Mary Does she want you? Sophie, come here. Here: two hundred and fifty guineas.

She throws her the sack of money.

Sophie Oh, no, I can't.

Mrs Temptwell Take it.

Sophie Thank you, Miss Mary.

Mary Yes, but you must work for it.

Pause.

Nothing for nothing. That's their law. When they offer you money, you know what for. Well?

Sophie I don't understand.

Mary turns to Sophie and lifts up her skirts to her.

Mary Men don't know their way around there. You will.

Sophie I –

Mary Look. Surely it's more appealing than their drooping displays? Or do you share their prejudice?

Sophie kneels to Mary.

What is it, gentlemen, you turn away, you feel disgust? Why don't you look and see what it's like? When you talk of sulphurous pits, deadly darkness, it's your own imagination you see. Look. It's solid, rich, gently shaped, fully coloured. The blood flows there on the way to the heart. It answers tenderness with tenderness, there is no gaping void here, only soft bumps, corners, cool convexities. Ah, Sophie, how sweet you are, I understand why they love you. Such peace, Shall we sleep?

*Two **Old Women** shuffle on to the stage, very very slowly.*

No – look, over there, the spectres of passing time. I can't bear it. Wait. Mr Manners, a race? You cannot question my choice of opponent. Four thousand pounds.

Mrs Temptwell That's all our money.

Mr Hardlong (*to Sophie*) Let me take you away.

Mr Manners Set it up, Hardlong.

The two Old Women are placed side by side.

Mr Hardlong Gentlemen! last chance to win your fortune in this unique event.

He takes the bets.

Mr Manners' hag is favourite.

All get ready. Lord Gordon raises his arm. The two Old Women stand.

Go! Go!

The two old women start to run as fast as they can, which is extremely slowly. They cough, spit, stumble, pant, covering just a few feet.

Mrs Temptwell Four thousand pounds. We'll go hungry if she loses.

Sophie We've been well fed.

Mr Manners Faster, faster. There's a good girl.

Lord Exrake I've put money on Miss Mary's hag, her ankles look firm.

Lord Gordon Mr Manners' hag is taking the lead. Miss Mary's hag having a little trouble.

Mary A cane to your back if you stumble again. Pick your feet up!

Mr Manners Come on, girl, you can do it.

Lord Gordon Miss Mary's hag catching up. Is she? Yes she is. No, she's just tripped.

Mary Your hag tripped mine, Mr Manners. I saw.

Lord Gordon No, there was no foul play. Mr Manners' hag still in the lead, and gaining.

Lord Exrake Get up, girl, get up. Go.

Mr Hardlong She's too broad in the back, bad for balance.

Mr Manners Faster, faster.

Lord Gordon Miss Mary's hag a little winded. Making an effort, yes, she's closing the gap. Yes. Will she do it?

Mr Manners Steady, girl, steady.

Lord Gordon Miss Mary's hag pulling ahead, yes, Mr Manners' hag slowing down.

Mary Go on, you can do it.

Sophie She's ahead, she'll win. Faster. Faster.

Mrs Temptwell You're cheering yourself on. That could be us.

Sophie You cheer her on.

Lord Gordon Miss Mary's hag now well in the lead. Yes. Mr Manners' hag stumbles.

They cheer.

Lord Exrake I've always been a good judge of ankles.

Lord Gordon Only a few steps to the finishing line. It looks like Miss Mary's hag will win. But no. Look. Oh, what a jump. Look at that, what an effort and is it? Yes it is. It's Mr Manners' hag first, what a superb effort, what a close race, but it's Mr Manners' hag.

More cheers.

Mary I saw him give her brandy.

Mr Manners That is not against the rules.

Lord Gordon Mr Manners never breaks the rules. You owe him four thousand pounds.

Mrs Temptwell Don't give it to him. He likes you. Burst into tears.

Mary What? Turn female now?

Mrs Temptwell (*to Sophie*) We go hungry for her vanity.

Mary Here, Mr Manners. I've lost.

Mr Manners I have that effect on people.

Lord Exrake I lost two thousand pounds on a woodlice race. No one wants to know you when you've lost, but they forget. A few weeks in Ipswich always helps.

Mr Manners Where's my hag? Here's a shilling for you, you ran well.

The other Old Woman approaches Mary who ignores her.

Old Woman Please, Miss.

Mary Let go.

Old Woman I ran for you.

Mary And lost. Don't touch me.

Old Woman I've been ill. Be kind.

Mary Why? Look around. Do you see kindness anywhere? Where is it?

Old Woman Give me something.

Mary I'll give you something priceless. Have you heard of knowledge?

She takes the whip and beats her.

There is no kindness. The world is a dry place.

Old Woman Please.

Mary What, you want more?

She beats her again. The Old Woman falls.

Have I hurt her?

She bends over her.

I've seen her before. Or was it her sister? Why do you all stare at me? She was standing outside church. My father told me to give her some money. He gave me a coin. I gave her the coin, smiling. She smiled. I smiled more kindly. My father smiled. I followed his glance and saw a lady and a young man, her son. They were smiling. My father gave me another coin. I moved closer to her, my steps lit by everyone's smiles. I remember watching the movement of my wrist as I put the coin in her hand., I smiled at its grace. (*Pause.*) Was that better? Tell me, was that better?

Interval.

Act Three

SCENE ONE

Vauxhall Gardens at night. Mary and Mrs Temptwell stand in the dark, waiting. Music and lights in the background. Mary has a rounded stomach under dirty clothes.

Mrs Temptwell Voices. Coming this way.

They listen.

Mary They've turned down another path.

Mrs Temptwell They're coming closer.

Mary They've turned away. Your hearing's blunt.

They listen.

Mrs Temptwell Footsteps on the grass.

Mary They're not his.

Mrs Temptwell You can't know that. Shht.

Mary Those footsteps bounded my happiness for eighteen years. I'd recognize them now. Damn. This itch.

She scratches herself. Listens.

Shht. No.

Mrs Temptwell Are you miserable?

Mary You're waiting for my yes, aren't you? You'll chew on that yes like a hungry dog, spit it up and chew again. Well, you can beg for your yes. Do a trick for me, Mrs Temptwell. Say something interesting. You know I hate silence. And stop smiling.

Mrs Temptwell You're seeing things.

Mary I saw your evil grin through the darkness. Cover up your teeth, please, they make me ill.

Mrs Temptwell It's your condition. I told you to sit.

Mary Damn this leech in my stomach, sucking at my blood, determined to wriggle into life. Why can't you do something about it, you old wizard?

Mrs Temptwell If I was the devil we wouldn't be shivering in Vauxhall Gardens waiting for our supper.

Mary I could kill the man who did this. I found him in the Haymarket, he looked strong, seemed to have some wit and the night was soft and thick. We went to Westminster Bridge, I liked that, the water rushing beneath me, cool air through my legs, until I discovered he was wearing a pigskin. New invention from Holland, he explained. He wouldn't catch my itching boils and I'd be protected from this. Fair exchange. So I had this piece of bookbinding scratching inside me and his words scratching at my intelligence. I'd mistaken talkativeness for wit. I hope he caught my infection. Footsteps. No. Why is it the one time I had no pleasure my body decided to give life? What's the meaning of that? Why don't you answer? Why do you never say anything? Has it ever happened to you? Were you ever young? Answer my questions, damn you. Who are you?

Mrs Temptwell It won't interest you.

Mary You don't know what interests me.

Mrs Temptwell If you had an interest in anybody else, you wouldn't have thrown all your money away.

Mary I was only trying to determine whether greed was the dominant worm in the human heart. I admit the experiment was costly. You didn't have to stay.

Mrs Temptwell I hear something.

Mary Let's rob the first person who comes.

Mrs Temptwell Don't you want to see him? Find out how deeply he's mourning his dear dead daughter?

Mary How easily he cancelled my existence.

Mrs Temptwell He's in the Cabinet now. He's happy.

Mary Tell me a story.

Mrs Temptwell I don't know any.

Mary Go away then. Do you enjoy this misery? Distract me, damn you. Tell me your story. Where were you born? Don't you dare not answer.

Mrs Temptwell The country.

Mary The country. The country. There are trees here.

Mrs Temptwell The North.

Mary I know that from your granite face. Where?

Mrs Temptwell Don't shout or they'll hear us.

Mary Then talk. Remember something.

Mrs Temptwell I had a grandmother.

Mary I had a father.

Mrs Temptwell She was hanged as a witch.

Mary That's better.

Mrs Temptwell That's all.

Mary Aren't there laws against hanging witches?

Mrs Temptwell It depends on the magistrate.

Mary And she taught you to cast spells?

Mrs Temptwell She was an old woman, and poor. She talked to herself because she was angry and no one listened.

Mary Tell me more. Tell me everything.

Mrs Temptwell They put a nail through her tongue.

Mary And then?

Mrs Temptwell She was naked. I remember how thin she was. And the hair, the hair between her legs. It was white. That's all I remember.

Mary Did people cry?

Mrs Temptwell They laughed. I laughed too once I'd forgotten she was my grandmother. The magistrate laughed loudest. She'd been on his land and he'd taken her cottage but she stayed at his gates, wouldn't leave. She asked for justice, he heard a witch's spell.

Mary How interesting to have so much power and still so much fear.

Mrs Temptwell He also enjoyed humiliating her. Everyone did. It's an unusual experience . . .

Mary Tell me, Mrs Temptwell, are we imitators by nature wishing to do what we see and hear? Or is every crime already in the human heart, dormant, waiting only to be tickled out?

Mrs Temptwell Footsteps.

Mary His.

Giles and Sophie appear. She is leading him.

Giles Where are you taking me, my sweet? No need to come this far.

Sophie I'm afraid of being seen, Sir.

Giles Let's stop at this tree.

Sophie This way, Sir.

Giles I'm in such a hurry.

Mary Here, Sir.

Giles Who's that?

Mrs Temptwell A woman, Sir.

Giles Sophie, where are you?

Mrs Temptwell Forget Sophie, Sir, she's docile but dull.
Look here.

Giles I can't see anything.

Mary Here, Sir, I'll entertain you.

Mrs Temptwell She's fanciful and clever and I'm practical
and knowing, if not so young.

Giles I want a woman, not a personality. Sophie . . .

Mrs Temptwell A drawbridge: the treasures are here.

Mary Here, Sir.

Mrs Temptwell Go to Mary.

Giles Mary . . .

Mrs Temptwell Lovely name, Mary, isn't it?

Giles Sophie's young. I want someone very young.

Mary I'm young, Sir, and know things Sophie does not
know. Don't turn away, Sir, rejection is so painful. Come
here.

Giles If it means that much to you . . . this isn't a trick?
You're not the more expensive?

Mrs Temptwell Labour is cheap, there's too much of it. And it's not as good as the machines. Perhaps one day this too will be done by machines. Would you like that, Sir?

Giles At least machines don't talk.

Mary But my conversation, Sir, is my greatest charm. Come.

Giles It's so dark.

Mary Isn't light the greatest mistake of this century? We light the streets only to stare at dirt. As for the lantern we poke into nature's crevasses, what has it revealed? Beauty? Or the most terrifying chaos? And if I take a close look at nature now, I mean your nature, what will I find?

As she talks she unbuttons Giles.

That it's tame, Sir, most tame, but our gardeners have taught us to make it wild, with the help of a little art.

Giles (*feebly*) Must you talk so much?

Mary It's my father who taught me to talk, Sir. He didn't suspect he'd also be teaching me to think. He was not a sensitive man and didn't know how words crawl into the mind and bore holes that will never again be filled. What is a question, Sir, but a thought that itches? Some are mild, the merest rash but some are cankerous, infectious, without cure. Do you have children, Sir, to grace your old age? Men often tell me I remind them of their daughters. You look sad, Sir, is your daughter dead? Did she die of a chill? That happens with women of graceful breeding, the blood becomes too polite to flow through the body. As long as she died young, men prefer that. I've heard many confessions. One man told me he locked up his wife for seventeen years and she still had the vulgarity not to die. Age, after all, is a manly quality. But even manly age, it seems, needs a little help if we're to get anywhere. A rub, will that do?

She begins to massage him.

It helps men to think of their daughters when I do this.
You didn't kill yours, did you? Ah, I see it works. We're
ready. Front or back? Oh, the bird's already flown the
cage. Happens. Must have been the thrill of my
conversation. Or thinking of your daughter.

Mary uncovers her face.

But you recognized your daughter some time ago, Papa,
by the grace of her conversation.

Pause.

How did you say your daughter died? Did you starve her
with your puny rations of approval? Immolate her to the
country's future? But she's here. Look.

Giles I have no daughter.

Mary My name is Mary Traverse. Your wife had little
chance of fathering me elsewhere.

Giles You're a whore.

Mary Is a daughter not a daughter when she's a whore?
Or can she not be your daughter? Which words are at war
here: whore, daughter, my? I am a daughter, but not yours,
I am your whore but not your daughter. You dismiss the
'my' with such ease, you make fatherhood an act of grace,
an honour I must buy with my graces, which you
withdraw as soon as I disgrace you.

Giles What do you want from me?

Mary Two things. Look at me.

Giles Tell me what you want.

Mary I'm here, Papa, Here. Look at me.

Pause, Giles looks.

Good.

Giles Why? I gave you everything.

Mary Except experience.

Giles You could have married a lord.

Mary I said experience, not a pose. The world outside, all of it. This.

Giles This! I did everything to keep you from this! I didn't live in a beautiful house like you as a child. I had to work hard. Very hard. Not just with my hands. I didn't mind that. But with people. I had to work at not being despised. I was able. I made money, started the potteries, bought land, made more money. Everything I make sells now. And I'm listened to. I wanted you to have the ease, the delights I never knew. I wanted you to protect you from what I had experienced, the slights, the filth, protect you even from the knowledge I had experienced it.

Mary It wasn't what I wanted.

Giles Whenever I looked at you I could forget my first twenty years.

Mary Yes, you took my future to rewrite your past. Oh Father, don't you see that's worse than Saturn eating his own children?

Giles I let you read too much, it's maddened you.

Mary And when I try to explain you threaten me with a madhouse? How dare you!

Giles I forbid you to speak to me in that manner!

Mary You have no power over me, Papa. Your daughter's dead. Now for the second thing. I want money.

Giles Here's fifteen guineas.

Mary Money, Papa. Not its frayed edges.

Giles It's the agreed price for a whore.

Mary If I wanted to make money lying on my back, I would have married your lord, Papa.

Giles But – you –

Mary I learn. I do not whore.

Giles I don't understand.

Mary You don't try.

Giles Why? But – if you – if you're not – we could forget – I'll find a way to bring you back. Some questions, it wouldn't matter. If you would come back . . . as you were . . .

Mary As your graceful daughter?

Giles My beautiful and witty daughter.

Mary Open your eyes. Look at me.

Giles looks. Silence.

Do you want me back?

Silence.

The father I want cannot be the father of 'your' daughter. And yet, I want a father. Could you not be 'my' father? Could you not try?

Giles I'll send you a little money.

Mary I see. (*Pause.*) I want half your money.

Giles No.

Mary A small price to keep me dead, Papa. Your powerful friends are supping in these gardens. Shall I walk through the tables and cry you've whored your daughter? I'll be believed. I talk well. People love to think ill. Don't try to cheat me. I know how much you have, the factories, the shops, your share of the canal.

Giles What's made you like this?

Mary Experience is expensive and precise.

Giles I can tell you one thing, Mary. At the end of all this, you'll find nothing. Nothing. I know. Goodbye.

He leaves. Mrs Temptwell steps out of the shadows.

Mary The only time he says my name, it's to curse me. One more denial. And he can still make the world grow cold.

Mrs Temptwell Did you see the humiliation on his face? I loved it.

Mary Why?

Mrs Temptwell He made his younger brother a magistrate. It was that magistrate who hanged my grandmother.

Mary Ah.

Mrs Temptwell It's not something you need understand.

Mary I no longer understand anything.

Mrs Temptwell At least you've experienced cruelty. Their cruelty.

Mary Is that what it is?

Mrs Temptwell Didn't it give you pleasure?

Mary No. Sadness. And then, nothing. Nothing. The withering of the night. I'm cold.

SCENE TWO

Vauxhall Gardens. Sophie by herself. Then **Jack.**

Jack By yourself?

Sophie Yes.

Jack Always by yourself?

Sophie Yes!

Jack Want company?

Sophie Yes.

Jack No one to look after you?

Sophie No.

Jack Not here for the toffs!

Sophie No!

Jack I hate them.

Sophie Yes?

Jack Fat. We go hungry.

Sophie Yes.

Jack Hungry?

Sophie Yes.

He gives her some bread.

Jack Here. Good?

Sophie Yes.

Jack Stole it.

Sophie Yes?

Jack Dangerous. But not wrong.

Sophie No.

Jack Ever seen them work?

Sophie No.

Jack Come here.

Sophie Yes.

Jack Jack.

Sophie Jack. Yes. Jack.

They kiss.

SCENE THREE

Vauxhall Gardens. Mr Manners, Lord Gordon.

Mr Manners The mob can be good or the mob can be bad, Lord Gordon, it depends on whether they do what you want them to do.

Lord Gordon I could lead them, I could lead anything if I were made into a leader. It's getting there I find difficult.

Mr Manners Real power prefers to remain invisible.

Lord Gordon I wouldn't mind not having power. Just make me visible. Notorious.

Mr Manners What can I do? I'm no more than a servant.

Lord Gordon You, Mr Manners? The man most feared in Parliament?

Mr Manners A mere servant, I assure you. I serve, however, an awesome power.

Lord Gordon The King.

Mr Manners The King's only a human being, Gordon, a German one at that. No, I serve a divine power.

Lord Gordon You don't mean God, you haven't become a Methodist?

Mr Manners Order, Gordon, order: the very manifestation of God in the universe. Have you studied the planets?

Lord Gordon Can't say I have, no. I look at 'em.

Mr Manners Ordered movement, perfect, everything in its place, for ever. That's why I like men who make machines. They understand eternal principles, as I do. As you must.

Lord Gordon I'm good at adding.

Mr Manners When you ride in your carriage, you mustn't sit back and loll in your own comfort, no, you must study and love the smooth functioning of the vehicle. And if a wheel falls off, you must take it as a personal affront. Do you understand?

Lord Gordon Check the wheels of my carriage . . .

Mr Manners So with the country. Our duty is to watch that no wheel falls off.

Lord Gordon Do we wear splendid livery?

Mr Manners What?

Lord Gordon I would like to serve the country.

Mr Manners Good.

Lord Gordon When can I start?

Mr Manners We must wait. The times are restless.

Lord Gordon (*triumphantly*) The roads are bumpy!

Mr Manners And dangerous.

Lord Gordon Highwaymen lurking behind every tree!

Mr Manners I think we've exhausted that, Gordon. It is clear we must find something new, and entertaining to the people.

Lord Gordon Me!

Mr Manners Who knows? Someone . . . inevitably appears, usually thrown up by the mob itself. And then one must be vigilant . . . persuasive . . .

Lord Gordon Be good to have me. Keep them quiet.

Mr Manners Who?

Lord Gordon The families, you know, my uncle. The other old families.

Mr Manners What do they say?

Lord Gordon That they wouldn't invite you to their house. Have to invite me. I'm a relative.

Mr Manners What else do they say?

Lord Gordon Nothing much. Used to rule England, time to rule again, better at it, born to it, look at the mess, all that. I don't listen.

Mr Manners In times such as these, Lord Gordon, many different people make claims for themselves. The good servant must look for what fits best into the order of things. It is not always obvious. It can be even surprising.

Lord Gordon I'm here, Mr Manners, as soon as you want a change.

Mr Manners No, no, Gordon, you haven't understood: whatever happens, nothing must change.

SCENE FOUR

Elegant lodgings. Mary and Sophie, well dressed, sit in silence.

Mary I'm cold.

Sophie Are you ill, Miss Mary?

Mary In which part of the anatomy does sadness sit, do you know, Sophie? It's not the heart because the heart's a machine. So tell me how in this perfectly ordered universe you explain the chaos of the human soul. My father's right. I'm too clever. The inside of my skin hurts.

Sophie Here's Mrs Temptwell with your milk.

Mrs Temptwell comes on.

Mary Take it from her and tell her to go.

Mrs Temptwell Mary –

Mary Make her go, Sophie.

Mrs Temptwell Mary –

Sophie Mary wants you to go, Mrs Temptwell. Go away.

Mrs Temptwell leaves. Silence.

Mary How's your child?

Sophie He died.

Mary Did he? I didn't know. (*Pause.*) I'm sorry. (*Pause.*) Am I? Are you? (*Pause.*) You can have mine.

Sophie Oh yes, Miss Mary, I'd like that. Please.

Mary Why?

Sophie Why what?

Mary No. I don't want to know why. What's that noise?

Sophie Shouting. The price of white bread has gone up again.

Mary I thought you people ate brown bread.

Sophie We don't like it. My teeth aren't strong enough to eat brown bread. The merchants are hiding sacks of flour to make the prices go up so the people have decided to find the sacks and take them by force. Then they'll buy the sacks at a fair price. Jack says it's happening all over the country. They've beaten some merchants.

Mary Would you do that if you were hungry?

Sophie Oh no.

Mary If you were very hungry? I would. But I don't have to. Do you ever think about that?

Sophie About what?

Mary Come here. Closer. We're the same age. Why do you never look at me? (*Pause.*) Look into my eyes.

Sophie They're very beautiful, Miss Mary.

Mary What do you think of me?

Sophie You're feverish, Miss Mary. I'll bring you a brandy.

Mary I asked you a question. What do you think of me?

Sophie I don't understand.

Mary You have a mind. Tell me what it sees.

Sophie The country, Miss Mary. Fields. The fields I used to walk in as a child. That's what it sees. Green.

Mary What questions does it ask?

Sophie Questions? Yes. How can I be less tired? Why does my belly hurt? Is that what you call thinking? And how good white bread is. Sometimes I think about the baby, but not much.

Mary What do you think about my life?

Sophie I hope it will be a long one.

Mary Are you pretending to be stupid?

Sophie I don't understand, Miss Mary. (*Pause.*) I feel things.

Mary What do you feel for me? Hatred? Contempt? Don't be afraid, Sophie, answer.

Sophie I don't feel – that way. I feel the cold. And the heat even more than the cold.

Mary Sophie!

Sophie I don't have time to think the way you do. Please, Miss Mary, let me get you some wine.

Mary Do I disgust you?

Sophie You found me in the streets. I had nothing.

Mary I pushed you on the streets as well. You took my place with Lord Gordon. What did you feel then? What did you feel in the gambling den, servicing my pleasures? What did you feel?

Sophie I don't know. I can't remember. Sometimes I don't feel I'm there. It could be someone else. And I'm walking in the fields. So I don't mind much. My brother used to touch me. He was strong and I learned to make it not me. I was somewhere else. But when I want to, with Jack, I'm there. And then not. It's not difficult.

Mary I see. I'm not sorry then. Perhaps I never was. Tell Mrs Temptwell to come to me with some ideas.

Mrs Temptwell comes on immediately.

Mrs Temptwell I knew our quiet Sophie wouldn't entertain you long. You can go, Sophie.

Mary No, let her stay.

Pause.

Well?

Mrs Temptwell I've seen some beautiful jewels we could acquire.

Mary Jewels.

Mrs Temptwell There are women wrestling in Clerkenwell. You like that.

Mary Do I?

Silence.

Will I have to kill myself to make the time pass?

Something. Something. And I can't sleep. Do you have dreams, Sophie?

Sophie I dream of a little cottage . . .

Mary Oh stop.

Mrs Temptwell Why don't you go, Sophie?

Sophie Jack dreams of a new world.

Mary A new world? Does he? A new world . . . who's Jack?

Sophie He's – Jack. He's very handsome.

Mary All men are handsome when we drape them with our longings. A new world . . . even Sophie's Jack has more interesting thoughts than I do. Why?

Mrs Temptwell We'll think of something tomorrow.

Mary Another endless round of puny, private vice? This isn't experience, Mrs Temptwell, this is another bounded room. You promised more, remember? They must have more than this. What? Yes . . . they go to war. They go to war . . .

Mrs Temptwell We could go to America.

Mary Or they dream of new worlds. They let their imaginations roam freely over the future, yes, they think about the country, and then they rule the country. What sort of a new world does Jack dream of, Sophie? Who is Jack?

SCENE FIVE

A cobbler's basement in Southwark. Jack, then Mary, Sophie, Mrs Temptwell.

Jack A travelling preacher taught me how to read. I was sixteen. He wanted me to spread the word of God. But I didn't like the word of God. Fear and obedience. Obedience and fear. I heard another word. Freedom. The preacher said God would punish me for such devilish rebellion. And he did. I can't talk. I want to tell people about freedom. I can't explain it. I have other words: equality, justice, right, but they're rough stones that won't stand together to make a house. I have a new world, in my head, I can't make it come out, I can't give it to anyone. I look across the river at those houses of tyrants. I know the world needs me, but I'm cursed. Silent.

Mary I can talk, Jack, but until now I had nothing to say. I understand what it is to need freedom. I thought it was something only I wanted, but now I know it is a longing in every human heart. I have watched freedom, beautiful freedom, hunted from every street and I know what it is to bang at the doors of tyranny. I could speak for you, Jack, if you taught me what to say.

Jack You?

Mary Why not?

Sophie She can help us, Jack.

Jack You wouldn't understand about equality.

Mary I know the humiliation of being denied equality, Jack, and that it is a dignity due to all, men and women, rich and poor.

Jack There should be no poor. Government makes people poor. Do you understand about natural rights?

Mary I used to talk about nature.

Jack Everyone is born with them. Born.

Mary Yes. Nature has given us certain unquestionable, inalienable rights but these have been taken from us by those who set themselves above us.

Jack We have to get them back.

Mary Wrench back from a usurping, base and selfish government what is ours by right.

Jack And the new world – the new world –

Mary Will be a world ruled by us, for our delight, a world of hope for all. Oh Jack, that's beautiful. Let's go tell everyone.

Jack The tyrants: show them up.

Mary We'll explain to the people that they worship an authority that mocks, abuses and eventually kills them.

Jack That's it, Mary.

Mary Let's go, let's go quickly.

Mrs Temptwell Where are you going?

Mary There, where the power sits. Parliament.

Mrs Temptwell You're mad.

Mary If you wish to talk like my father, go home.

Mrs Temptwell She only wants power, Jack.

Sophie No, she wants our good.

Mary In the new world, they will be identical. Let's go.

SCENE SIX

In front of the Houses of Parliament. Jack and Mary try to get by the **Guard**. *A* **Spy** *in dark clothes comes on during the exchange, then two* **Old Women**, *then the* **Locksmith**, *then* **Giles**.

Jack Listen to her.

Guard I told you: no petticoats in the Houses of Parliament.

Mary I'll unpetticoat myself if it's my underwear you object to. What I have to say is without frills.

Jack We have the right to be heard.

Guard I know you: you're the one who keeps bringing petitions.

Mary No petticoats, no petitions, what do you allow in that house which is supposed to represent us all?

Jack Thieves and hangmen. Let the working man in.

Spy (*to an Old Woman*) Do you know that woman?

Mary We'll change history if we go in there. Don't you want a change?

Guard No.

Mary Wouldn't you like a world where everyone was free to choose their future?

Guard Not much.

Mary Oh the precious maidenhead of a young man. No virgin shuts her legs as tight as you your mind. No new thought will penetrate to make you bleed.

Guard Watch your language, Miss.

Mary What are they doing for you in there? What?

Jack Nothing, that's what.

Spy (*to the* Old Woman) Has she ever spoken here before?

Guard And what would your world do for me, eh?

Mary It would do what you asked because it would be a world you would have made. What have those in there done to deserve their power? Nothing.

Jack They stole it from us, that's what.

Spy (*to the* Old Woman) You don't know her name, do you?

Mary Our sons and daughters will share the land.

Old Woman I'm not giving anything to my daughter. She's a whore.

Mary In the new world, there will be no whores, there won't have to be.

Locksmith If I want a whore and I can pay for her, I have a right to that whore.

Mary No one has the right to pleasure at the cost of another's pain. In the new world, everyone will have their natural, just, share of pleasure. Think of a world where there is no hoarding of ill-begotten riches, no more theft –

Locksmith What happens to the locksmiths?

Mary A world where there are no longer any families living in greed –

Locksmith I'm a locksmith. What good are locks without thieves?

Mary You will make keys for all of us.

Locksmith Oh. No. You get paid more for locks than keys.

Jack The working man pays for everything and gets nothing.

Mary Do you know how much our King costs us?

Spy This is sedition.

Mary Eight hundred thousand pounds sterling a year.

Spy (*to the Old Woman*) Remember what she says, will you.

The Spy leaves quickly.

Mary How much bread does eight hundred thousand pounds a year buy?

Old Woman I saw the King the other day. He looks ever such a gentleman.

Locksmith Why don't you go to America if you don't like it here? They make you pick cotton in the heat there and you die in two weeks.

Mary Who was the first King of England? A French bandit.

Old Woman I didn't know that. Is that why he speaks so different from us?

Jack A King's privilege is an insult to the working people.

Mary What does the King do for us?

Locksmith If that was my daughter, I'd have her locked up.

Giles Why? She speaks well. What she says is wrong, of course.

Mary Let us share in the building of a new world.

Jack All men will be brothers.

Mary A world that is gentle, wise, free, uncircumscribed.

Giles I used to have dreams like that.

Mary Imagine how you would run this world and now, ask yourselves this: why have we no bread to eat?

Old Woman I've asked that before. No one tells me.

Mary Ask yourselves why our children are born to hunger and toil.

Old Woman Why?

Mr Manners comes on from the Houses of Parliament.

Mary Ask yourselves why they are indifferent to our needs.

Old Woman/Locksmith Why?

Mary Ask yourselves why they won't let us speak out.

All Why?

Mr Manners Why do you say all this out here and not in there?

Mary/All Yes. Why?

Mr Manners They'd like to have you in there. They are interested in what you have to say.

Jack They don't let people in there.

Mr Manners That can change.

Mary You'll let us into the House?

Mr Manners Not the House, exactly, but there are many rooms.

Mary Let's go.

Mr Manners Just you – for the moment.

Jack Go in, Mary. Talk to them about the people.

Mary I'll see what they have to say and come back.

Mary and Mr Manners leave.

Guard She was better out here.

Giles People were listening to her. She made them listen.

Jack She'll talk to them and come back.

Guard I've seen people go in there and come out very different.

Jack Even they will have to listen to common sense.

Guard Are you going to this new world?

Locksmith I'm not having a world without locks.

SCENE SEVEN

Preparations for a midnight conversation. Mrs Temptwell and Sophie set out the chairs.

Mrs Temptwell We must stop her.

Sophie Why? She's so gay.

Mrs Temptwell And us?

Sophie She said I could go to the country and look after her child.

Mrs Temptwell No!

Sophie Please don't stop me from having the child.

Mrs Temptwell She had you raped, she made you a whore, she caused the misery that killed your child and now you'll slave to bring up her reject?

Sophie She said we could have a cottage.

Mrs Temptwell Until she takes it to make way for some roses. Don't you know what they're like?

Sophie Who?

Mrs Temptwell Listen to these words, Sophie: freeborn Englishman. Aren't they sweet?

Sophie I suppose so.

Mrs Temptwell My father was a freeborn Englishman. So was yours.

Sophie I never knew him.

Mrs Temptwell But us? I'm a servant. Nothing my own, no small piece of ground, no hour, no sleep she can't break with a bell. Do you understand, girl?

Sophie Did you suffer misfortune?

Mrs Temptwell He was our misfortune, her father. I had to watch my mother grow thin as hunger and die. I curse the whole family.

Sophie You could get another place.

Mrs Temptwell She'll be as low as us when I'm finished. And you could help, Sophie.

Sophie I don't feel low.

Mrs Temptwell When you know all I know, you'll be angry too.

Sophie When I've been angry, it's only made it all worse. No, I won't be angry. Is that all the chairs?

Mrs Temptwell We could work together. I'll be your friend.

Sophie You said that when you brought me into the house.

Mrs Temptwell I didn't know how vicious she was. And now she'll do us even more harm with these ideas of hers.

Sophie I like it when she speaks of the new world. So does Jack.

Mrs Temptwell New world? This is no way to get rid of the old.

SCENE EIGHT

A midnight conversation: the last stages of a drunken dinner. Sophie, Mrs Temptwell, Mary, Mr Manners, Jack, the Guard, Lord Gordon.

Mary Sophie, more wine for the gentlemen and for me.

Mr Manners No more for me.

Mary Moderation in all things, Mr Manners?

Mr Manners Historical moments need level heads.

Mary Why? The future is intoxicating.

Jack I'm a working man. I drink gin.

Mrs Temptwell And gin for me.

Mary I forgot you, Mrs Temptwell.

Mrs Temptwell That's what happens to working people, Jack.

Guard It's all going to change now.

Mrs Temptwell Is it?

Mary I have asked you all here this evening that we may hammer out our common cause. Mr Manners tells me it's a good time to be heard.

Jack We want bread. Bread for everyone.

Mary We have to ask for more than bread.

Jack Every man has a right to eat.

Mary It's a right remembered only by the hungry. No, we need something big enough to net the future.

Jack All men are born equal.

Mr Manners Too general. We don't listen to abstractions in England.

Mary But we do need a good cry as our banner. I remember my father talking about the frenzy caused by the cry Wilkes and Liberty.

Lord Gordon What about Silks and Tyranny? (*Pause.*) Milk and Bigotry?

    Silence.

There's a Wilkes in the House. Tory chap isn't he?

Mr Manners He's calmed down since the sixties. The House does that.

Jack Liberty. We'd go for that.

Mary Yes. Liberty is a beautiful word.

Mr Manners Dangerous, Mary.

Guard Will there be liberty in the new world?

Mary Oh yes. (*to Mr Manners*) Why dangerous? It's what we want.

Mr Manners It's been heard before and no one understands it. People were shouting for Wilkes, not for liberty.

Lord Gordon Gordon . . . What about Gordon and Drollery? I do so wish to hear my name shouted.

Mary Let us start again: to build a new world, one must know what is wrong with the old. What do you most want to be rid of, Jack?

Jack Tyranny. I want to kill the tyrants.

Mr Manners That won't do, Mary.

Mary Shouldn't we hear the people?

Mr Manners One must interpret to lead.

Lord Gordon You said I could be the leader in this, Mr Manners, you said I could make myself known in history.

Mr Manners You will, Lord Gordon.

Lord Gordon I know: the French!

Mary What about the French?

Lord Gordon What I most want to be rid of. Hate them. Riot against them. No French!

Mr Manners That's called war and we already have one.

Mary Sophie, what do you most dislike?

Sophie Me? I don't know. Bad smells.

Jack That's my sweet lass.

Lord Gordon Told you it was the French. No French food. That'll rouse 'em.

Mr Manners (*to Mary*) There's actually a clue in all that.

Mary Where? We're not getting anywhere.

Mr Manners What makes a smell good or bad?

Lord Gordon I don't know, but I know it when I smell it.

Guard What do smells have to do with the new world?

Mrs Temptwell There won't be a new world.

Jack I don't understand any of this. I want to organize for bread and liberty.

Mrs Temptwell Go quickly before it's too late.

Sophie No, Jack. Mary will help us. She's thinking for us.

Mary Listen: our lives ought by nature to be pleasant and free, but are not. Why? We have been invaded by unnatural practices and beliefs: the bad smells. What are they?

Mr Manners Or: who are they?

Mary Yes.

Mr Manners The Dutch . . . but one could hardly get emotional about the Dutch. The Jews . . . not enough of them. The Irish . . .

Jack I hate the Irish, they take lower wages.

Mrs Temptwell They work, like you. They're turning you against your own kind.

Mary We must not turn against working people. What do all foreigners have in common?

Lord Gordon They're not English.

Mr Manners And not Church of England.

Jack We hate the Church.

Mary Yes. Anything that encourages superstition, hierarchy and prejudice is vile.

Mr Manners That's not the Church of England. After all, the Church of England is more England than Church. The superstitions are unfortunate remains from former times . . . when we were under the Catholics. Yes. The Catholics . . .

Lord Gordon I'm to lead a mob of Catholics?

Mr Manners You can't lead any mob, Gordon, you're in Parliament, remember? But you can present petitions . . .

Mary We've done all that. We're wasting time.

Mr Manners Did you know there's a bill about to be presented to the House which will give back to all Catholics their right to own property? There's already fear it will cause trouble. After all, the more Catholics take, the less for people like Jack.

Mary What do you think of the Catholics, Jack?

Jack I don't know much. They do smoky things on Sundays and come out smelling funny.

Mr Manners It's much worse than that, isn't it, Mary?

Mary Is it?

Mr Manners Tell Jack about the Catholics. Tell him how they stuff themselves with white bread on Sundays.

Mary Ah, yes. They buy it all up and hoard it in their chapels, that's why there's none left for you. Mr Manners –

Mr Manners Tell Jack about the Pope.

Mary He is the tyrant of tyrants –

Mr Manners The Pope has stores of bread in his palaces. He ships the bread secretly from England. He delights in eating Protestant bread. He would like to eat Protestants.

Mary He makes them starve instead. Every day the number of hungry Protestants is read out to him and it makes him laugh.

Jack Where is this Pope? I'll kill him.

Mary All Catholics are the Pope's slaves. If he tells them to drink the blood of Protestant children with their wine, they do.

Mr Manners Protestant children have been known to disappear near Catholic chapels.

Sophie Help!

Mary It's the Catholics who've enclosed all the common land so they could build their chapels underground.

Mrs Temptwell Oh!

Mr Manners That's right, Mary.

Mary The Pope builds his palaces of luxury and depravity with the bones of murdered Protestants.

Mr Manners Actually, the Pope is a woman. Her red robe is dyed anew every year in putrid blood.

Lord Gordon That's disgusting.

Mary The Pope washes his hands in the blood of tortured Protestant babes and drinks the tears of English mothers.

Sophie Mothers against the Pope!

Mr Manners That's not quite right.

Mary Popery is the beast who claws at our freedom.

Jack No to Popery, yes to Liberty.

Mr Manners Excellent. I suggest we leave out liberty for the moment.

Lord Gordon No Popery! Follow me.

Mr Manners You, Lord Gordon, must present a petition to Parliament. It will be for the repeal of the Catholic Relief Act.

Lord Gordon How do you spell Relief?

Mary You'll say the people don't want Catholics back in power. We'll explain all that later, but now we must rouse the people. Stop English babies from being roasted. No Popery!

Sophie Save the children. No Hopery.

Mary No. It's no Popery.

Jack Save the working man. No Popery!

Guard This new world . . .

Mary Later, later. No Poverty! No Popery!

Mrs Temptwell No fences. No Popery!

All No Popery!

They knock over the chairs. They chant.

NO POPERY. NO POPERY. NO POPERY.

SCENE NINE

The streets of London. Mary, Mr Manners, Lord Gordon.

Mary There are at least sixty thousand.

Mr Manners Assembling in Lambeth.

Mary A headless snake winding its way towards Westminster Bridge. I'm breathless.

Lord Gordon I'm a little nervous, too.

Mary It's time for you to go, Lord Gordon.

Mr Manners Do you have the petition ready?

Lord Gordon Here. In my hand. Both hands.

Mr Manners Present it at half past two. Parliament is certain to delay any consideration of such a petition. Announce this to the crowd.

Mary Tell them Parliament is on the side of the Catholics.

Lord Gordon There are so many. I won't be hurt, will I?

Mary Hurry, Lord Gordon, they're moving fast.

Lord Gordon I never liked crowds.

Mary Once they've surrounded Parliament, you won't get through.

Lord Gordon It's not an easy thing to become a historical figure.

He leaves.

Mary Thousands and I've roused them. Oh, this is a delight beyond anything. Aren't you enjoying yourself?

Mr Manners No. I like quiet. I'll be happy when it's over.

Mary But this is a beginning. A new surge, which I shall lead.

Mr Manners To what?

Mary Freedom.

Mr Manners You could be very useful, Mary, but you have a lot to learn. Power, however, is a brilliant master. Ah, listen. Shouts. The crowd's beginning to be unruly. It usually takes an hour or two, a few well-placed rumours . . .

Sophie and Jack run on.

Sophie Parliament won't save us from the Catholics.

Jack We'll save ourselves from the Catholics.

Sophie We went to Duke Street.

Jack Where there are many Catholics.

Sophie We found the chapel of the ambassador from Gardenia.

Mary Gardenia?

Sophie It's a Poperist island, they capture ships and make shoes from the bones of sailors. They speak horrible spells in ill-Latin.

Mary Sardinia!

Jack No Popery and wooden shoes! We burnt the chapel.

Sophie No Popery!

Jack We're looking for the Bavarian chapel.

Sophie Burn it! No Popery!

Both No Popery!

They go off.

Mary Let's go. Let's go and lead them.

Mr Manners Power always moves from behind. Let the bodies move forward.

Mary I'm drunk with what I've done: glory!

The Guard runs on. Increasing noise of riot in the background.

Guard We're thousands but act like one. We have the strength to build the new world. Yes, we'll have all we want, we'll share it, we're one.

Mary Yes, Yes. And it's by my command. I've done it all.

Jack and Sophie come on.

Jack The Bavarian embassy: burnt. On to Wapping. Find the Catholic houses and throw all the contents on to the street. Burn, burn it all. There's a house belongs to a Protestant manufacturer, we're going to leave it but someone shouts: why? Catholic or not, why should anyone be possessed of more than a thousand pounds a year? Yes. Why? Burn it to the ground.

Sophie No Popery. Freedom for all. Set the Protestant prisoners free. To Newgate.

Jack To Bridewell.

Both No Popery. To Clerkenwell.

They rush off.

Mary This burning makes me a little uneasy, Mr Manners.

Mr Manners If you want to chop wood, you must expect the chips to fly. Are you afraid?

Mary No indeed.

Mr Manners It has never been possible to define freedom.

Mary What?

Mr Manners Nothing. It's getting dark. Shapes lose their firmness.

Jack comes on, followed by Sophie. Noise and fire in the background.

Sophie Lord Gordon has presented the petition five times and Parliament has refused to consider it five times. And now they want to go home and sleep. We're rough handling the ones we catch. They're afraid to come out.

Jack We're collecting for the poor mob. Give to the poor mob. For the poor mob.

Sophie Here. Here's a penny for the poor mob. But I am the poor mob.

The Guard runs on.

Guard No Popery and wooden shoes. To Holborn.

Jack To Holborn!

Sophie To Holborn!

They run off.

Mary Why Holborn?

Mr Manners Streets and streets of distilleries. And they all belong to Catholics – or so the rumour goes.

Mary I don't understand. I feel so powerful I can't think any more. Look. Fire.

Mr Manners There are twenty thousand gallons of gin in Holborn.

Mary Oh God!

Mr Manners God?

Silence. Mrs Temptwell comes on slowly, charred. She speaks coldly and quietly to Mary.

Mrs Temptwell It was dark, only a few thousand of us left. Prisoners, enthusiasts, those who couldn't free themselves from the throe of the crowd. We heard 'to Holborn'. We moved, step by step, pushed, pushing. Torches were at the front. We heard there was gin inside the houses, gin to refresh the mob. We rushed in, we fell in, pressed against the houses, torches high. I was pushed, I dropped, on my knees, drank the liquid, warm, then burning, looked up to see all coated in flames, fire rippling along the gin, houses, people, clothes, all burning.

Pause.

Bodies pushed each other into the burning river, slid, still trying to drink, lapped at the fire. Women, children, tearing off their clothes, people laughed. Laughed. A man next to me found a girl, rolled her into the fire, pulled up her skirts. A wall crumbled over them.

Mary Stop.

Mrs Temptwell Arms, arms waved underneath bodies. Faces, shouting, mouths black, teeth chattering: dogs snapping at the edge of hell. A woman grabbed me. 'I was just looking,' she said, 'why me?' Her cindered scalp peeled off.

Mary Stop it!

Mrs Temptwell The smell. It was the smell. I fainted, slept. All quiet, the fire on to other houses. Moved a leg, shoved a body off me, crawled on cushion of corpses, soft, nothing much left.

Mary It's not true. It didn't happen.

Mrs Temptwell opens a bundle she's been carrying, ashes and bones, and throws them over Mary.

Mrs Temptwell Look carefully through the teeth and you'll find some gold.

Mary No! No! It cannot have happened.

Jack runs on, his clothes are smouldering.

Jack Water. I'm burning. Gin. the working man's in flames. Help me.

Sophie rushes to him.

Sophie Jack! Jack! (*She laughs, drunk.*) We've burnt everything. No Popery. No nothing. Jack. Damn them. Damn everything. Jack!

She punches him, laughing. They fall over and roll off, together.

Mary Oh my sweet Sophie. No.

The Guard comes on.

Guard Where's my new world, where is it? Where?

He leaves. Giles Traverse comes on.

Giles They're moving towards the Bank of England, Mr Manners.

Mr Manners Ah. That must be stopped.

Giles (*to Mary*) So you've been involved in this horror?

Mary I didn't want it to be like this. Please believe me. I wanted something good. I had dreams.

Giles I could have told you how quickly private dreams become public nightmares.

Mary Why didn't you warn me?

Giles Would you have listened?

Mary Help me.

Giles How can I, Mary? You're accountable now.

Mr Manners Tell them to send the soldiers, Giles. And for the soldiers to shoot.

Mary No!

Giles You can't do that, Mr Manners.

Mr Manners If you don't agree with our policies, Giles, you need not stay with us.

Giles This isn't policy, this is crime.

Mr Manners Do what I ask or you will be suspected of condoning this horror and encouraging these criminals.

Mary This isn't what I wanted!

Giles Do we ever know what we want?

He leaves.

Mary Don't let them shoot, don't.

Mr Manners There is nothing so cleansing as massive death, Mary. People return with relief to their private little pains and stop barking at the future. It's what they want. This will last forty years at least, forty years of rule and order.

Mary Damn your order and your rules.

Mr Manners Don't damn the rules, Mary. Rules keep you from horror and emptiness. They bring peace to the heart, they're clear and simple, they hide the lengthening shadows. I'll do anything to keep the rules safe, not only for myself but for the good of the world. One day all men will understand the beauty of rules.

Lord Gordon rushes on.

Lord Gordon They say it's my fault. They want to arrest me. Save me.

Mr Manners We will. Give us time. Go to them now.

Lord Gordon (*to Mary*) I've just remembered where I saw you. I didn't mean to, that is, I didn't know – it didn't seem to matter. They're coming for me. It was better to be nobody.

Lord Gordon runs off. The shooting starts.

Mary Please, please tell me it isn't so.

She screams. The shooting continues.

Mrs Temptwell (*she has been piling the bones into a neat little pile*) One, two, twelve, one hundred, two hundred and forty thousand, three million, six million, twenty million, thirty-eight, two, eighteen, one, four, one.

Mary Please tell me it did not happen.

Act Four

Lodgings in Oxford Street, near Tyburn. Sophie has a baby in her arms. Mrs Temptwell tries to get near her.

Sophie I love her.

Mrs Temptwell That's a title to nothing. Give her to me.

Sophie I've looked after her well.

Mrs Temptwell You always were a fool.

Sophie I want to see Miss Mary.

Mrs Temptwell Do as you're told.

Mary comes on. She's half-dressed, a mess. She drags herself to a chair and collapses.

Mary Find a shoe for my right foot, Mrs Temptwell.

Mrs Temptwell I don't know where they are.

Mary kicks off her one shoe.

Mary There. Order. No.

She stares vacantly at one of her legs, then rolls down her one stocking. She stops.

Leave it. (*to Sophie*) What are you doing here?

Sophie You wanted to see your child.

Mary Did I?

Mrs Temptwell The future citizen of the new world.

Mary Stop. Yes: the last act.

Sophie Let me take her back to the country. We're very happy. Jack is coming soon.

Mary Jack.

Sophie They'll let him go, he didn't do anything.

Mrs Temptwell You don't have to do anything to get yourself killed. Give us the child.

Sophie Why?

Mary Don't use that fateful word. Has that woman tempted you as well? Run.

Mrs Temptwell You did what you wanted.

Mary Did I? I wanted knowledge, but I didn't know what it was. Even God wouldn't love this world if he existed, and I know he doesn't because Voltaire said so and Voltaire is a wit and the truth can only be funny. (*to Sophie*) You never laugh.

Sophie What will you do with her?

Mary Look at us – crumbling. Too charred to scavenge for more hope. Soon we can stop breathing – last intake of the future. But it's not enough: our death won't redeem what's been. I am human. I know the world. I've shared its acts. And I would like to pour poison down the throat of this world, burn out its hideous memories. A white cloud to cancel it all. How? I don't know. But I can start here. I can look after what I've generated. Stop it.

Sophie You want to poison your daughter.

Mrs Temptwell We're all poisoned anyway.

Sophie You can't do that.

Mary Is there anything of which we are not capable?

Sophie You don't know.

Mrs Temptwell She knows everything.

Sophie You're wrong. You don't know how to think, Mary. You think at a distance – too ahead or far back. If you just looked, from near.

Mrs Temptwell Our Sophie's found her tongue.

Mary Just when I want silence.

Mrs Temptwell Must be that country air. Pink cheeks. Pink thoughts.

Sophie Stop, Mrs Temptwell, don't you dare. Listen to me, Mary. I know – about mornings.

Mary The mornings?

Sophie The first light of the morning. It's fresh, new. And I feel a kind of hunger in the mornings, but without the pain. Cold water on the skin. It makes her laugh too. Think about the mornings.

Mrs Temptwell Corpses look very fresh in the morning. You can go.

Sophie In London too, the windows, the crisscross of the panes. You walk and then suddenly you're in one of the new squares, light, Don't you understand?

Mrs Temptwell We don't need an upstart bumpkin preaching to us. Go.

Sophie I will not. Miss Mary is unhappy about the world, but you, Mrs Temptwell, are only full of hate. She hates you, Mary, she always did. (*Pause.*) She only wants to hurt you. Then she'll be happy.

Mary Is that true?

(*Pause.*)

I suppose it's fair.

Sophie No. It's wrong.

Mary Not wrong, but small. As small as everything else. The world is made up of small particles of unspeakable ugliness. Why should I have the arrogance to claim a shared despair? (*to Mrs Temptwell*) Couldn't you have just strangled me in my cradle?

Mrs Temptwell I hate you, Mary, I hate your father, I hate your child, but she's wrong, it's no longer for what you did to me, no, it's for what you are. I know who you are, now, your kind. You're the evil spirits of the world, you keep us bound. Everything you touch goes wrong, but you always save yourselves and then go all poetic over other people's bodies. I know all we need is your death and then it won't go wrong again. Then there can be a new world. I'm starting here, but we'll get all of you.

Mary More burning, more bones.

Mrs Temptwell The right bones this time. I'll laugh when I touch the ashes of thy kind, Mary Traverse.

Mary I see. (*Pause.*) Perhaps you're right. But you could simply become addicted to counting bodies. And greed can attach itself to anyone. So. (*Pause.*) Let me have the child.

Sophie You can't decide for anyone, Mary.

Mary The child is mine.

Sophie She's not yours. You gave her birth, that's all. Let her decide, when she's ready, when she knows.

Mary Give her to me.

Sophie She likes to watch the street.

Mrs Temptwell She'll see men on their way to be hanged at Tyburn. That's why we took these lodgings. It's the best attended amusement in London.

Over this Sophie has begun to sing an incredibly beautiful song. She moves away from both of them and goes on singing.

Mary Listen.

Mrs Temptwell Shouts for death.

Mary Listen to Sophie. Ha. A grace note there.

Sophie sings, watching the street.

What are you looking at, Sophie, what is it you see?

Sophie Look at the stone. The carved stone.

Mary The new houses. Soft grey lines sloping against the London sky.

Sophie sings.

Do I have it all wrong? Sing, Sophie. If I were God your song would appease me and I would forgive the history of the world.

Sophie (*giving Mary the child*) Touch a baby's skin. It's the same thing.

Mrs Temptwell There's a cart. See who's in there, Sophie, and then sing to us.

Sophie (*screams*) Jack!

SCENE TWO

*Tyburn. Sophie, Mrs Temptwell and Mary holding her baby. A **Man** pulls a cart. Jack is inside, alone. Lord Exrake follows the cart.*

Sophie Jack!

Mary I thought it would be Lord Gordon.

Sophie Jack!

Mrs Temptwell You don't like to hang lords.

Sophie Jack. Speak to me. Jack.

Jack is silent.

Man Let the cart pass.

Lord Exrake Is he going to say something?

Mary Lord Exrake!

Lord Exrake Hello, my dear. Who are you? Forgive me
. . . my memory. What a sweet child. Not mine, I hope.
No: too young. These days . . .

Sophie Jack. It's me. Sophie. Speak to me.

Jack is silent.

Lord Exrake Sophie . . . means wisdom. I have loved . . .
Did you ask why I'm here? I've found a way to go to sleep.
I listen to what they say before they're hanged. I repeat
their last words and it makes me sleep. Try it.

Mary Is there no grace, somewhere?

Lord Exrake (*to the Man*) When will he talk?

Man Don't know. Some of them make jokes at the end.
Some tell their lives, give speeches. I've never seen one who
wouldn't talk.

Lord Exrake Silence. Silence at the very end. Would that
make me sleep?

Sophie (*to Mary*) You know he didn't do anything. Tell
them!

Mary Who will listen?

Mrs Temptwell Sing to her, Sophie.

Man (*to Jack*) Look, I know how you feel. Animals out there, aren't they? But you have a wife, right? Someone, anyway. Children? Well, there's a way you can take care of them when you're dead. Nothing magic. I work for this man: all you have to do is say this word we tell you and we'll look after your widow and any woman. What about it?

Sophie Jack!

Man Look, she's crying for you. You don't want her to go hungry, do you? All you have to do is say, before the man – you know. Just before. All you say is: Drink Olvitie. Got it? Drink Olvitie. That's all.

Lord Exrake That's what a man said a few weeks ago. Drink Olvitie. I've been drinking it ever since.

Man Remember that: Drink Olvitie, and she'll be looked after.

Sophie (*to Mary*) You did all this. You should be up there. Go on. Kill your child. Here, I'll put her under the wheel for you.

Mary Sophie, no. Not now. Not from you. I know we can . . . we will find.

Mrs Temptwell You won't.

Lord Exrake Have you lost something, my dear? Perhaps I can help you. What won't she find?

Mrs Temptwell Grace. She hasn't the right.

Sophie Jack!

Mary Come with me, Sophie. We will grieve, but we won't despair. Come.

> *Mary takes Sophie in her arms and turns away her head. Jack stares, impassive. Silence.*

Lord Exrake Silence. Not even a curse.

*Schubert's Adagio in E flat major op. post. 148
'Notturno'.*

SCENE THREE

A garden in the Potteries. Mary, Sophie, Giles, Little Mary.

Mary Beauty. Seen, unseen. I want to touch the light on the river. But we can't even see light. Perhaps one day we'll understand it.

Giles Are you still trying to understand everything?

Sophie When you told me the world was made up of little particles, Mary, I cried for days.

Giles I was unhappy when I found out how old the world was.

Mary I love your wrinkles, Father.

Giles Are there not things it is better not to know? Others it is best to forget?

Sophie No. We must not forget.

Mary And now the light lifts itself, streaks the chimneys. Gone.

Giles Where's little Mary? I'll take her in.

Mrs Temptwell comes on.

Mrs Temptwell This is my father's land. Try to throw me off.

Giles No. That much I have learned. Other things too . . . but I'm old. Speak to them.

Mary I'm certain that when we understand it all, it'll be simpler, not more confusing. One day we'll know how to love this world.

Mrs Temptwell Will you know how to make it just?

Giles Mary!

Mary There she is.

Blackout.

OUR COUNTRY'S GOOD

In memory of John Price

Preface

In the summer of 1988, I went to HMP Wormwood
Scrubs with the actors of *Our Country's Good*, the
director Max Stafford-Clark and Philip Howard, the
assistant director. We went to see a performance of
Howard Barker's *The Love of a Good Man*, performed by
long-term prisoners, that is, prisoners convicted of the
most serious crimes. It was an unforgettable evening. We
huddled in the forecourt as the prison gates closed behind
us, and then were led through the courtyard: high walls,
barbed wire – upstairs to the barking of guard dogs and
finally into a small room. But, once the play began, we
were at the theatre: the intensity of the performances, the
extremely good acting of some of the prisoners, the
understanding they seemed to have of this complex play,
made it a riveting evening. Afterwards, they were as happy
and eager for praise as any actors after a good
performance, but we only had five minutes before we
watched them being led back to their cells.

That night was pivotal for the acting and writing of *Our
Country's Good*: it confirmed all our feelings about the
power and the value of theatre.

Some months later I received the first letter from Joe
White. Other letters followed, from other prisoners. (I
have printed these in full, unedited.) Joe White then asked
me if he could put on *Our Country's Good* at Blundeston
prison, Lowestoft, where he had been transferred. Philip
Howard and I went to see it. It seemed to me the play had
come full circle, performed in that prison room with an
intensity and accuracy playwrights dream of and I

remember relishing the wit with which the prisoners portrayed the officers of the play.

As I write this, many Education Departments of prisons are being cut – theatre comes under the Education Department – and the idea of tough punishment as justice seems to be gaining ground in our increasingly harsh society. I hope these letters speak for themselves and, indeed, for our world.

T. W.
London, June 1991

LETTERS FROM JOE WHITE

N55463 J. WHITE
D WING
HMP BLUNDESTON
LOWESTOFT
SUFFOLK NR32 5BG
APRIL 1989

Dear Timberlake,

It seems an age since the production of 'The Love Of A Good Man' at the 'Scrubs'. Within a couple of months the 'inside' cast was split up and moved to various far flung parts of the country.

Firstly a belated congratulations on your award for 'Our Country's Good'. I did manage to have a read of the script, Eve White – one of the actresses – brought a copy in for us to read. Of course I'd much rather have been able to see a performance, but, there you go. Reading through the play, there were moments of ghostly familiarity, uncanny likeness.

Secondly, the compliments you gave to our play in the various reviews of 'Our Country's Good', did not pass unnoticed. Not to mention the 'plug' you gave us all on actually receiving your award. It is difficult for me to explain the sense of achievement and feelings of pride it gave not only myself and the rest of the cast, but also to our families and friends. It spoke volumes. Thank you.

Mac, who played the Prince of Wales in 'The Love Of . . .' was moved to a prison on the Isle of Shepey, where he is making moves to start a drama group. Here at Blundeston, I was lucky enough to meet up with a fellow 'lifer' that I'd previously acted with in another Scrubs production, Steven Berkoff's 'East'. Lee subsequently wrote a play 'Timecycles' about prison life, based around some of Steve's material. We set to work getting it put on here. I had a bash at directing, and I'm happy to say the first (of many hopefully) Blundeston plays was performed last month to the rest of the guys in here. It was quite an experience for all concerned. You wouldn't believe the amount of energy and patience needed to get it all together. Maybe you would – a universal aspect of the theatre?

Basically the spirit lives on. Prison is about failure normally, and how we are reminded of it each day of every year. Drama, and self-expression in general, is a refuge and one of the only real weapons against the hopelessness of these places. I believe you gained the insight to recognize this, it is evident in your writing.

Theatre is, of course, an essential part of all society, and I'm glad to say that it is alive and kicking within these walls. Long may it do so. Again many, many thanks, and I look forward to reading more of your work.

Yours sincerely,

Joe White

(Hacker)

Dear Timberlake,

Thank you for your letter, I had meant to reply sooner but its been a particularly hectic few weeks for me, both emotionally and physically.

Firstly, I'm sorry that I was unable to speak to you on the phone, in prison, the other week. I'm afraid it's one of those infuriating procedures that it does no one any good trying to fathom out. I thought it worth a try though, to see if (by some miracle) you could have got away at such short notice. Perhaps in the future, if you were interested and given a little more pre-warning, you could come to our next production.

'TIMECYCLES' has finally come to a close. We've just finished editing a video of the invited audience performance. It's proved not only an interesting experience but has also served as a great tonic against the Post-Production Blues.

'TIMECYCLES' was a play that attempted to face the realities of prison life, by focusing on the effects of prison on individuals – rather than on the political quagmire that surrounds these institutions. During the brief opportunity I had to talk to the audience afterwards, it soon became apparent that they were more concerned with the actual event itself and the constituent parts of the production, rather than the subject matter. I wonder if you have experienced anything similar, with view to your own work? Maybe it was a case of the audience's attention to the play, merging with their impressions of entering a prison, and that the real impact of the play would register once outside again?

It obviously means a great deal to receive praise for a performance as an actor, but I can't help feeling this should be secondary to the reaction the play has, or has failed, to provoke in the audience. I felt like pointing out that most of what they had seen portrayed in drama, was actually happening, at that very moment, not a hundred yards away. In this respect I still feel that the play failed, in that this connection was not seen to be made. Am I expecting too much do you think? Could it be that a play's impact on an audience is more subtle? I'm sure, having directed the play and its subject being so poignant for me, has had a lot to do with this stress on the importance of meaning. I feel it is an instructive lesson though, as long as it doesn't lead to excessive depression!

As for the future, I have been in contact with Snoo Wilson and would dearly love to produce 'The Glad Hand' here, hopefully early in the new year. I believe it was first produced at the Royal Court and directed by Max in 78. It really is such a challenging play and so different from 'TIMECYCLES'. It would allow full rein to both the actors and the stage crew's imagination, as opposed to the excessive amounts of personal experience needed for 'TIMECYCLES'. Snoo has expressed a wish to attend rehearsals, and what with the chances of a director being employed here still being slim, I would be doubly keen to have him present, if only sporadically. I am very excited about this new project.

Charles Vance came to see 'TIMECYCLES' and has promised us a piece in the Amateur Stage. He also offered his services to take a couple of 'master acting classes' – I wish I knew what they were! I must admit to being a little dubious about this, as I'm not entirely sure we're on the same wavelength. I suppose it would be a good experience either way though?

I'm really pleased that 'Our Country's Good' is back at the Court. Some of my family are hoping to get to see it. I did write to Max ages ago, giving him my whole-hearted permission to re-print my letter to you in the programme, if he so wished. I fear, though, that it is possible my letter failed to reach him, prison mail being almost as undependable as the telephone system is unreachable!

Anyway, I trust all is going well and I look forward to reading the new script. If you do wish to send Stanislavsky's book it would be gratefully received. There is no problem, thank goodness, about books being sent into prison. They are a lifeline to me. I hope to hear from you soon.

Best wishes,

Joe x.

Dear Timberlake,

Thank you for your letter, bearing the good news enabling us to set to work on 'Our Country's Good'. I can't believe that was over a month ago. I really have meant to write sooner. It has been such a busy month. Hopefully, Frances will have conveyed to you my, and the rest of the cast's great pleasure and excitement at the news. I was particularly touched by your own enthusiasm for the production, and I am looking forward immensely to hearing your responses to our work.

Initially, I found it strange to be working on a play that I already held a strong emotional attachment to and involvement with. Combined with the fact that I was working with a director again – therefore having to relinquish the reins of artistic control, albeit willingly – has led to feelings of uncertainty as to how much I should contribute to rehearsals. I was very conscious of not wanting to tread on our director's toes. It's possible that I've been cautious about writing to you about the play because of this.

Everything has come together extremely well I feel. There have been wonderful moments of sharing experiences among the cast. Everyone has brought something important to the play. There have also been, seemingly, strange tricks of reality when the play and our situation have overlapped merging the borders of the creative process and actuality.

I am finding the character of Ralph Clark a challenging and an enjoyable role. His naivete is perhaps akin to my own when first entering the prison system. There is also the touch of the romantic about him I feel and maybe in spite of his seriousness, a comic element too. Anyway you shall judge for yourself.

The Royal Court, namely Max Stafford-Clark and Jennifer Cook, have been wonderfully helpful, with press contacts and the loan of costumes. All in all I feel strongly that this production was meant to be.

I look forward to seeing you.

With Best Wishes,

Joe White.

Dear Timberlake,

Of course you have my permission to use any extracts from my letters that you think might be suitable to use in an introduction to 'Our Country's Good'.

I have always been lucky in that I have always discovered close affinities with the various scripts I've worked on. 'Our Country's Good', though, is a play I feel I developed a very special relationship with and I am extremely happy to be involved in this way. Billy, I have spoken to and he is delighted at the prospect – I believe he intends to write to you himself. Perhaps you could send me a copy of the republished edition somewhere, as my present one shows all the signs of a well-worked script!

I shall be moving to Norwich in the early N. Year to an annexed section of Norwich Prison. It is a more open prison, with, I'm informed, 'a very progressive attitude'. We shall soon see. The place certainly sports an impressively heraldic name, Britannia! I'm hopeful of establishing links with the nearby University and possibly the Maddermarket Theatre, where I once worked on a voluntary basis many moons ago.

A production company is showing enormous interest – perhaps too much – in making possibly two programmes for Channel 4, regarding the proposed Crime and Punishment project. Firstly, in the form of an Art documentary, with the idea of following a prison production through various stages of rehearsal and secondly, a full blown television drama of the finished production to run alongside the documentary. Considering Norwich hasn't even a drama group as yet, it's still *very* early days – it is all very exciting none the less, I hope something comes of it all.

Yes, I would be interested in reading 'The Possessed', I have a great deal of spare time these days.

Best Wishes,

Joe

LETTER FROM GREG STABLER-SMITH

G. STABLER-SMITH
N56002 D. WING
HMP WORMWOOD SCRUBS
DU CANE ROAD
LONDON W12 0AE

11.2.89

Deat Timberlake,

Just a few lines to thank you, for mentioning us the drama group, I'm sure that Joe, Mac, Colin and Rick all join me in saying thankyou.

Being able to do the play alone was an unbelievable insight and experience for us all, but the feedback completely blew our minds.

Memories from prison are on the whole negative but having the part of Clout is one positive memory I won't forget.

Eve one of the actresses from 'A Good Man' first brought in Our Country's Good which we read as a group and really enjoyed, but now we have the same problem. Joe Mac and Colin have moved on to other nicks and I shall be on my way soon.

What you said to the Guardian and on the Olivia awards (our director videoed it) was really special to us, it will take me a long time to forget and as they say, I've got plenty of time (laughter.)

Must close now thanks and takecare

Greg.

15.2.89
P.S. I've just been told I'll be moving to Lewes prison in a few weeks so that's put the clamp on another play here for

174

me, but I've heard there's a drama group down there, I'll have to see what the material is like, I don't really want to go back to Ray Cooney after Berkoff & Barker.

Bye.

In replying to this letter, please write on the envelope:
Number L15979   Name Reid – Billy M.C.

> B WING 124
> HMP BLUNDESTON
> LOWESTOFT
> SUFFOLK NR32 5BG
>
> 7 June 90

Hullo Timberlake,

Billy Reid here (I played Harry in O.C's.G.). I had a read of your letter. Thanx for the compliments, and Thanx again for making it all possible. I'm sorry I didn't get to Thank you personally after our performance, not that I feel it matters now, but I just thot I'd mention it.

It's good to know you were happy with our interpretation of O.C's.G. It was all a Bran U scene to me, I mean where I come from in Glasgow there isn't any Drama or Theatre. Wot a pity! Maybe after my release I could go back and spread the script. I should've picked up enough exp by then. In Glasgow theres so much mischanneled energy you wouldn't believe. Youngsters with real potential who want to be good or the best at something. Usually, because of the options, they become good at stealing, chatting up Girls or fighting, or, like me, getting the jail, HA! HA!

I'm glad I took the plunge into Drama when I did. Initially I joined to refine my speech and learn how to communicate with other people. Those reasons must come across really stupid to someone like yourself who knows a lot about the theatrical world, well wotever I got a lot-lot more than wot I'd expected. That wasn't all down to the acting side of it but more down to O.C's.G. and the part of Harry. I got so much out of that I play. I was already on the Road but doing O.C's.G. gave me the opportunity to take a short cut on my own Road to Reality. I mean just tying my hair back or getting it cut out of my face would've taken me yonx to do wot with the scars and blind left eye. I've since put my hair back to it's natural state, wild'n'curly, tying it back served a purpose because now if I get a part that calls for me to have short-looking hair I won't hesitate to tie and gel it back, I aint so weak in that area no more. That was the first time in 9 years the top $\frac{1}{2}$ of my face had seen the light of day.

Thanx again

Billy

Timberlake
PS. I KNOW YOU'RE BUSY OUT THERE SO DON'T BOTHER WORRYING ABOUT WRITING BACK. I JUST WANTED TO SAY THANX.

Hullo Again Timberlake,

Billy Reid here. I hope all is well with you and yours out there. I'm doing allright back here.

I was out on a 4 day home leave, when I came back Joe let me see your letter. Sorry I haven't replied any sooner than now. Anyway Timberlake I'd be honoured to give my permission for you to publish my letter in whole or in part for the republication of O.C's.G.

Since doing O.C's.G. I haven't been into any thing to do with the Drama, that don't mean I'm giving up on it, I quit the Drama because I was going thru a particularly difficult phase and didn't want to draw any heat towards the Drama Group, as it happened anyway, the Group weren't getting any real encouragement because of the internal scene. It's a real pity the people who make the rules can't, or wont, see the sort of benifit a person can get from acting while doing a sentence. I thot after doing O.C's.G. with all its possitive feedback, we'd have gotten a lot more help. We couldn't have asked for any better than the Guardian gave us. Obviously it didn't go down too well with someone with enough weight to block the Drama Groups progress, it's real sad when people like THAT are allowed to make such decisions.

Before I went on home leave I did hear there'd been a discussion about the Drama Group, music group and the prison magazine, which was an idea of mine, I've yet to find out the result of the discussion.

Well that's about it for now, all the best for the future,

Billy H. C. Reid

PS. Good luck with your new project.

Twenty per cent of the children in a certain elementary school were reported to their teachers as showing unusual potential for intellectual growth. The names of these twenty per cent of the children were drawn by means of a table of random numbers, which is to say that the names were drawn out of a hat. Eight months later these unusual or 'magic' children showed significantly greater gains in IQ than did the remaining children who had not been singled out for the teachers' attention. The change in the teachers' expectations regarding the intellectual performance of these allegedly 'special' children had led to an actual change in the intellectual performance of these randomly selected children . . . who were also described as more interesting, as showing greater intellectual curiosity and as happier.

R. Rosenthal and L. Jacobsen *Pygmalion in the Classroom*

Characters

Captain Arthur Phillip
Major Robbie Ross
Captain David Collins
Captain Watkin Tench
Captain Jemmy Campbell
Reverend Johnson
Lieutenant George Johnston
Lieutenant Will Dawes
Second Lieutenant Ralph Clark
Second Lieutenant William Faddy
Midshipman Harry Brewer
The Aborigine
John Arscott
Black Caesar
Ketch Freeman
Robert Sideway
John Wisehammer
Mary Brenham
Dabby Bryant
Liz Morden
Duckling Smith
Meg Long

Our Country's Good was premièred at the Royal Court Theatre, London on 10 September 1988 with the following cast:

Captain Arthur Phillip, RN (*Governor-in-Chief of New South Wales*) Ron Cook
Major Robbie Ross, RM Mark Lambert
Captain David Collins, RM (*Advocate General*) Nick Dunning
Captain Watkin Tench, RM Jude Akuwudike
Captain Jemmy Campbell, RM Jim Broadbent
Reverend Johnson Lesley Sharp
Lieutenant George Johnstone, RM Alphonsia Emmanuel
Lieutenant Will Dawes, RM Linda Bassett
Second Lieutenant Ralph Clark, RM David Haig
Second Lieutenant William Faddy, RM Mossie Smith
Midshipman Harry Brewer, RN (*Provost Marshal*) Jim Broadbent
The Aborigine Jude Akuwudike
John Arscott Jim Broadbent
Black Caesar Jude Akuwudike
Ketch Freeman Mark Lambert
Robert Sideway Nick Dunning
John Wisehammer Ron Cook
Mary Brenham Lesley Sharp
Dabby Bryant Mossie Smith
Liz Morden Linda Bassett
Duckling Smith Alphonsia Emmanuel
Meg Long Lesley Sharp

Directed by Max Stafford-Clark
Décor by Peter Hartwell
Lighting by Jenny Cane
Sound by Bryan Bowen
Fights by Terry King

Note: The play takes place in Sydney, Australia in 1788–9.

Act One

SCENE ONE. THE VOYAGE OUT

The hold of a convict ship bound for Australia, 1787. The convicts huddle together in the semi-darkness. On deck, the convict **Robert Sideway** *is being flogged.* **Second Lieutenant Ralph Clark** *counts the lashes in a barely audible, slow and monotonous voice.*

Ralph Clark Forty-four, forty-five, forty-six, forty-seven, forty-eight, forty-nine, fifty.

> *Sideway is untied and dumped with the rest of the convicts. He collapses. No one moves. A short silence.*

John Wisehammer At night? The sea cracks against the ship. Fear whispers, screams, falls silent, hushed. Spewed from our country, forgotten, bound to the dark edge of the earth, at night what is there to do but seek English cunt, warm, moist, soft, oh the comfort, the comfort of the lick, the thrust into the nooks, the crannies of the crooks of England. Alone, frightened, nameless in this stinking hole of hell, take me, take me inside you, whoever you are. Take me, my comfort and we'll remember England together.

John Arscott Hunger. Funny. Doesn't start in the stomach, but in the mind. A picture flits in and out of a corner. Something you've eaten long ago. Roast beef with salt and grated horseradish.

Mary Brenham I don't know why I did it. Love, I suppose.

SCENE TWO. A LONE ABORIGINAL AUSTRALIAN DESCRIBES THE ARRIVAL OF THE FIRST CONVICT FLEET IN BOTANY BAY ON JANUARY 20, 1788

The Aborigine A giant canoe drifts on to the sea, clouds billowing from upright oars. This is a dream which has lost its way. Best to leave it alone.

SCENE THREE. PUNISHMENT

Sydney Cove. **Governor Captain Arthur Phillip, Judge Captain David Collins, Captain Watkin Tench, Midshipman Harry Brewer.** *The men are shooting birds.*

Phillip Was it necessary to cross fifteen thousand miles of ocean to erect another Tyburn?

Tench I should think it would make the convicts feel at home.

Collins This land is under English law. The court found them guilty and sentenced them accordingly. There: a bald-eyed corella.

Phillip But hanging?

Collins Only the three who were found guilty of stealing from the colony's stores. And that, over there on the Eucalyptus, is a flock of *Cacatua galerita* – the sulphur-crested cockatoo. You have been made Governor-in-Chief of a paradise of birds, Arthur.

Phillip And I hope not a human hell, Davey. Don't shoot yet, Watkin, let's observe them. Could we not be more humane?

Tench Justice and humaneness have never gone hand in hand. The law is not a sentimental comedy.

Phillip I am not suggesting they go without punishment. It is the spectacle of hanging I object to. The convicts will feel nothing has changed and will go back to their ways.

Tench The convicts never left their old ways, Governor, nor do they intend to.

Phillip Three months is not long enough to decide that. You're speaking too loud, Watkin.

Collins I commend your endeavour to oppose the baneful influence of vice with the harmonizing acts of civilization, Governor, but I suspect your edifice will collapse without the mortar of fear.

Phillip Have these men lost all fear of being flogged?

Collins John Arscott has already been sentenced to 150 lashes for assault.

Tench The shoulder-blades are exposed at about 100 lashes and I would say that somewhere between 250 and 500 lashes you are probably condemning a man to death anyway.

Collins With the disadvantage that the death is slow, unobserved and cannot serve as a sharp example.

Phillip Harry?

Harry The convicts laugh at hangings, Sir. They watch them all the time.

Tench It's their favourite form of entertainment, I should say.

Phillip Perhaps because they've never been offered anything else.

Tench Perhaps we should build an opera house for the convicts.

Phillip We learned to love such things because they were offered to us when we were children or young men. Surely no one is born naturally cultured? I'll have the gun now.

Collins We don't even have any books here, apart from the odd play and a few Bibles. And most of the convicts can't read, so let us return to the matter in hand, which is the punishment of the convicts, not their education.

Phillip Who are the condemned men, Harry?

Harry Thomas Barrett, aged seventeen. Transported seven years for stealing one ewe sheep.

Phillip Seventeen!

Tench It does seem to prove that the criminal tendency is innate.

Phillip It proves nothing.

Harry James Freeman, age twenty-five, Irish, transported fourteen years for assault on a sailor at Shadwell Dock.

Collins I'm surprised he wasn't hanged in England.

Harry Handy Baker, marine and the thieves' ringleader.

Collins He pleaded that it was wrong to put the convicts and the marines on the same rations and that he could not work on so little food. He almost swayed us.

Tench I do think that was an unfortunate decision. My men are in a ferment of discontent.

Collins Our Governor-in-Chief would say it is justice, Tench, and so it is. It is also justice to hang these men.

Tench The sooner the better, I believe. There is much

excitement in the colony about the hangings. It's their theatre, Governor, you cannot change that.

Phillip I would prefer them to see real plays: fine language, sentiment.

Tench No doubt Garrick would relish the prospect of eight months at sea for the pleasure of entertaining a group of criminals and the odd savage.

Phillip I never liked Garrick, I always preferred Macklin.

Collins I'm a Kemble man myself. We will need a hangman.

Phillip Harry, you will have to organize the hanging and eventually find someone who agrees to fill that hideous office.

Phillip shoots.

Collins Shot.

Tench Shot.

Harry Shot, Sir.

Collins It is my belief the hangings should take place tomorrow. The quick execution of justice for the good of the colony, Governor.

Phillip The good of the colony? Oh, look! We've frightened a kankaroo.

They look.

All Ah!

Harry There is also Dorothy Handland, eighty-two, who stole a biscuit from Robert Sideway.

Phillip Surely we don't have to hang an eighty-two-year-old woman?

Collins That will be unnecessary. She hanged herself this morning.

SCENE FOUR. THE LONELINESS OF MEN

Ralph Clark's tent. It is late at night. Ralph stands, composing and speaking his diary.

Ralph Dreamt, my beloved Alicia, that I was walking with you and that you was in your riding-habit – oh my dear woman when shall I be able to hear from you –

All the officers dined with the Governor – I never heard of any one single person having so great a power vested in him as Captain Phillip has by his commission as Governor-in-Chief of New South Wales – dined on a cold collation but the Mutton which had been killed yesterday morning was full of maggots – nothing will keep twenty-four hours in this dismal country I find –

Went out shooting after breakfast – I only shot one cockatoo – they are the most beautiful birds –

Major Ross ordered one of the Corporals to flog with a rope Elizabeth Morden for being impertinent to Captain Campbell – the Corporal did not play with her but laid it home which I was very glad to see – she has long been fishing for it –

On Sunday as usual, kissed your dear beloved image a thousand times – was very much frightened by the lightning as it broke very near my tent – several of the convicts have run away.

He goes to his table and writes in his journal.

If I'm not made 1st Lieutenant soon . . .

Harry Brewer has come in.

Ralph Harry –

Harry I saw the light in your tent –

Ralph I was writing my journal.

Silence.

Is there any trouble?

Harry No. (*Pause.*) I just came.
Talk, you know. If I wrote a journal about my life it would fill volumes. Volumes. My travels with the Captain – His Excellency now, no less, Governor-in-Chief, power to raise armies, build cities – I still call him plain Captain Phillip. He likes it from me. The war in America and before that, Ralph, my life in London. That would fill a volume on its own. Not what you would call a good life.

Pause.

Sometimes I look at the convicts and I think, one of those could be you, Harry Brewer, if you hadn't joined the navy when you did. The officers may look down on me now, but what if they found out that I used to be an embezzler?

Ralph Harry, you should keep these things to yourself.

Harry You're right, Ralph.

Pause.

I think the Captain suspects, but he's a good man and he looks for different things in a man –

Ralph Like what?

Harry Hard to say. He likes to see something unusual. Ralph, I saw Handy Baker last night.

Ralph You hanged him a month ago, Harry.

Harry He had a rope – Ralph, he's come back.

Ralph It was a dream. Sometimes I think my dreams are real – But they're not.

Harry We used to hear you on the ship, Ralph, calling for your Betsey Alicia.

Ralph Don't speak her name on this iniquitous shore!

Harry Duckling's gone silent on me again. I know it's because of Handy Baker. I saw him as well as I see you. Duckling wants me, he said, even if you've hanged me. At least your poker's danced its last shindy, I said. At least it's young and straight, he said, she likes that. I went for him but he was gone. But he's going to come back, I know it. I didn't want to hang him, Ralph, I didn't.

Ralph He did steal that food from the stores.

Pause.

I voted with the rest of the court those men should be hanged, I didn't know His Excellency would be against it.

Harry Duckling says she never feels anything. How do I know she didn't feel something when she was with him? She thinks I hanged him to get rid of him, but I didn't, Ralph.

Pause.

Do you know I saved her life? She was sentenced to be hanged at Newgate for stealing two candlesticks but I got her name put on the transport lists. But when I remind her of that she says she wouldn't have cared. Eighteen years old, and she didn't care if she was turned off.

Pause.

These women are sold before they're ten. The Captain says we should treat them with kindness.

Ralph How can you treat such women with kindness? Why does he think that?

Harry Not all the officers find them disgusting, Ralph – haven't you ever been tempted?

Ralph Never! (*Pause.*) His Excellency never seems to notice me.

Pause.

He finds time for Davey Collins, Lieutenant Dawes.

Harry That's because Captain Collins is going to write about the customs of the Indians here – and Lieutenant Dawes is recording the stars.

Ralph I could write about the Indians.

Harry He did suggest to Captain Tench that we do something to educate the convicts, put on a play or something, but Captain Tench just laughed. He doesn't like Captain Tench.

Ralph A play? Who would act in a play?

Harry The convicts of course. He is thinking of talking to Lieutenant Johnston, but I think Lieutenant Johnston wants to study the plants.

Ralph I read *The Tragedy of Lady Jane Grey* on the ship. It is such a moving and uplifting play. But how could a whore play Lady Jane?

Harry Some of those women are good women, Ralph, I believe my Duckling is good. It's not her fault – if only she would look at me, once, react. Who wants to fuck a corpse!

Silence.

I'm sorry. I didn't mean to shock you, Ralph, I have shocked you, haven't I? I'll go.

Ralph Is His Excellency serious about putting on a play?

Harry When the Captain decides something, Ralph.

Ralph If I went to him – no. It would be better if you did, Harry, you could tell His Excellency how much I like the theatre.

Harry I didn't know that Ralph, I'll tell him.

Ralph Duckling could be in it, if you wanted.

Harry I wouldn't want her to be looked at by all the men.

Ralph If His Excellency doesn't like *Lady Jane* we could find something else.

Pause.

A comedy perhaps . . .

Harry I'll speak to him, Ralph. I like you.

Pause.

It's good to talk . . .

Pause.

You don't think I killed him then?

Ralph Who?

Harry Handy Baker.

Ralph No, Harry. You did not kill Handy Baker.

Harry Thank you, Ralph.

Ralph Harry, you won't forget to talk to His Excellency about the play?

SCENE FIVE. AN AUDITION

Ralph Clark, **Meg Long.** *Meg Long is very old and very smelly. She hovers over Ralph.*

Meg We heard you was looking for some women, Lieutenant. Here I am.

Ralph I've asked to see some women to play certain parts in a play.

Meg I can play, Lieutenant, I can play with any part you like. There ain't nothing puts Meg off. That's how I got my name: Shitty Meg.

Ralph The play has four particular parts for young women.

Meg You don't want a young woman for your peculiar, Lieutenant, they don't know nothing. Shut your eyes and I'll play you as tight as a virgin.

Ralph You don't understand, Long. Here's the play. It's called *The Recruiting Officer*.

Meg Oh, I can do that too.

Ralph What?

Meg Recruiting. Anybody you like. (*She whispers*.) You want women: you ask Meg. Who do you want?

Ralph I want to try some out.

Meg Good idea, Lieutenant, good idea. Ha! Ha! Ha!

Ralph Now if you don't mind –

Meg doesn't move.

Long!

Meg (*frightened but still holding her ground*) We thought you was a madge cull.

Ralph What?

Meg You know, a fluter, a mollie. (*impatiently*) A prissy cove, a girl! You having no she-lag on the ship. Nor here, neither. On the ship maybe you was seasick. But all these months here. And now we hear how you want a lot of women, all at once. Well, I'm glad to hear that, Lieutenant, I am. You let me know when you want Meg, old Shitty Meg.

She goes off quickly and Robert Sideway comes straight on.

Sideway Ah, Mr Clark.

He does a flourish.

I am calling you Mr Clark as one calls Mr Garrick Mr Garrick, we have not had the pleasure of meeting before.

Ralph I've seen you on the ship.

Sideway Different circumstances, Mr Clark, best forgotten. I was once a gentleman. My fortune has turned. The wheel . . . You are doing a play, I hear, ah, Drury Lane, Mr Garrick, the lovely Peg Woffington. (*conspiratorially*) He was so cruel to her. She was so pale –

Ralph You say you were a gentleman, Sideway?

Sideway Top of my profession, Mr Clark, pickpocket, born and bred in Bermondsey. Do you know London, Sir, don't you miss it? In these my darkest hours, I remember my happy days in that great city. London Bridge at dawn – hand on cold iron for good luck. Down Cheapside with the market traders – never refuse a mince pie. Into St Paul's churchyard – I do love a good church – and begin work in Bond Street. There, I've spotted her, rich, plump, not of the best class, stands in front of the shop, plucking up courage, I pluck her. Time for coffee until five o'clock and the pinnacle, the glory of the day: Drury Lane. The coaches, the actors scuttling, the gentlemen watching, the ladies tittering, the perfumes, the clothes, the handkerchiefs.

He hands Ralph the handkerchief he has just stolen from him.

Here, Mr Clark, you see the skill. Ah, Mr Clark, I beg you, I entreat you, to let me perform on your stage, to let me feel once again the thrill of a play about to begin. Ah, I see ladies approaching: our future Woffingtons, Siddons.

Dabby Bryant *comes on, with a shrinking Mary Brenham in tow. Sideway bows.*

Ladies.

I shall await your word of command, Mr Clark, I shall be in the wings.

Sideway scuttles off.

Dabby You asked to see Mary Brenham, Lieutenant. Here she is.

Ralph Yes – the Governor has asked me to put on a play. (*to Mary*) You know what a play is?

Dabby I've seen lots of plays, Lieutenant, so has Mary.

Ralph Have you, Brenham?

Mary (*inaudibly*) Yes.

Ralph Can you remember which plays you've seen?

Mary (*inaudibly*) No.

Dabby I can't remember what they were called, but I always knew when they were going to end badly. I knew right from the beginning. How does this one end, Lieutenant?

Ralph It ends happily. It's called *The Recruiting Officer*.

Dabby Mary wants to be in your play, Lieutenant, and so do I.

Ralph Do you think you have a talent for acting, Brenham?

Dabby Of course she does, and so do I. I want to play Mary's friend.

Ralph Do you know *The Recruiting Officer*, Bryant?

Dabby No, but in all those plays, there's always a friend. That's because a girl has to talk to someone and she talks to her friend. So I'll be Mary's friend.

Ralph Silvia – that's the part I want to try Brenham for – doesn't have a friend. She has a cousin. But they don't like each other.

Dabby Oh. Mary doesn't always like me.

Ralph The Reverend Johnson told me you can read and write, Brenham?

Dabby She went to school until she was ten. She used to read to us on the ship. We loved it. It put us to sleep.

Ralph Shall we try reading some of the play?

Ralph hands her the book. Mary reads silently, moving her lips.

I meant read it aloud. As you did on the ship. I'll help you, I'll read Justice Balance. That's your father.

Dabby Doesn't she have a sweetheart?

Ralph Yes, but this scene is with her father.

Dabby What's the name of her lover?

Ralph Captain Plume.

Dabby A Captain! Mary!

Ralph Start here, Brenham.

Mary begins to read.

Mary 'Whilst there is life there is hope, Sir.'

Dabby Oh, I like that, Lieutenant. This is a good play, I can tell.

Ralph Shht. She hasn't finished. Start again, Brenham, that's good.

Mary 'Whilst there is life there is hope, Sir; perhaps my brother may recover.'

Ralph That's excellent, Brenham, very fluent. You could read a little louder. Now I'll read.
'We have but little reason to expect it. Poor Owen! But the decree is just; I was pleased with the death of my father, because he left me an estate, and now I'm punished with the loss of an heir to inherit mine.'

Pause. He laughs a little.

This is a comedy. They don't really mean it. It's to make people laugh. 'The death of your brother makes you sole heiress to my estate, which you know is about twelve hundred pounds a year.'

Dabby Twelve hundred pounds! It must be a comedy.

Mary 'My desire of being punctual in my obedience requires that you would be plain in your commands, Sir.'

Dabby Well said, Mary, well said.

Ralph I think that's enough. You read very well, Brenham. Would you also be able to copy the play? We have only two copies.

Dabby Course she will. Where do I come in, Lieutenant? The cousin.

Ralph Can you read, Bryant?

Dabby Not those marks in the books, Lieutenant, but I can read other things. I read dreams very well, Lieutenant. Very well.

Ralph I don't think you're right for Melinda. I'm thinking of someone else. And if you can't read . . .

Dabby Mary will read me the lines, Lieutenant.

Ralph There's Rose . . .

Dabby Rose. I like the name. I'll be Rose. Who is she?

Ralph She's a country girl . . .

Dabby I grew up in Devon, Lieutenant. I'm perfect for Rose. What does she do?

Ralph She – well, it's complicated. She falls in love with Silvia.

Mary begins to giggle but tries to hold it back.

But it's because she thinks Silvia's a man. And she – they – she sleeps with her. Rose. With Silvia. Euh. Silvia too. With Rose. But nothing happens.

Dabby It doesn't? Nothing?

Dabby bursts out laughing.

Ralph Because Silvia is pretending to be a man, but of course she can't –

Dabby Play the flute? Ha! She's not the only one around here. I'll do Rose.

Ralph I would like to hear you.

Dabby I don't know my lines yet, Lieutenant. When I know my lines, you can hear me do them. Come on, Mary –

Ralph I didn't say you could – I'm not certain you're the right – Bryant, I'm not certain I want you in the play.

Dabby Yes you do, Lieutenant. Mary will read me the lines and I, Lieutenant, will read you your dreams.

There's a guffaw. It's **Liz Morden**.

Ralph Ah. Here's your cousin.

There is a silence. Mary shrinks away. Dabby and Liz stare at each other, each holding her ground, each ready to pounce.

Melinda. Silvia's cousin.

Dabby You can't have her in the play, Lieutenant.

Ralph Why not?

Dabby You don't have to be able to read the future to know that Liz Morden is going to be hanged.

Liz looks briefly at Dabby, as if to strike, then changes her mind.

Liz I understand you want me in your play, Lieutenant. Is that it?

She snatches the book from Ralph and strides off.

I'll look at it and let you know.

SCENE SIX. THE AUTHORITIES DISCUSS THE MERITS OF THE THEATRE

Governor Arthur Phillip, **Major Robbie Ross,** *Judge David Collins, Captain Watkin Tench,* **Captain Jemnmy Campbell, Reverend Johnson, Lieutenant George Johnston, Lieutenant Will Dawes,** *Second Lieutenant Ralph Clark,* **Second Lieutenant William Faddy.**
It is late at night, the men have been drinking, tempers

are high. They interrupt each other, overlap, make jokes under and over the conversation but all engage in it with the passion for discourse and thought of eighteenth-century men.

Ross A play! A f –

Revd Johnson Mmhm.

Ross A frippery frittering play!

Campbell Aheeh, aeh, here?

Ralph (*timidly*) To celebrate the King's birthday, on June the fourth.

Ross If a frigating ship doesn't appear soon, we'll all be struck with stricturing starvation – and you – a play!

Collins Not putting on the play won't bring us a supply ship, Robbie.

Ross And you say you want those contumelious convicts to act in this play. The convicts!

Campbell Eh, kev, weh, discipline's bad. Very bad.

Ralph The play has several parts for women. We have no other women here.

Collins Your wife excepted, Reverend.

Revd Johnson My wife abhors anything of that nature. After all, actresses are not famed for their morals.

Collins Neither are our women convicts.

Revd Johnson How can they be when some of our officers set them up as mistresses?

He looks pointedly at Lieutenant George Johnston.

Ross Filthy, thieving, lying whores and now we have to watch them flout their flitty wares on the stage!

Phillip No one will be forced to watch the play.

Dawes I believe there's a partial lunar eclipse that night. I shall have to watch that. The sky of this southern hemisphere is full of wonders. Have you looked at the constellations?

Short pause.

Ross Constellations. Plays! This is a convict colony, the prisoners are here to be punished and we're here to make sure they get punished. Constellations! Jemmy? Constellations!

He turns to Jemmy Campbell for support.

Campbell Tss, weh, marines, marines: war, phoo, discipline. Eh? Service – His Majesty.

Phillip We are indeed here to supervise the convicts who are already being punished by their long exile. Surely they can also be reformed?

Tench We are talking about criminals, often hardened criminals. They have a habit of vice and crime. Many criminals seem to have been born that way. It is in their nature.

Phillip Rousseau would say that we have made them that way, Watkins: 'Man is born free, and everywhere he is in chains.'

Revd Johnson But Rousseau was a Frenchman.

Ross A Frenchman! What can you expect? We're going to listen to a foraging Frenchman now –

Collins He was Swiss actually.

Campbell Eeh, eyeh, good soldiers, the Swiss.

Phillip Surely you believe man can be redeemed, Reverend?

Revd Johnson By the grace of God and a belief in the true church, yes. But Christ never proposed putting on plays to his disciples. However, he didn't forbid it either. It must depend on the play.

Johnston He did propose treating sinners, especially women who have sinned, with compassion. Most of the convict women have committed small crimes, a tiny theft –

Collins We know about your compassion, not to say passion, for the women convicts, George.

Tench A crime is a crime. You commit a crime or you don't. If you commit a crime, you are a criminal. Surely that is logical? It's like the savages here. A savage is a savage because he behaves in a savage manner. To expect anything else is foolish. They can't even build a proper canoe.

Phillip They can be educated.

Collins Actually, they seem happy enough as they are. They do not want to build canoes or houses, nor do they suffer from greed and ambition.

Faddy (*looking at Ralph*) Unlike some.

Tench Which can't be said of our convicts. But really, I don't see what this has to do with a play. It is at most a passable diversion, an entertainment to wile away the hours of the idle.

Campbell Ttts, weh, heh, the convicts, bone idle.

Dawes We're wiling away precious hours now. Put the play on, don't put it on, it won't change the shape of the universe.

Ralph But it could change the nature of our little society.

Faddy Second Lieutenant Clark change society!

Phillip William!

Tench My dear Ralph, a bunch of convicts making fools of themselves, mouthing words written no doubt by some London ass, will hardly change our society.

Ralph George Farquhar was not an ass! And he was from Ireland.

Ross An Irishman! I have to sit there and listen to an Irishman!

Campbell Tss, tt. Irish. Wilde. Wilde.

Revd Johnson The play doesn't propagate Catholic doctrine, does it, Ralph?

Ralph He was also an officer.

Faddy Crawling for promotion.

Ralph Of the Grenadiers.

Ross Never liked the Grenadiers myself.

Campbell Ouah, pheuee, grenades, pho. Throw and run. Eh. Backs.

Ralph The play is called *The Recruiting Officer*.

Collins I saw it in London I believe. Yes. Very funny if I remember. Sergeant Kite. The devious ways he used to serve his captain . . .

Faddy Your part, Ralph.

Collins William, if you can't contribute anything useful to the discussion, keep quiet!

Silence.

Revd Johnson What is the plot, Ralph?

Ralph It's about this recruiting officer and his friend, and they are in love with these two young ladies from

Shrewsbury and after some difficulties, they marry them.

Revd Johnson It sanctions Holy Matrimony then?

Ralph Yes, yes, it does.

Revd Johnson That wouldn't do the convicts any harm. I'm having such trouble getting them to marry instead of this sordid cohabitation they're so used to.

Ross Marriage, plays, why not a ball for the convicts!

Campbell Euuh. Boxing.

Phillip Some of these men will have finished their sentence in a few years. They will become members of society again, and help create a new society in this colony. Should we not encourage them now to think in a free and responsible manner?

Tench I don't see how a comedy about two lovers will do that, Arthur.

Phillip The theatre is an expression of civilization. We belong to a great country which has spawned great playwrights: Shakespeare, Marlowe, Jonson, and even in our own time, Sheridan. The convicts will be speaking a refined, literate language and expressing sentiments of a delicacy they are not used to. It will remind them that there is more to life than crime, punishment. And we, this colony of a few hundred, will be watching this together, for a few hours we will no longer be despised prisoners and hated gaolers. We will laugh, we may be moved, we may even think a little. Can you suggest something else that will provide such an evening, Watkin?

Dawes Mapping the stars gives me more enjoyment, personally.

Tench I'm not sure it's a good idea having the convicts laugh at officers, Arthur.

Campbell No. Pheeoh, insubordination, heh, ehh, no discipline.

Ross You want this vice-ridden vermin to enjoy themselves?

Collins They would only laugh at Sergeant Kite.

Ralph Captain Plume is a most attractive, noble fellow.

Revd Johnson He's not loose, is he Ralph? I hear many of these plays are about rakes and encourage loose morals in women. They do get married? Before, that is, before. And for the right reasons.

Ralph They marry for love and to secure wealth.

Revd Johnson That's all right.

Tench I would simply say that if you want to build a civilization there are more important things than a play. If you want to teach the convicts something, teach them to farm, to build houses, teach them a sense of respect for property, teach them thrift so they don't eat a week's rations in one night, but above all, teach them how to work, not how to sit around laughing at a comedy.

Phillip The Greeks believed that it was a citizen's duty to watch a play. It was a kind of work in that it required attention, judgement, patience, all social virtues.

Tench And the Greeks were conquered by the more practical Romans, Arthur.

Collins Indeed, the Romans built their bridges, but they also spent many centuries wishing they were Greeks. And they, after all, were conquered by barbarians, or by their own corrupt and small spirits.

Tench Are you saying Rome would not have fallen if the theatre has been better?

Ralph (*very loud*) Why not? (*Everyone looks at him and he continues, fast and nervously.*) In my own small way, in just a few hours, I have seen something change. I asked some of the convict women to read me some lines, these women who behave often no better than animals. And it seemed to me, as one or two – I'm not saying all of them, not at all – but one or two, saying those well-balanced lines of Mr Farquhar, they seemed to acquire a dignity, they seemed – they seemed to lose some of their corruption. There was one, Mary Brenham, she read so well, perhaps this play will keep her from selling herself to the first marine who offers her bread –

Faddy (*under his breath*) She'll sell herself to him, instead.

Ross So that's the way the wind blows –

Campbell Hooh. A tempest. Hooh.

Ralph (*over them*) I speak about her, but in a small way this could affect all the convicts and even ourselves, we could forget our worries about the supplies, the hangings and the floggings, and think of ourselves at the theatre, in London with our wives and children, that is, we could, euh –

Phillip Transcend –

Ralph Transcend the darker, euh – transcend the –

Johnston Brutal –

Ralph The brutality – remember our better nature and remember –

Collins England.

Ralph England.

A moment.

Ross Where did the wee Lieutenant learn to speak?

Faddy He must have had one of his dreams.

Tench (*over them*) You are making claims that cannot be substantiated, Ralph. It's two hours, possibly of amusement, possibly of boredom, and we will lose the labour of the convicts during the time they are learning to play. It's a waste, an unnecessary waste.

Revd Johnson I'm still concerned about the content.

Tench The content of a play is irrelevant.

Ross Even if it teaches insubordination, disobedience, revolution?

Collins Since we have agreed it can do no harm, since it might, possibly, do some good, since the only person violently opposed to it is Major Ross for reasons he has not made quite clear, I suggest we allow Ralph to rehearse his play. Does anyone disagree?

Ross I – I –

Collins We have taken your disagreement into account, Robbie.

Campbell Ah, eeh, I – I – (*He stops.*)

Collins Thank you, Captain Campbell. Dawes? Dawes, do come back to earth and honour us with your attention for a moment.

Dawes What? No? Why not? As long as I don't have to watch it.

Collins Johnston?

Johnston I'm for it.

Collins Faddy?

Faddy I'm against it.

Collins Could you tell us why?

Faddy I don't trust the director.

Collins Tench?

Tench Waste of time.

Collins The Reverend, our moral guide, has no objections.

Revd Johnson Of course I haven't read it.

Tench Davey, this is not an objective summing up, this is typical of your high-handed manner –

Collins (*angrily*) I don't think you're the one to accuse others of a high-handed manner, Watkin.

Phillip Gentlemen, please.

Collins Your Excellency, I believe, is for the play and I myself am convinced it will prove a most interesting experiment. So let us conclude with our good wishes to Ralph for a successful production.

Ross I will not accept this. You willy-wally wobbly words, Greeks, Romans, experiment, to get your own way. You don't take anything seriously, but I know this play – this play – order will become disorder. The theatre leads to threatening theory and you, Governor, you have His Majesty's commission to build castles, raise armies, administer a military colony, not fandangle about with a lewdy play! I am going to write to the Admiralty about this.

He goes.

Phillip You're out of turn, Robbie.

Campbell Aah – eeh – a. Confusion. (*He goes.*)

Dawes Why is Robbie so upset? So much fuss over a play.

Johnston Major Ross will never forgive you, Ralph.

Collins I have summed up the feelings of the assembled company, Arthur, but the last word must be yours.

Phillip The last word will be the play, gentlemen.

SCENE SEVEN. HARRY AND DUCKLING
GO ROWING

Harry Brewer, **Duckling Smith**. *Harry is rowing, Duckling is sulking.*

Harry It's almost beginning to look like a town. Look, Duckling, there's the Captain's house. I can see him in his garden.

Harry waves. Duckling doesn't turn around.

Sydney. He could have found a better name. Mobsbury. Lagtown. Duckling Cove, eh?

Harry laughs. Duckling remains morose.

The Captain said it had to be named after the Home Secretary. The courthouse looks impressive all in brick. There's Lieutenant Dawes' observatory. Why don't you look, Duckling?

Duckling glances, then turns back.

The trees look more friendly from here. Did you know the eucalyptus tree can't be found anywhere else in the world? Captain Collins told me that. Isn't that interesting? Lieutenant Clark says the three orange trees on his island are doing well. It's the turnips he's worried about, he thinks they're being stolen and he's too busy with his play to go and have a look. Would you like to see the orange trees, Duckling?

Duckling glowers.

I thought you'd enjoy rowing to Ralph's island. I thought it would remind you of rowing on the Thames. Look how blue the water is. Duckling. Say something. Duckling!

Duckling If I was rowing on the Thames, I'd be free.

Harry This isn't Newgate, Duckling.

Duckling I wish it was.

Harry Duckling!

Duckling At least the gaoler of Newgate left you alone and you could talk to people.

Harry I let you talk to the women.

Duckling (*with contempt*) Esther Abrahams, Mary Brenham!

Harry They're good women.

Duckling I don't have anything to say to those women, Harry. My friends are in the women's camp –

Harry It's not the women you're after in the women's camp, it's the marines who come looking for buttock, I know you, who do you have your eye on now, who, a soldier? Another marine, a corporal? Who, Duckling, who?

Pause.

You've found someone already, haven't you? Where do you go, on the beach? In my tent, like with Handy Baker, eh? Where, under the trees?

Duckling You know I hate trees, don't be so filthy.

Harry Filthy, you're filthy, you filthy whore.

Pause.

I'm sorry, Duckling, please. Why can't you? – can't you just be with me? Don't be angry. I'll do anything for you, you know that. What do you want, Duckling?

Duckling I don't want to be watched all the time. I wake up in the middle of the night and you're watching me. What do you think I'm going to do in my sleep, Harry? Watching, watching, watching. JUST STOP WATCHING ME.

Harry You want to leave me. All right, go and live in the women's camp, sell yourself to a convict for a biscuit. Leave if you want to. You're filthy, filthy, opening your legs to the first marine –

Duckling Why are you so angry with your Duckling, Harry? Don't you like it when I open my legs wide to you? Cross them over you – the way you like? What will you do when your little Duckling isn't there any more to touch you with her soft fingertips, Harry, where you like it? First the left nipple and then the right. Your Duckling doesn't want to leave you, Harry.

Harry Duckling . . .

Duckling I need freedom sometimes, Harry.

Harry You have to earn your freedom with good behaviour.

Duckling Why didn't you let them hang me and take my corpse with you, Harry? You could have kept that in chains. I wish I was dead. At least when you're dead, you're free.

Silence.

Harry You know Lieutenant Clark's play?

Duckling is silent.

Do you want to be in it?

Duckling laughs.

Dabby Bryant is in it too and Liz Morden. Do you want to be in it? You'd rehearse in the evenings with Lieutenant Clark.

Duckling And he can watch over me instead of you.

Harry I'm trying to make you happy, Duckling, if you don't want to –

Duckling I'll be in the play.

Pause.

How is Lieutenant Clark going to manage Liz Morden?

Harry The Captain wanted her to be in it.

Duckling On the ship we used to see who could make Lieutenant Clark blush first. It didn't take long, haha.

Harry Duckling, you won't try anything with Lieutenant Clark, will you?

Duckling With that Mollie? No.

Harry You're talking to me again. Will you kiss your Harry?

They kiss.

I'll come and watch the rehearsals.

SCENE EIGHT. THE WOMEN LEARN THEIR LINES

Dabby Bryant is sitting on the ground muttering to herself with concentration. She could be counting. Mary Brenham comes on.

Mary Are you remembering your lines, Dabby?

Dabby What lines? No. I was remembering Devon. I was on my way back to Bigbury Bay.

Mary You promised Lieutenant Clark you'd learn your lines.

Dabby I want to go back. I want to see a wall of stone. I want to hear the Atlantic breaking into the estuary. I can bring a boat into any harbour, in any weather. I can do it as well as the Governor.

Mary Dabby, what about your lines?

Dabby I'm not spending the rest of my life in this flat, brittle burnt-out country. Oh, give me some English rain.

Mary It rains here.

Dabby It's not the same. I could recognize English rain anywhere. And Devon rain, Mary, Devon rain is the softest in England. As soft as your breasts, as soft as Lieutenant Clark's dimpled cheeks.

Mary Dabby, don't!

Dabby You're wasting time, girl, he's ripe for the plucking. You can always tell with men, they begin to walk sideways. And if you don't –

Mary Don't start. I listened to you once before.

Dabby What would you have done without that lanky sailor drooling over you?

Mary I would have been less of a whore.

Dabby Listen, my darling, you're only a virgin once. You can't go to a man and say, I'm a virgin except for this one lover I had. After that, it doesn't matter how many men go through you.

Mary I'll never wash the sin away.

Dabby If God didn't want women to be whores he shouldn't have created men who pay for their bodies. While you were with your little sailor there were women in that stinking pit of a hold who had three men on them at once, men with the pox, men with the flux, men biting like dogs.

Mary But if you don't agree to it, then you're not a whore, you're a martyr.

Dabby You have to be a virgin to be a martyr, Mary, and you didn't come on that ship a virgin. 'A. H. I love thee to the heart', ha, tattooed way up there –

Dabby begins to lift Mary's skirt to reveal a tattoo high up on the inner thigh. Mary leaps away.

Mary That was different. That was love.

Dabby The second difficulty with being a martyr is that you have to be dead to qualify. Well, you didn't die, thanks to me, you had three pounds of beef a week instead of two, two extra ounces of cheese.

Mary Which you were happy to eat!

Dabby We women have to look after each other. Let's learn the lines.

Mary You sold me that first day so you and your husband could eat!

Dabby Do you want me to learn these lines or not?

Mary How can I play Silvia? She's brave and strong. She couldn't have done what I've done.

Dabby She didn't spend eight months and one week on a convict ship. Anyway, you can pretend you're her.

Mary No. I have to *be* her.

Dabby Why?

Mary Because that's acting.

Dabby No way I'm being Rose, she's an idiot.

Mary It's not such a big part, it doesn't matter so much.

Dabby You didn't tell me that before.

Mary I hadn't read it carefully. Come on, let's do the scene between Silvia and Rose. (*She reads*.) 'I have rested but indifferently, and I believe my bedfellow was as little pleased; poor Rose! Here she comes –

Dabby I could have done something for Rose. Ha! I should play Silvia.

Mary 'Good morrow, my dear, how d'ye this morning?' Now you say: 'Just as I was last night, neither better nor worse for you.'

Liz Morden comes on.

Liz You can't do the play without me. I'm in it! Where's the Lieutenant.

Dabby She's teaching me some lines.

Liz Why aren't you teaching me the lines?

Mary We're not doing your scenes.

Liz Well do them.

Dabby You can read. You can read your own lines.

Liz I don't want to learn them on my own.

Liz thrusts Dabby away and sits by Mary.

I'm waiting.

Dabby What are you waiting for, Liz Morden, a blind man to buy your wares?

Mary (*quickly*) We'll do the first scene between Melinda and Silvia, all right?

Liz Yea. The first scene.

Mary gives Liz the book.

Mary You start.

Liz looks at the book.

You start. 'Welcome to town, cousin Silvia' –

Liz 'Welcome to town, cousin Silvia' –

Mary Go on – 'I envied you' –

Liz 'I envied you' – You read it first.

Mary Why?

Liz I want to hear how you do it.

Mary Why?

Liz Cause then I can do it different.

Mary 'I envied you your retreat in the country; for Shrewsbury, methinks, and all your heads of shires' –

Dabby Why don't you read it? You can't read!

Liz What?

She lunges at Dabby.

Mary I'll teach you the lines.

Dabby Are you her friend now, is that it? Mary the holy innocent and thieving bitch –

Liz and Dabby seize each other. **Ketch Freeman** *appears.*

Ketch (*with nervous affability*) Good morning, ladies. And why aren't you at work instead of at each other's throats?

Liz and Dabby turn on him.

Liz I wouldn't talk of throats if I was you, Mr Hangman Ketch Freeman.

Dabby Crap merchant.

Liz Crapping cull. Switcher.

Mary Roper.

Ketch I was only asking what you were doing, you know, friendly like.

Liz Stick to your ropes, my little galler, don't bother the actresses.

Ketch Actresses? You're doing a play?

Liz Better than dancing the Paddington frisk in your arms – noser!

Ketch I'll nose on you, Liz, if you're not careful.

Liz I'd take a leap in the dark sooner than turn off my own kind. Now take your whirligigs out of our sight, we have lines to learn.

Ketch slinks away as Liz and Dabby spit him off.

Dabby (*after him*) Don't hang too many people, Ketch, we need an audience!

Mary 'Welcome to town, cousin Silvia.' It says you salute.

Liz (*giving a military salute*) 'Welcome to town, cousin – Silvia.'

SCENE NINE. RALPH CLARK TRIES TO KISS HIS DEAR WIFE'S PICTURE

Ralph's tent. Candlelight. Ralph paces.

Ralph Dreamt my beloved Betsey that I was with you and that I thought I was going to be arrested.

He looks at his watch.

I hope to God that there is nothing the matter with you my tender Alicia or that of our dear boy –

He looks at his watch.

My darling tender wife I am reading Proverbs waiting till midnight, the Sabbath, that I might kiss your picture as usual.

He takes his Bible and kneels. Looks at his watch.

The Patrols caught three seamen and a boy in the women's camp.

He reads.

'Let thy fountain be blessed: and rejoice with the wife of thy youth.'
Good God what a scene of whoredom is going on there in the women's camp.

He looks at his watch. Gets up. Paces.

Very hot this night.
Captain Shea killed today one of the kankaroos – it is the most curious animal I ever saw.

He looks at his watch.

Almost midnight, my Betsey, the Lord's day –

He reads.

'And behold, there met him a woman with the attire of an harlot, and subtle of heart.

So she caught him, and kissed him with an impudent face.'

Felt ill with the toothache my dear wife my God what pain.

Reads.

'So she caught him, and kissed him with an impudent face . . .'

'I have perfumed my bed with myrrh, aloes, cinnamon – '

Sarah McCormick was flogged today for calling the doctor a c– midnight –

This being Sunday took your picture out of its prison and kissed it – God bless you my sweet woman.

He now proceeds to do so. That is, he goes down on his knees and brings the picture to himself. Ketch Freeman comes into the tent. Ralph jumps.

Ketch Forgive me, Sir, please forgive me, I didn't want to disturb your prayers. I say fifty Hail Marys myself every night, and 200 on the days when – I'll wait outside, Sir.

Ralph What do you want?

Ketch I'll wait quietly, Sir, don't mind me.

Ralph Why aren't you in the camp at this hour?

Ketch I should be, God forgive me, I should be. But I'm not. I'm here. I have to have a word with you, Sir.

Ralph Get back to the camp immediately, I'll see you in the morning, Ketch.

Ketch Don't call me that, Sir, I beg you, don't call me by that name, that's what I came to see you about, Sir.

Ralph I was about to go to sleep.

Ketch I understand, Sir, and your soul in peace, I won't take up your time, Sir, I'll be brief.

Pause.

Ralph Well?

Ketch Don't you want to finish your prayers? I can be very quiet. I used to watch my mother, may her poor soul rest in peace, I used to watch her say her prayers, every night.

Ralph Get on with it!

Ketch When I say my prayers I have a terrible doubt. How can I be sure God is forgiving me? What if he will forgive me, but hasn't forgiven me yet? That's why I don't want to die, Sir. That's why I can't die. Not until I am sure. Are you sure?

Ralph I'm not a convict: I don't sin.

Ketch To be sure. Forgive me, Sir. But if we're in God's power, then surely he makes us sin. I was given a guardian angel when I was born, like all good Catholics, why didn't my guardian angel look after me better? But I think he must've stayed in Ireland. I think the devil tempted my mother to London and both our guardian angels stayed behind. Have you ever been to Ireland, Sir? It's a beautiful country. If I'd been an angel I wouldn't have left it either. And when we came within six fields of Westminster, the devils took over. But it's God's judgement I'm frightened of. And the women's. They're so hard. Why is that?

Ralph Why have you come here?

Ketch I'm coming to that, Sir.

Ralph Hurry up, then.

Ketch I'm speaking as fast as I can, Sir –

Ralph Ketch –

Ketch James, Sir, James, Daniel, Patrick, after my three uncles. Good men they were too, didn't go to London. If my mother hadn't brought us to London, may God give peace to her soul and breathe pity into the hearts of hard women – because the docks are in London and if I hadn't worked on the docks, on that day, May 23rd, 1785, do you remember it, Sir? Shadwell Dock. If only we hadn't left, then I wouldn't have been there, then nothing would have happened, I wouldn't have become a coal heaver on Shadwell Dock and been there on the 23rd of May when we refused to unload because they were paying us so badly, Sir. I wasn't even near the sailor who got killed. He shouldn't have done the unloading, that was wrong of the sailors, but I didn't kill him, maybe one blow, not to look stupid, you know, just to show I was with the lads, even if I wasn't, but I didn't kill him. And they caught five at random, Sir, and I was among the five, and they found the cudgel, but I just had that to look good, that's all, and when they said to me later you can hang or you can give the names, what was I to do, what would you have done, Sir?

Ralph I wouldn't have been in that situation, Freeman.

Ketch To be sure, forgive me, Sir. I only told on the ones I saw, I didn't tell anything that wasn't true. Death is a horrible thing, that poor sailor.

Ralph Freeman, I'm going to go to bed now –

Ketch I understand, Sir, I understand. And when it happened again, here! And I had hopes of making a good life here. It's because I'm so friendly, see, so I go along, and then I'm the one who gets caught. That theft, I didn't do it, I was just there, keeping a look out, just to help some friends, you know. But when they say to you, hang or be

hanged, what do you do? Someone has to do it. I try to do
it well. God had mercy on the whore, the thief, the lame,
surely he'll forgive the hang– it's the women – they're
without mercy – not like you and me, Sir, men. What I
wanted to say, Sir, is that I heard them talking about the
play.

    Pause.

Some players came into our village once. they were loved
like the angels, Lieutenant, like the angels. And the way
the women watched them – the light of a spring dawn in
their eyes.
    Lieutenant –
    I want to be an actor.

SCENE TEN. JOHN WISEHAMMER AND MARY BRENHAM EXCHANGE WORDS

Mary is copying The Recruiting Officer *in the afternoon
light. John Wisehammer is carrying bricks and piling them
to one side. He begins to hover over her.*

Mary 'I would rather counsel than command; I don't
propose this with the authority of a parent, but as the
advice of your friend' –

Wisehammer Friend. That's a good word. Short, but full
of promise.

Mary 'That you would take the coach this moment and
go into the country.'

Wisehammer Country can mean opposite things. It
renews you with trees and grass, you go rest in the
country, or it crushes you with power: you die for your
country, your country doesn't want you, you're thrown
out of your country.

Pause.

I like words.

Pause.

My father cleared the houses of the dead to sell the old clothes to the poorhouses by the Thames. He found a dictionary – Johnson's dictionary – it was as big as a bible. It went from A to L. I started with the A's. Abecedarian: someone who teaches the alphabet or rudiments of literature. Abject: a man without hope.

Mary What does indulgent mean?

Wisehammer How is it used?

Mary (*reads*) 'You have been so careful, so indulgent to me' –

Wisehammer It means ready to overlook faults.

Pause.

You have to be careful with words that begin with 'in'. It can turn everything upside down. Injustice. Most of that word is taken up with justice, but the 'in' twists it inside out and makes it the ugliest word in the English language.

Mary Guilty is an uglier word.

Wisehammer Innocent ought to be a beautiful word, but it isn't, it's full of sorrow. Anguish.

Mary goes back to her copying.

Mary I don't have much time. We start this in a few days.

Wisehammer looks over her shoulder.

I have the biggest part.

Wisehammer You have a beautiful hand.

Mary There is so much to copy. So many words.

Wisehammer I can write.

Mary Why don't you tell Lieutenant Clark? He's doing it.

Wisehammer No . . . no . . . I'm –

Mary Afraid?

Wisehammer Diffident.

Mary I'll tell him. Well, I won't. My friend Dabby will. She's –

Wisehammer Bold.

Pause.

Shy is not a bad word, it's soft.

Mary But shame is a hard one.

Wisehammer Words with two L's are the worst. Lonely, loveless.

Mary Love is a good word.

Wisehammer That's because it only has one L. I like words with one L: Luck. Latitudinarian.

Mary laughs.

Laughter.

SCENE ELEVEN. THE FIRST REHEARSAL

Ralph Clark, Robert Sideway, John Wisehammer, Mary Brenham, Liz Morden, Dabby Bryant, Duckling Smith, Ketch Freeman.

Ralph Good afternoon, ladies and gentlemen –

Dabby We're ladies now. Wait till I tell my husband I've become a lady.

Mary Sshht.

Ralph It is with pleasure that I welcome you –

Sideway Our pleasure, Mr Clark, our pleasure.

Ralph We have many days of hard word ahead of us.

Liz Work! I'm not working. I thought we was acting.

Ralph Now, let me introduce the company –

Dabby We've all met before, Lieutenant, you could say we know each other, you could say we'd know each other in the dark.

Sideway It's a theatrical custom, the company is formally introduced to each other, Mrs Bryant.

Dabby Mrs Bryant? Who's Mrs Bryant?

Sideway It's the theatrical form of address, Madam. You may call me Mr Sideway.

Ralph If I may proceed –

Ketch Shhh! You're interrupting the director.

Dabby So we are, Mr Hangman.

The women all hiss and spit at Ketch.

Ralph The ladies first: Mary Brenham who is to play Silvia. Liz Morden who is to play Melinda. Duckling Smith who is to play Lucy, Melinda's maid.

Duckling I'm not playing Liz Morden's maid.

Ralph Why not?

Duckling I live with an officer. He wouldn't like it.

Dabby Just because she lives chained up in that old toss pot's garden.

Duckling Don't you dare talk of my Harry –

Ralph You're not playing Morden's maid, Smith, you're playing Melinda's. And Dabby Bryant, who is to play Rose, a country girl.

Dabby From Devon.

Duckling (*to Dabby*) Screw jaws!

Dabby (*to Duckling*) Salt bitch!

Ralph That's the ladies. Now, Captain Plume will be played by Henry Kable.

He looks around.

Who seems to be late. That's odd. I saw him an hour ago and he said he was going to your hut to learn some lines, Wisehammer?

Wisehammer is silent.

Sergeant Kite is to be played by John Arscott, who did send a message to say he would be kept at work an extra hour.

Dabby An hour! You won't see him in an hour!

Liz (*under her breath*) You're not the only one with new wrinkles in your arse, Dabby Bryant.

Ralph Mr Worthy will be played by Mr Sideway.

Sideway takes a vast bow.

Sideway I'm here.

Ralph Justice Balance by James Freeman.

Duckling No way I'm doing a play with a hangman. The

words would stick in my throat.

More hisses and spitting. Ketch shrinks.

Ralph You don't have any scenes with him, Smith. Now if I could finish the introductions. Captain Brazen is to be played by John Wisehammer.

The small parts are still to be cast. Now. We can't do the first scene until John Arscott appears.

Dabby There won't be a first scene.

Ralph Bryant, will you be quiet please! The second scene. Wisehammer, you could read Plume.

Wisehammer comes forward eagerly.

No, I'll read Plume myself. So, Act One, Scene Two, Captain Plume and Mr Worthy.

Sideway That's me. I'm at your command.

Ralph The rest of you can watch and wait for your scenes. Perhaps we should begin by reading it.

Sideway No need, Mr Clark. I know it.

Ralph Ah, I'm afraid I shall have to read Captain Plume.

Sideway I know that part too. Would you like me to do both?

Ralph I think it's better if I do it. Shall we begin? Kite, that's John Arscott, has just left –

Dabby Running.

Ralph Bryant! I'll read the line before Worthy's entrance: 'None at present. 'Tis indeed the picture of Worthy, but the life's departed.' Sideway? Where's he gone?

Sideway has scuttled off. He shouts from the wings.

Sideway I'm preparing my entrance, Mr Clark, I won't be

a minute. Could you read the line again, slowly?

Ralph ''Tis indeed the picture of Worthy, but the life's departed. What, arms-a-cross, Worthy!'

Sideway comes on, walking sideways, arms held up in a grandiose eighteenth-century theatrical pose. He suddenly stops.

Sideway Ah, yes, I forgot. Arms-a-cross. I shall have to start again.

He goes off again and shouts.

Could you read the line again louder please?

Ralph 'What, arms-a-cross, Worthy!'

Sideway rushes on.

Sideway My wiper! Someone's buzzed my wiper! There's a wipe drawer in this crew, Mr Clark.

Ralph What's the matter?

Sideway There's a pickpocket in the company.

Dabby Talk of the pot calling the kettle black.

Sideway stalks around the company threateningly.

Sideway My handkerchief. Who prigged my handkerchief?

Ralph I'm sure it will turn up, Sideway, let's go on.

Sideway I can't do my entrance without my handkerchief. (*furious*) I've been practising it all night. If I get my mittens on the rum diver I'll –

He lunges at Liz, who fights back viciously. They jump apart, each taking threatening poses and Ralph intervenes with speed.

Ralph Let's assume Worthy has already entered, Sideway. Now, I say: 'What arms-a-cross, Worthy! Methinks you should hold 'em open when a friend's so near. I must expel this melancholy spirit.'

Sideway has dropped to his knees and is sobbing in a pose of total sorrow.

What are you doing down there, Sideway?

Sideway I'm being melancholy. I saw Mr Garrick being melancholy once. That is what he did. *Hamlet* it was.

He stretches his arms to the ground and begins to repeat.

'Oh that this too, too solid flesh would melt. Oh that this too too solid flesh would melt. Oh that this too too – '

Ralph This is a comedy. It is perhaps a little lighter. Try simply to stand normally and look melancholy. I'll say the line again. (*Sideway is still sobbing.*) The audience won't hear Captain Plume's lines if your sobs are so loud, Sideway.

Sideway I'm still establishing my melancholy.

Ralph A comedy needs to move quite fast. In fact, I think we'll cut that line and the two verses that follow and go straight to Worthy greeting Plume.

Wisehammer I like the word melancholy.

Sideway A greeting. Yes. A greeting looks like this.

He extends his arms high and wide.

'Plume!' Now I'll change to say the next words. 'My dear Captain', that's affection isn't it? If I put my hands on my heart, like this. Now, 'Welcome'. I'm not quite sure how to do 'Welcome'.

Ralph I think if you just say the line.

Sideway Quite. Now.

He feels Ralph.

Ralph Sideway! What are you doing?

Sideway I'm checking that you're safe and sound returned. That's what the line says: 'Safe and sound returned.'

Ralph You don't need to touch him. You can see that!

Sideway Yes, yes. I'll check his different parts with my eyes. Now, I'll put it all together, 'Plume! My dear Captain, welcome. Safe and sound returned!'

He does this with appropriate gestures.

Ralph Sideway – it's a very good attempt. It's very theatrical. But you could try to be a little more – euh – natural.

Sideway Natural! On the stage! But Mr Clark!

Ralph People must – euh – believe you. Garrick after all is admired for his naturalness.

Sideway Of course. I thought I was being Garrick – but never mind. Natural. Quite. You're the director, Mr Clark.

Ralph Perhaps you could look at me while you're saying the lines.

Sideway But the audience won't see my face.

Ralph The lines are said to Captain Plume. Let's move on. Plume says: 'I 'scaped safe from Germany', shall we say – America? It will make it more contemporary –

Wisehammer You can't change the words of the playwright.

Ralph Mm, well, 'and sound, I hope, from London: you see I have – '

Black Caesar *rushes on.*

Ralph Caesar, we're rehearsing – would you –

Caesar I see that well, Monsieur Lieutenant. I see it is a piece of theatre, I have seen many pieces of theatre in my beautiful island of Madagascar so I have decided to play in your piece of theatre.

Ralph There's no part for you.

Caesar There is always a part for Caesar.

Sideway All the parts have been taken.

Caesar I will play his servant.

He stands next to Sideway.

Ralph Farquhar hasn't written a servant for Worthy.

Duckling He can have my part. I want to play something else.

Caesar There is always a black servant in a play, Monsieur Lieutenant. And Caesar is that servant. So, now I stand here just behind him and I will be his servant.

Ralph There are no lines for it, Caesar.

Caesar I speak in French. That makes him a more high up gentleman if he has a French servant, and that is good. Now he gets the lady with the black servant. Very chic.

Ralph I'll think about it. Actually, I would like to rehearse the ladies now. They have been waiting patiently and we don't have much time left. Freeman, would you go and see what's happened to Arscott. Sideway, we'll come back to this scene another time, but that was very good, very good. A little, a little euh, but very good.

Sideway bows out, followed by Caesar.

Now we will rehearse the first scene between Melinda and Silvia. Morden and Brenham, if you would come and stand here. Now the scene is set in Melinda's apartments. Silvia is already there. So, if you stand here, Morden. Brenham, you stand facing her.

Liz (*very, very fast*) 'Welcome to town cousin Silvia I envied you your retreat in the country for Shrewsbury methinks and all your heads of shires are the most irregular places for living – '

Ralph Euh, Morden –

Liz Wait, I haven't finished yet. 'Here we have smoke noise scandal affectation and pretension in short everything to give the spleen and nothing to divert it then the air is intolerable – '

Ralph Morden, you know the lines very well.

Liz Thank you, Lieutenant Clark.

Ralph But you might want to try and act them.

Pause.

Let's look at the scene.

Liz looks.

You're a rich lady. You're at home. Now a rich lady would stand in a certain way. Try to stand like a rich lady. Try to look at Silvia with a certain assurance.

Liz Assurance.

Wisehammer Confidence.

Ralph Like this. You've seen rich ladies, haven't you?

Liz I robbed a few.

Ralph How did they behave?

Liz They screamed.

Ralph I mean before you – euh – robbed them.

Liz I don't know. I was watching their purses.

Ralph Have you ever seen a lady in her own house?

Liz I used to climb into the big houses when I was a girl, and just stand there, looking. I didn't take anything. I just stood. Like this.

Ralph But if it was your own house, you would think it was normal to live like that.

Wisehammer It's not normal. It's not normal when others have nothing.

Ralph When acting, you have to imagine things. You have to imagine you're someone different. So, now, think of a rich lady and imagine you're her.

Liz begins to masticate.

What are you doing?

Liz If I was rich I'd eat myself sick.

Dabby Me too, potatoes.

The convicts speak quickly and over each other.

Sideway Roast beef and Yorkshire pudding.

Caesar Hearts of palm.

Wisehammer Four fried eggs, six fried eggs, eight fried eggs.

Liz Eels, oysters –

Ralph Could we get on with the scene, please? Brenham, it's your turn to speak.

Mary 'Oh, Madam, I have heard the town commended for its air.'

Liz 'But you don't consider Silvia how long I have lived in't!'

Ralph (*to Liz*) I believe you would look at her.

Liz She didn't look at me.

Ralph Didn't she? She will now.

Liz 'For I can assure you that to a lady the least nice in her constitution no air can be good above half a year change of air I take to be the most agreeable of any variety in life.'

Mary 'But prithee, my dear Melinda, don't put on such an air to me.'

Ralph Excellent, Brenham. You could be a little more sharp on the 'don't'.

Mary 'Don't.' (*Mary now tries a few gestures.*) 'Your education and mine were just the same, and I remember the time when we never troubled our heads about air, but when the sharp air from the Welsh mountains made our noses drop in a cold morning at the boarding-school.'

Ralph Good! Good! Morden?

Liz 'Our education cousin was the same but our temperaments had nothing alike.'

Ralph That's a little better, Morden, but you needn't be quite so angry with her. Now go on Brenham.

Liz I haven't finished my speech!

Ralph You're right, Morden, please excuse me.

Liz (*embarrassed*) No, no, there's no need for that, Lieutenant. I only meant – I don't have to.

Ralph Please do.

Liz 'You have the constitution of a horse.'

Ralph Much better, Morden. But you must always remember you're a lady. What can we do to help you? Lucy.

Dabby That's you, Duckling.

Ralph See that little piece of wood over there? Take it to Melinda. That will be your fan.

Duckling I'm not fetching nothing for Liz.

Ralph She's not Morden, she's Melinda, your mistress. You're her servant, Lucy. In fact, you should be in this scene. Now take her that fan.

Duckling (*gives the wood to Liz*) Here.

Liz Thank you, Lucy, I do much appreciate your effort.

Ralph No, you would nod your head.

Wisehammer Don't add any words to the play.

Ralph Now, Lucy, stand behind Morden.

Duckling What do I say?

Ralph Nothing.

Duckling How will they know I'm here? Why does she get all the lines? Why can't I have some of hers?

Ralph Brenham, it's your speech.

Mary 'So far as to be troubled with neither spleen, colic, nor vapours –

> *The convicts slink away and sink down, trying to make themselves invisible as Major Ross, followed by Captain Campbell, come on.*

'I need no salt for my stomach, no – '

She sees the officers herself and folds in with the rest of the convicts.

Ralph Major Ross, Captain Campbell, I'm rehearsing.

Ross Rehearsing! Rehearsing!

Campbell Tssaach. Rehearsing.

Ross Lieutenant Clark is rehearsing. Lieutenant Clark asked us to give the prisoners two hours so he could rehearse, but what has he done with them? What?

Campbell Eeh. Other things, eh.

Ross Where are the prisoners Kable and Arscott, Lieutenant.

Campbell Eh?

Ralph They seem to be late.

Ross While you were rehearsing, Arscott and Kable slipped into the woods with three others, so five men have run away and it's all because of your damned play and your so-called thespists. And not only have your thespists run away, they've stolen food from the stores for their renegade escapade, that's what your play has done.

Ralph I don't see that the play –

Ross I said it from the beginning. The play will bring down calamity on this colony.

Ralph I don't see –

Ross The devil, Lieutenant, always comes through the mind, here, worms its way, idleness and words.

Ralph Major Ross, I can't agree –

Ross Listen to me, my lad, you're a Second Lieutenant and you don't agree or disagree with Major Ross.

Campbell No discipline, tcchhha.

Ross looks over the convicts.

Ross Caesar! He started going with them and came back.

Ralph That's all right, he's not in the play.

Caesar Yes I am, please Lieutenant, I am a servant.

Ross John Wisehammer!

Wisehammer I had nothing to do with it!

Ross You're Jewish, aren't you? You're guilty. Kable was last seen near Wisehammer's hut. Liz Morden! She was observed next to the colony's stores late last night in the company of Kable who was supposed to be repairing the door. (*to Liz*) Liz Morden, you will be tried for stealing from the stores. You know the punishment? Death by hanging. (*Pause.*) And now you may continue to rehearse, Lieutenant.

Ross goes. Campbell lingers, looking at the book.

Campbell Ouusstta. *The Recruiting Officer*. Good title. Arara. But a play, tss, a play.

He goes. Ralph and the convicts are left in the shambles of their rehearsal. A silence.

Act Two

SCENE ONE. VISITING HOURS

Liz, Wisehammer, Arscott, Caesar all in chains. Arscott is bent over, facing away.

Liz Luck? Don't know the word. Shifts its bob when I comes near. Born under a ha'penny planet I was. Dad's a nibbler, don't want to get crapped. Mum leaves. Five brothers, I'm the only titter. I takes in washing. Then. My own father. Lady's walking down the street, he takes her wiper. She screams, he's shoulder-clapped, it's not me, Sir, it's Lizzie, look, she took it. I'm stripped, beaten in the street, everyone watching. That night, I take my dad's cudgel and try to kill him. I prig all his clothes and go to my older brother. He don't want me. Liz he says, why trine for a make, when you can wap for a winne? I'm no dimber mort, I says. Don't ask you to be a swell mollisher, Sister, men want Miss Laycock, don't look at your mug. So I begin to sell my mother of saints. I thinks I'm in luck when I meet the swell cove. He's a bobcull: sports a different wiper every day of the week. He says to me, it's not enough to sell your mossie face, Lizzie, it don't bring no shiners no more. Shows me how to spice the swells. So Swell has me up the wall, flashes a pocket watch, I lifts it. But one time, I stir my stumps too slow, the swell squeaks beef, the snoozie hears. I'm nibbed. It's up the ladder to rest, I thinks when I goes up before the fortune teller, but no, the judge's a bobcull, I nap the King's pardon and it's seven years across the herring pond. Jesus Christ the hunger on the ship, sailors won't touch me: no rantum scantum, no food. But here, the Governor says, new life. You could nob it here, Lizzie, I thinks, bobcull Gov, this

niffynaffy play, not too much work, good crew of rufflers,
Kable, Arscott, but no, Ross don't like my mug, I'm
nibbed again and now it's up the ladder to rest for good.
Well. Lizzie Morden's life. And you, Wisehammer, how did
you get here?

Wisehammer Betrayal. Barbarous falsehood. Intimidation.
Injustice.

Liz Speak in English, Wisehammer.

Wisehammer I am innocent. I didn't do it and I'll keep
saying I didn't.

Liz It doesn't matter what you say. If they say you're a
thief, you're a thief.

Wisehammer I am not a thief. I'll go back to England to
the snuff shop of Rickett and Loads and say, see, I'm back,
I'm innocent.

Liz They won't listen.

Wisehammer You can't live if you think that way.

   Pause.

I'm sorry. Seven years and I'll go back.

Liz What do you want to go back to England for? You're
not English.

Wisehammer I was born in England. I'm English. What
do I have to do to make people believe I'm English?

Liz You have to think English. I hate England. But I think
English. And him, Arscott, he's not said anything since
they brought him in but he's thinking English, I can tell.

Caesar I don't want to think English. If I think English I will
die. I want to go back to Madagascar and think Malagasy. I
want to die in Madagascar and join my ancestors.

Liz It doesn't matter where you die when you're dead.

Caesar If I die here, I will have no spirit. I want to go home. I will escape again.

Arscott There's no escape!

Caesar This time I lost my courage, but next time I ask my ancestors and they will help me escape!

Arscott (*shouts*) There's no escape!

Liz See. That's English. You know things.

Caesar My ancestors will know the way.

Arscott There's no escape I tell you.

Pause.

You go in circles out there, that's all you do. You go out there and you walk and walk and you don't reach China. You come back on your steps if the savages don't get you first. Even a compass doesn't work in this foreign upside-down desert. Here. You can read. Why didn't it work? What does it say?

He hands Wisehammer a carefully folded, wrinkled piece of paper.

Wisehammer It says north.

Arscott Why didn't it work then? It was supposed to take us north of China, why did I end up going in circles?

Wisehammer Because it's not a compass.

Arscott I gave me only shilling to a sailor for it. He said it was a compass.

Wisehammer It's a piece of paper with north written on it. He lied. He deceived you, he betrayed you, he betrayed you.

Sideway, Mary and Duckling come on.

Sideway Madam, gentleman, fellow players, we have come to visit, to commiserate, to offer our humble services.

Liz Get out!

Mary Liz, we've come to rehearse the play.

Wisehammer Rehearse the play?

Duckling The Lieutenant has gone to talk to the Governor. Harry said we could come see you.

Mary The Lieutenant has asked me to stand in his place so we don't lose time. We'll start with the first scene between Melinda and Brazen.

Wisehammer How can I play Captain Brazen in chains?

Mary This is the theatre. We will believe you.

Arscott Where does Kite come in?

Sideway (*bowing to Liz*) Madam I have brought you your fan. (*He hands her the 'fan', which she takes.*)

SCENE TWO. HIS EXCELLENCY EXHORTS RALPH

Phillip, Ralph.

Phillip I hear you want to stop the play, Lieutenant.

Ralph Half of my cast is in chains, Sir.

Phillip That is a difficulty, but it can be overcome. Is that your only reason, Lieutenant?

Ralph So many people seem against it, Sir.

Phillip Are you afraid?

Ralph No, Sir, but I do not wish to displease my superior officers.

Phillip If you break conventions, it is inevitable you make enemies, Lieutenant. This play irritates them.

Ralph Yes and I –

Phillip Socrates irritated the state of Athens and was put to death for it.

Ralph Sir –

Phillip Would you have a world without Socrates?

Ralph Sir, I –

Phillip In the Meno, one of Plato's great dialogues, have you read it, Lieutenant, Socrates demonstrates that a slave boy can learn the principles of geometry as well as a gentleman.

Ralph Ah –

Phillip In other words, he shows that human beings have an intelligence which has nothing to do with the circumstances into which they are born.

Ralph Sir –

Phillip Sit down, Lieutenant. It is a matter of reminding the slave of what he knows, of his own intelligence. And by intelligence you may read goodness, talent, the innate qualities of human beings.

Ralph I see – Sir.

Phillip When he treats the slave boy as a rational human being, the boy becomes one, he loses his fear, and he becomes a competent mathematician. A little more encouragement and he might become an extraordinary mathematician. Who knows? You must see your actors in that light.

Ralph I can see some of them, Sir, but there are others . . .
John Arscott –

Phillip He has been given 200 lashes for trying to escape.
It will take time for him to see himself as a human being
again.

Ralph Liz Morden –

Phillip Liz Morden – (*He pauses.*) I had a reason for
asking you to cast her as Melinda. Morden is one of the
most difficult women in the colony.

Ralph She is indeed, Sir.

Phillip Lower than a slave, full of loathing, foul mouthed,
desperate.

Ralph Exactly, Sir. And violent.

Phillip Quite. To be made an example of.

Ralph By hanging?

Phillip No, Lieutenant, by redemption.

Ralph The Reverend says he's given up on her, Sir.

Phillip The Reverend's an ass, Lieutenant. I am speaking
of redeeming her humanity.

Ralph I am afraid there may not be much there, Sir.

Phillip How do we know what humanity lies hidden
under the rags and filth of a mangled life? I have seen
soldiers given up for dead, limbs torn, heads cut open,
come back to life. If we treat her as a corpse, of course she
will die. Try a little kindness, Lieutenant.

Ralph But will she be hanged, Sir?

Phillip I don't want a woman to be hanged. You will have
to help, Ralph.

Ralph Sir!

Phillip I had retired from His Majesty's Service, Ralph. I was farming. I don't know why they asked me to rule over this colony of wretched souls, but I will fulfil my responsibility. No one will stop me.

Ralph No, Sir, but I don't see –

Phillip What is a statesman's responsibility? To ensure the rule of law. But the citizens must be taught to obey the law of their own will. I want to rule over responsible human beings, not tyrannize over a group of animals. I want there to be a contract between us, not a whip on my side, terror and hatred on theirs. And you must help me, Ralph.

Ralph Yes, Sir. The play –

Phillip Won't change much, but it is the diagram in the sand that may remind – just remind the slave boy – Do you understand?

Ralph I think so.

Phillip We may fail. I may have a mutiny on my hands. They are trying to convince the Admiralty that I am mad.

Ralph Sir!

Phillip And they will threaten you. You don't want to be a Second Lieutenant all your life.

Ralph No, Sir!

Phillip I cannot go over the head of Major Ross in the matter of promotion.

Ralph I see.

Phillip But we have embarked, Ralph, we must stay afloat. There is a more serious threat and it may capsize us all. If a ship does not come within three months, the supplies will be exhausted. In a month, I will cut the rations again. (*Pause.*) Harry is not well. Can you do something? Good luck with the play, Lieutenant. Oh, and Ralph –

Ralph Sir –

Phillip Unexpected situations are often matched by unexpected virtues in people, are they not?

Ralph I believe they are, Sir.

Phillip A play is a world in itself, a tiny colony we could almost say.

Pause.

And you are in charge of it. That is a great responsibility.

Ralph I will lay down my life if I have to, Sir.

Phillip I don't think it will come to that, Lieutenant. You need only do your best.

Ralph Yes, Sir, I will, Sir.

Phillip Excellent.

Ralph It's a wonderful play, Sir. I wasn't sure at first, as you know, but now –

Phillip Good, Good. I shall look forward to seeing it. I'm sure it will be a success.

Ralph Thank you, Sir. Thank you.

SCENE THREE. HARRY BREWER SEES THE DEAD

Harry Brewer's tent. Harry sits, drinking rum, speaking in the different voices of his tormenting ghosts and answering in his own.

Harry Duckling! Duckling! 'She's on the beach, Harry,

waiting for her young Handy Baker.' Go away, Handy, go away! 'The dead never go away, Harry. You thought you'd be the only one to dance the buttock ball with your trull, but no one owns a whore's cunt, Harry, you rent.' I didn't hang you. 'You wanted me dead.' I didn't. 'You wanted me hanged.' All right, I wanted you hanged. Go away! (*Pause.*) 'Death is horrible, Mr Brewer, it's dark, there's nothing.' Thomas Barrett! You were hanged because you stole from, the stores. 'I was seventeen, Mr Brewer.' You lived a very wicked life. 'I didn't.' That's what you said that morning, 'I have led a very wicked life.' 'I had to say something, Mr Brewer, and make sense of dying. I'd heard the Reverend say we were all wicked, but it was horrible, my body hanging, my tongue sticking out.' You shouldn't have stolen that food! 'I wanted to live, go back to England, I'd only be twenty-four. I hadn't done it much, not like you.' Duckling! 'I wish I wasn't dead, Mr Brewer I had plans. I was going to have my farm, drink with friends and feel the strong legs of a girl around me – ' You shouldn't have stolen. 'Didn't you ever steal?' No! Yes. But that was different. Duckling! 'Why should you be alive after what you've done?' Duckling! Duckling!

Duckling rushes on.

Duckling What's the matter, Harry?

Harry I'm seeing them.

Duckling Who?

Harry All of them. The dead. Help me.

Duckling I've heard your screams from the beach. You're having another bad dream.

Harry No. I see them.

Pause.

Let me come inside you.

Duckling Now?

Harry Please.

Duckling Will you forget your nightmares?

Harry Yes.

Duckling Come then.

Harry Duckling . . .

She lies down and lifts her skirts. He begins to go down over her and stops.

What were you doing on the beach? You were with him, he told me, you were with Handy Baker.

SCENE FOUR. THE ABORIGINE MUSES ON THE NATURE OF DREAMS

The Aborigine Some dreams lose their way and wander over the earth, lost. But this is a dream no one wants. It has stayed. How can we befriend this crowded, hungry and disturbed dream?

SCENE FIVE. THE SECOND REHEARSAL

Ralph Clark, Mary Benham and Robert Sideway are waiting. Major Ross and Captain Campbell bring the three prisoners Caesar, Wisehammer and Liz Morden. They are still in chains. Ross shoves them forward.

Ross Here is some of your caterwauling cast, Lieutenant.

Campbell The Governor, chhht, said, release, tssst. Prisoners.

Ross Unchain Wisehammer and the savage, Captain Campbell. (*Points to Liz.*) She stays in chains. She's being tried tomorrow, we don't want her sloping off.

Ralph I can't rehearse with one of my players in chains, Major.

Campbell Eeh. Difficult, Mmmm.

Ross We'll tell the Governor you didn't need her and take her back to prison.

Ralph No. We shall manage. Sideway, go over the scene you rehearsed in prison with Melinda, please.

Caesar I'm in that scene too, Lieutenant.

Ralph No, you're not.

Liz and Sideway Yes he is, Lieutenant.

Sideway He's my servant.

Ralph nods.

Ralph The rest of us will go from Silvia's entrance as Wilful. Where's Arscott?

Ross We haven't finished with Arscott yet, Lieutenant.

Campbell Punishment, eeh, for escape. Fainted. Fifty-three lashes left. Heeeh.

Ross (*pointing to Caesar*) Caesar's next. After Morden's trial.

Caesar cringes.

Ralph Brenham, are you ready? Wisehammer? I'll play Captain Plume.

Ross The wee Lieutenant wants to be in the play too. He wants to be promoted to convict. We'll have you in the chain gang soon, Mr Clark, haha. (*A pause. Ross and*

Campbell stand, watching. The Convicts are frozen.)

Ralph Major, we will rehearse now.

Pause. No one moves.

We wish to rehearse.

Ross No one's stopping you, Lieutenant.

Silence.

Ralph Major, rehearsals need to take place in the utmost euh – privacy, secrecy you might say. The actors are not yet ready to be seen by the public.

Ross Not ready to be seen?

Ralph Major, there is a modesty attached to the process of creation which must be respected.

Ross Modesty? Modesty! Sideway, come here.

Ralph Major, Sideway – stay –

Ross Lieutenant. I would not try to countermand the orders of a superior officer.

Campbell Obedience. Ehh, first euh, rule.

Ross Sideway.

Sideway comes up to Ross.

Take your shirt off.

Sideway obeys Ross turns him and shows his scarred back to the company.

One hundred lashes on the *Sirius* for answering an officer. Remember, Sideway? Three hundred lashes for trying to strike the same officer.

I have seen the white of this animal's bones, his wretched blood and reeky convict urine have spilled on my boots and he's feeling modest? Are you feeling modest, Sideway?

He shoves Sideway aside.

Modesty.
Bryant. Here.

Dabby comes forward.

On all fours.

Dabby goes down on all fours.

Now wag your tail and bark, and I'll throw you a biscuit. What? You've forgotten? Isn't that how you begged for your food on the ship? Wag your tail, Bryant, bark! We'll wait.
Brenham.

Mary comes forward.

Where's your tattoo, Brenham? Show us. I can't see it. Show us.

Mary tries to obey, lifting her skirt a little.

If you can't manage. I'll help you. (*Mary lifts her skirt a little higher.*) I can't see it.

But Sideway turns to Liz and starts acting, boldly, across the room, across everyone.

Sideway 'What pleasures I may receive abroad are indeed uncertain; but this I am sure of, I shall meet with less cruelty among the most barbarous nations than I have found at home.'

Liz 'Come, Sir, you and I have been jangling a great while; I fancy if we made up our accounts, we should the sooner come to an agreement.'

Sideway 'Sure, Madam, you won't dispute your being in

my debt – my fears, sighs, vows, promises, assiduities, anxieties, jealousies, have run for a whole year, without any payment.'

Campbell Mmhem, good, that. Sighs, vows, promises, hehem, mmm. Anxieties.

Ross Captain Campbell, start Arscott's punishment.

Campbell goes.

Liz 'A year! Oh Mr Worthy, what you owe to me is not to be paid under a seven years' servitude. How did you use me the year before – '

The shouts of Arscott are heard.

'How did you use me the year before – '

She loses her lines. Sideway tries to prompt her.

Sideway 'When taking advantage – '

Liz 'When taking the advantage of my innocence and necessity – '

But she stops and drops down, defeated. Silence, except for the beating and Arscott's cries.

SCENE SIX. THE SCIENCE OF HANGING

Harry, Ketch Freeman, Liz, sitting, staring straight ahead of her.

Ketch I don't want to do this.

Harry Get on with it, Freeman.

Ketch (*to Liz*) I have to measure you.

Pause.

I'm sorry.

Liz doesn't move.

You'll have to stand, Liz.

Liz doesn't move.

Please.

Pause.

I won't hurt you. I mean, now. And if I have the measurements right, I can make it quick. Very quick. Please.

Liz doesn't move.

She doesn't want to get up, Mr Brewer. I could come back later.

Harry Hurry up.

Ketch I can't. I can't measure her unless she gets up. I have to measure her to judge the drop. If the rope's too short, it won't hang her and if the rope is too long, it could pull her head off. It's very difficult, Mr Brewer, I've always done my best.

Pause.

But I've never hung a woman.

Harry (*in Tom Barrett's voice*) 'You've hung a boy.' (*to Ketch*) You've hung a boy.

Ketch That was a terrible mess, Mr Brewer, don't you remember. It took twenty minutes and even then he wasn't dead. Remember how he danced and everyone laughed. I don't want to repeat something like that, Mr Brewer, not now. Someone had to get hold of his legs to weigh him down and then –

Harry Measure her, Freeman!

Ketch Yes, Sir. Could you tell her to get up. She'll listen to you.

Harry (*shouts*) Get up you bitch.

Liz doesn't move.

Get up!

He seizes her and makes her stand.

Now measure her!

Ketch (*measuring the neck, etc., of Liz*) The Lieutenant is talking to the Governor again, Liz, maybe he'll change his mind. At least he might wait until we've done the play.

Pause.

I don't want to do this.
  I know, you're thinking in my place you wouldn't. But somebody will do it, if I don't, and I'll be gentle. I won't hurt you.

Liz doesn't move, doesn't look at him.

It's wrong, Mr Brewer. It's wrong.

Harry (*in Tom Barrett's voice*) 'It's wrong. Death is horrible.' (*in his own voice to Ketch*) There's no food left in the colony and she steals it and gives it to Kable to run away.

Ketch That's true, Liz, you shouldn't have stolen that food. Especially when the Lieutenant trusted us. That was wrong, Liz. Actors can't behave like normal people, not even like normal criminals. Still, I'm sorry. I'll do my best.

Harry 'I had plans.' (*to Ketch*) Are you finished?

Ketch Yes, yes. I have all the measurements I need. No, one more. I need to lift her. You don't mind, do you, Liz?

He lifts her.

She's so light. I'll have to use a very long rope. The fig tree would be better, it's higher. When will they build me some gallows, Mr Brewer? Nobody will laugh at you, Liz, you won't be ashamed, I'll make sure of that.

Harry 'You could hang yourself.' Come on, Freeman. Let's go.

Ketch Goodbye, Liz. You were a very good Melinda. No one will be as good as you.

They begin to go.

Liz Mr Brewer.

Harry 'You wanted me dead.' I didn't. You shouldn't've stolen that food!

Ketch Speak to her, please, Mr Brewer.

Harry What?

Liz Tell Lieutenant Clark I didn't steal the food. Tell him – afterwards. I want him to know.

Harry Why didn't you say that before? Why are you lying now?

Liz Tell the Lieutenant.

Harry 'Another victim of yours, another body. I was so frightened, so alone.'

Ketch Mr Brewer.

Harry 'It's dark. There's nothing.' Get away, get away!

Liz Please tell the Lieutenant.

Harry 'First fear, then a pain at the back of the neck. Then nothing.' I can't see. It's dark. It's dark.

Harry screams and falls.

SCENE SEVEN. THE MEANING OF PLAYS

The Aborigine Ghosts in a multitude have spilled from the dream. Who are they? A swarm of ancestors comes through unmended cracks in the sky? But why? What do they need? If we can satisfy them, they will go back. How can we satisfy them?

Mary, Ralph, Dabby, Wisehammer, Arscott. Mary and Ralph are rehearsing. The others are watching.

Ralph 'For I swear, Madam, by the honour of my profession, that whatever dangers I went upon, it was with the hope of making myself more worthy of your esteem, and if I ever had thoughts of preserving my life, 'twas for the pleasure of dying at your feet.'

Mary 'Well, well, you shall die at my feet, or where you will; but you know, Sir, there is a certain will and testament to be made beforehand.'
I don't understand why Silvia has asked Plume to make a will.

Dabby It's a proof of his love, he wants to provide for her.

Mary A will is a proof of love?

Wisehammer No. She's using will in another sense. He must show his willingness to marry her. Dying is used in another sense, too.

Ralph He gives her his will to indicate that he intends to take care of her.

Dabby That's right, Lieutenant, marriage is nothing, but will you look after her?

Wisehammer Plume is too ambitious to marry Silvia.

Mary If I had been Silvia, I would have trusted Plume.

Dabby When dealing with men, always have a contract.

Mary Love is a contract.

Dabby Love is the barter of perishable goods. A man's word for a woman's body.

Wisehammer Dabby is right. If a man loves a woman, he should marry her.

Ralph Sometimes he can't.

Wisehammer Then she should look for someone who can.

Dabby A woman should look after her own interests, that's all.

Mary Her interest is to love.

Dabby A girl will love the first man who knows how to open her legs. She's called a whore and ends up here. I could write scenes, Lieutenant, women with real lives, not these Shrewsbury prudes.

Wisehammer I've written something. The prologue of this play won't make any sense to the convicts: 'In ancient times, when Helen's fatal charms' and so on. I've written another one. Will you look at it, Lieutenant?

Ralph does so and Wisehammer takes Mary aside.

You mustn't trust the wrong people, Mary. We could make a new life together, here. I would marry you, Mary, think about it, you would live with me, in a house. He'll have to put you in a hut at the bottom of his garden and call you his servant in public, that is, his whore. Don't do it, Mary.

Dabby Lieutenant, are we rehearsing or not? Arscott and I have been waiting for hours.

Ralph It seems interesting. I'll read it more carefully later.

Wisehammer You don't like it.

Ralph I do like it. Perhaps it needs a little more work. It's not Farquhar.

Wisehammer It would mean more to the convicts.

Ralph We'll talk about it another time.

Wisehammer Do you think it should be longer?

Ralph I'll think about it.

Wisehammer Shorter? Do you like the last two lines? Mary helped me with them.

Ralph Ah.

Wisehammer The first lines took us days, didn't they, Mary?

Ralph We'll rehearse Silvia's entrance as Jack Wilful. You're in the scene, Wisehammer. We'll come to your scenes in a minute, Bryant. Now, Brenham, remember what I showed you yesterday about walking like a gentleman? I've ordered breeches to be made for you, you can practise in them tomorrow.

Mary I'll tuck my skirt in. (*She does so and takes a masculine pose.*) 'Save ye, save ye, gentlemen.'

Wisehammer 'My dear, I'm yours.'

He kisses her.

Ralph (*angrily*) It doesn't say Silvia is kissed in the stage directions!

Wisehammer Plume kisses her later and there's the line

about men kissing in the army. I thought Brazen would kiss her immediately.

Ralph It's completely wrong.

Wisehammer It's right for the character of Brazen.

Ralph No it isn't. I'm the director, Wisehammer.

Wisehammer Yes, but I have to play the part. They're equal in this scene. They're both captains and in the end fight for her. Who's playing Plume in our performance?

Ralph I will have to, as Kable hasn't come back. It's your line.

Wisehammer Will I be given a sword?

Ralph I doubt it. Let's move on to Kit's entrance, Arscott has been waiting too long.

Arscott 'Sir, if you please – '

Ralph Excellent, Arscott, but we should give you our last lines so you'll know when to come in. Wisehammer.

Wisehammer 'The fellow dare not fight.'

Ralph That's when you come in.

Arscott 'Sir, if you please – '

Dabby What about me? I haven't done anything either. You always rehearse the scenes with Silvia.

Ralph Let's rehearse the scene where Rose comes on with her brother Bullock. It's a better scene for you Arscott. Do you know it?

Arscott Yes.

Ralph Good. Wisehammer, you'll have to play the part of Bullock.

Wisehammer What? Play two parts?

Ralph Major Ross won't let any more prisoners off work. Some of you will have to play several parts.

Wisehammer It'll confuse the audience. They'll think Brazen is Bullock and Bullock Brazen.

Ralph Nonsense, if the audience is paying attention, they'll know that Bullock is a country boy and Brazen a captain.

Wisehammer What if they aren't paying attention?

Ralph People who can't pay attention should not go to the theatre.

Mary If you act well, they will have to pay attention.

Wisehammer It will ruin my entrance as Captain Brazen.

Ralph We have no choice and we must turn this necessity into an advantage. You will play two different characters and display the full range of your abilities.

Wisehammer Our audience won't be that discerning.

Ralph Their imagination will be challenged and trained. Let's start the scene. Bryant?

Dabby I think *The Recruiting Officer* is a silly play. I want to be in a play that has more interesting people in it.

Mary I like playing Silvia. She's bold, she breaks rules out of love for her Captain and she's not ashamed.

Dabby She hasn't been born poor, she hasn't had to survive, and her father's a Justice of the Peace. I want to play myself.

Arscott I don't want to play myself. When I say Kite's lines I forget everything else. I forgot the judge said I'm going to have to spend the rest of my natural life in this place getting beaten and working like a slave. I can forget that out there it's trees and burnt grass, spiders that kill you in four hours and snakes. I don't have to think about what happened to Kable, I don't have to remember the things I've done, when I speak Kite's lines I don't hate any more. I'm Kite. I'm in Shrewsbury. Can we get on with the scene, Lieutenant, and stop talking?

Dabby I want to see a play that shows life as we know it.

Wisehammer A play should make you understand something new. If it tells you what you already know, you leave it as ignorant as you went in.

Dabby Why can't we do a play about now?

Wisehammer It doesn't matter when a play is set. It's better if it's set in the past, it's clearer. It's easier to understand Plume and Brazen than some of the officers we know here.

Ralph Arscott, would you start the scene?

Arscott 'Captain, Sir, look yonder, a-coming this way, 'tis the prettiest, cleanest, little tit.'

Ralph Now Worthy – He's in this scene. Where's Sideway?

Mary He's so upset about Liz he won't rehearse.

Ralph I am going to talk to the Governor, but he has to rehearse. We must do the play, whatever happens. We've been rehearsing for five months! Let's go on. 'Here she comes, and what is that great country fellow with her?'

Arscott 'I can't tell, Sir.'

Wisehammer I'm not a great country fellow.

Ralph Act it, Wisehammer.

Dabby 'Buy chickens, young and tender, young and tender chickens?' This is a very stupid line and I'm not saying it.

Ralph It's written by the playwright and you have to say it. 'Here, you chickens!'

Dabby 'Who calls?'

Ralph Bryant, you're playing a pretty country wench who wants to entice the Captain. You have to say these lines with charm and euh – blushes.

Dabby I don't blush.

Ralph I can't do this scene without Sideway. Let's do another scene.

Pause.

Arscott, let's work on your big speeches. I haven't heard them yet. I still need Sideway. This is irresponsible, he wanted the part. Somebody go and get Sideway.

No one moves.

Arscott I'll do the first speech anyway, Sir. 'Yes, Sir, I understand my business, I will say it; you must know, Sir, I was born a gypsy, and bred among the crew till I was ten years old, there I learned canting and lying – '

Dabby That's about me!

Arscott 'I was bought from my mother Cleopatra by a certain nobleman, for three guineas, who liking my beauty made me his page – '

Dabby That's my story. Why do I have to play a silly milkmaid? Why can't I play Kite?

Mary You can't play a man, Dabby.

Dabby You're playing a man: Jack Wilful.

Mary Yes, but in the play, I know I'm a woman, whereas if you played Kite, you would have to think you were a man.

Dabby If Wisehammer can think he's a big country lad, I can think I'm a man. People will use their imagination and people with no imagination shouldn't go to the theatre.

Ralph Bryant, you're muddling everything.

Dabby No. I see things very clearly and I'm making you see clearly, Lieutenant. I want to play Kite.

Arscott You can't play Kite! I'm playing Kite! You can't steal my part!

Ralph You may have to play Melinda.

Dabby All she does is marry Sideway, that's not interesting.

Dabby stomps off. Ketch comes on.

Ketch I'm sorry I'm late, Lieutenant, but I know all my lines.

Ralph We'll rehearse the first scene between Justice Balance and Silvia. Brenham.

Arscott stomps off.

Mary 'Whilst there is life there is hope, Sir; perhaps my brother may recover.'

Ketch 'We have but little reason to expect it – '

Mary I can't. Not with him. Not with Liz – I can't.

She runs off.

Ralph One has to transcend personal feelings in the theatre.

Wisehammer runs after Mary.

(*to Ketch*) We're not making much progress today, let's end this rehearsal.

He goes. Ketch is left alone, bewildered.

SCENE EIGHT. DUCKLING MAKES VOWS

Night. Harry, ill. Duckling.

Duckling If you live, I will never again punish you with my silence. If you live, I will never again turn away from you. If you live, I will never again imagine another man when you make love to me. If you live, I will never tell you I want to leave you. If you live, I will speak to you. If you live, I will be tender with you. If you live, I will look after you. If you live, I will stay with you. If you live, I will be wet and open to your touch. If you live, I will answer all your questions. If you live, I will look after you. If you live, I will love you.

Pause.

If you die, I will never forgive you.

She leans over him. Listens. Touches. Harry is dead.

I hate you.
No. I love you.

She crouches into a foetal position, cries out.

How could you do this?

SCENE NINE. A LOVE SCENE

The beach. Night. Mary, then Ralph.

Mary (*to herself*)'Captain Plume, I despise your listing-money; if I do serve, 'tis purely for love – of that wench I mean. For you must know', etc. –

'So you only want an opportunity for accomplishing your designs upon her?'

'Well, Sir, I'm satisfied as to the point in debate; but now let me beg you to lay aside your recruiting airs, put on the man of honour, and tell me plainly what usage I must expect when I'm under your command.'

She tries that again, with a stronger and lower voice.
Ralph comes on, sees her. She sees him, but continues.

'And something tells me, that if you do discharge me 'twill be the greatest punishment you can inflict; for were we this moment to go upon the greatest dangers in your profession, they would be less terrible to me than to stay behind you. And now your hand – this lists me – and now you are my Captain.'

Ralph (*as Plume*) 'Your friend.' (*Kisses her.*) ''Sdeath! There's something in this fellow that charms me.'

Mary 'One favour I must beg – this affair will make some noise – '

Ralph Silvia –

He kisses her again.

Mary 'I must therefore take care to be impressed by the Act of Parliament – '

Ralph 'What you please as to that. Will you lodge at my quarters in the meantime? You shall have part of my bed.' Silvia. Mary.

Mary Am I doing it well? It's difficult to play a man. It's not the walk, it's the way you hold your head. A man doesn't bow his head so much and never at an angle. I must face you without lowering my head, Let's try it again.

Ralph 'What you please as to that. – Will you lodge at my quarters in the meantime? You shall have part of my bed.' Mary!

She holds her head straight. Pause.

Will you?

Pause.

Mary Yes.

They kiss.

Ralph Don't lower your head. Silvia wouldn't.

She begins to undress, from the top.

I've never looked at the body of a woman before.

Mary Your wife?

Ralph It wasn't right to look at her.
Let me see you.

Mary Yes.
Let me see you.

Ralph Yes.

He begins to undress himself.

SCENE TEN. THE QUESTION OF LIZ

Ralph, Ross, Phillip, Collins, Campbell.

Collins She refused to defend herself at the trial. She didn't say a word. This was taken as an admission of guilt and she was condemned to be hanged. The evidence against her, however, is flimsy.

Ross She was seen with Kable next to the food stores. That is a fingering fact.

Collins She was seen by a drunken sailor in the dark. He admitted he was drunk and that he saw her at a distance. He knew Kable was supposed to be repairing the door and she's known to be friends with Kable and Arscott. She won't speak, she won't say where she was. That is our difficulty.

Ross She won't speak because she's guilty.

Phillip Silence has many causes, Robbie.

Ralph She won't speak, Your Excellency, because of the convict code of honour. She doesn't want to beg for her life.

Ross Convict code of honour. This pluming play has muddled the muffy Lieutenant's mind.

Collins My only fear, Your Excellency, is that she may have refused to speak because she no longer believes in the process of justice. If that is so, the courts here will become travesties. I do not want that.

Phillip But if she won't speak, there is nothing more we can do. You cannot get at the truth through silence.

Ralph She spoke to Harry Brewer.

Phillip But Harry never regained consciousness before he died.

Ralph James Freeman was there and told me what she said.

Phillip Wasn't this used in the trial?

Collins Freeman's evidence wasn't very clear and as Liz Morden wouldn't confirm what he said, it was dismissed.

Ross You can't take the word of a crooked crawling hangman.

Phillip Why won't she speak?

Ross Because she's guilty.

Phillip Robbie, we may be about to hang the first woman in this colony. I do not want to hang the first innocent woman.

Ralph We must get at the truth.

Ross Truth! We have 800 thieves, perjurers, forgers, murderers, liars, escapers, rapists, whores, coiners in this scrub-ridden, dust-driven, thunder-bolted, savage-run, cretinous colony. My marines who are trained to fight are turned into ghouly gaolers, fed less than the prisoners –

Phillip The rations, Major, are the same for all, prisoners and soldiers.

Ross They have the right to more so that makes them have less. Not a ship shifting into sight, the prisoners running away, stealing, drinking and the wee ductile Lieutenant talks about the truth.

Phillip Truth is indeed a luxury, but its absence brings about the most abject poverty in a civilization. That is the paradox.

Ross This is a profligate prison for us all, it's a hellish hole we soldiers have been hauled to because they blame us for losing the war in America. This is a hateful, hary-scary, topsy-turvy outpost, this is not a civilization! I hate this possumy place.

Collins Perhaps we could return to the question of Liz Morden. (*Calls.*) Captain Campbell.

Campbell brings in Liz Morden.

Morden, if you don't speak, we will have to hang you: if you can defend yourself, His Excellency can overrule the court. We would not then risk a miscarriage of justice. But you must speak. Did you steal that food with the escaped prisoner Kable?

A silence.

Ralph She –

Collins It is the accused who must answer.

Phillip Liz Morden. You must speak the truth.

Collins We will listen to you.

Pause.

Ralph Morden. No one will despise you for telling the truth.

Phillip That is not so, Lieutenant. Tell the truth and accept the contempt. That is the history of great men. Liz, you may be despised, but you will have shown courage.

Ralph If that soldier has lied –

Ross There, there, he's accusing my soldiers of lying. It's that play, it makes fun of officers, it shows an officer lying and cheating. It shows a corrupt justice as well, Collins –

Campbell Good scene that, very funny, hah, scchhh.

Collins Et tu, Campbell?

Campbell What? Meant only. Hahah. 'If he be so good at gunning he shall have enough – he may be of use against the French, for he shoots flying,' hahaha. Good, and then there's this Constable ha –

Ross Campbell!

Phillip The play seems to be having miraculous effects

already. Don't you want to be in it, Liz?

Ralph Morden, you must speak.

Collins For the good of the colony.

Phillip And of the play.

A long silence.

Liz I didn't steal the food.

Collins Were you there when Kable stole it?

Liz No. I was there before.

Ross And you knew he was going to steal it?

Liz Yes.

Ross Guilty. She didn't report it.

Collins Failure to inform is not a hangable offence.

Ross Conspiracy.

Collins We may need a retrial.

Phillip Why wouldn't you say any of this before?

Ross Because she didn't have time to invent a lie.

Collins Major, you are demeaning the process of law.

Phillip Why, Liz?

Liz Because it wouldn't have mattered.

Phillip Speaking the truth?

Liz Speaking.

Ross You are taking the word of a convict against the word of a soldier –

Collins A soldier who was drunk and uncertain of what he saw.

Ross A soldier is a soldier and has a right to respect. You will have revolt on your hands, Governor.

Phillip I'm sure I will, but let us see the play first. Liz, I hope you are good in your part.

Ralph She will be, Your Excellency, I promise that.

Liz Your Excellency, I will endeavour to speak Mr Farquhar's lines with the elegance and clarity their own worth commands.

SCENE ELEVEN. BACKSTAGE

Night. The Aborigine.

The Aborigine Look: oozing pustules on my skin, heat on my forehead. Perhaps we have been wrong all this time and this is not a dream at all.

The Actors come on. They begin to change and make up. The Aborigine drifts off.

Mary Are the savages coming to see the play as well?

Ketch They come around the camp because they're dying: smallpox.

Mary Oh.

Sideway I hope they won't upset the audience.

Mary Everyone is here. All the officers too.

Liz (*to Duckling*) Dabby could take your part.

Duckling No. I will do it. I will remember the lines.

Mary I've brought you an orange from Lieutenant Clark's island. They've thrown her out of Harry Brewer's tent.

Wisehammer Why? He wouldn't have wanted that.

Duckling Major Ross said a whore was a whore and I was to go into the women's camp. They've taken all of Harry's things.

She bursts into tears.

Mary I'll talk to the Lieutenant.

Liz Let's go over your lines. And if you forget them, touch my foot and I'll whisper them to you.

Sideway (*who has been practising on his own*) We haven't rehearsed the bow. Garrick used to take his this way: you look up to the circle, to the sides, down, make sure everyone thinks you're looking at them. Get in a line.

They do so.

Arscott I'll be in the middle. I'm the tallest.

Mary No, Arscott. (*Mary places herself in the middle.*)

Sideway Dabby, you should be next to Mary.

Dabby I won't take a bow.

Sideway It's not the biggest part, Dabby, but you'll be noticed.

Dabby I don't want to be noticed.

Sideway Let's get this right. If we don't all do the same thing, it will look a mess.

They try. Dabby is suddenly transfixed.

Dabby Hurray, hurray, hurray.

Sideway No, they will be shouting bravo, but we're not in a line yet.

Dabby I wasn't looking at the bow, I saw the whole play, and we all knew our lines, and Mary, you looked so beautiful, and after that, I saw Devon and they were shouting bravo, bravo Dabby, hurray, you've escaped, you've sailed thousands and thousands of miles on the open sea and you've come back to your Devon, bravo Dabby, bravo.

Mary When are you doing this, Dabby?

Dabby Tonight.

Mary You can't.

Dabby I'll be in the play till the end, then in the confusion, when it's over, we can slip away. The tide is up, the night will be dark, everything's ready.

Mary The Lieutenant will be blamed, I won't let you.

Dabby If you say anything to the Lieutenant, I'll refuse to act in the play.

Arscott When I say my lines, I think of nothing else. Why can't you do the same?

Dabby Because it's only for one night. I want to grow old in Devon.

Mary They'll never let us do another play, I'm telling the Lieutenant.

All No, you're not.

Dabby Please, I want to go back to Devon.

Wisehammer I don't want to go back to England now. It's too small and they don't like Jews. Here, no one has more of a right than anyone else to call you a foreigner. I want to become the first famous writer.

Mary You can't become a famous writer until you're dead.

Wisehammer You can if you're the only one.

Sideway I'm going to start a theatre company. Who wants to be in it?

Wisehammer I will write you a play about justice.

Sideway Only comedies, my boy, only comedies.

Wisehammer What about a comedy about unrequited love?

Liz I'll be in your company, Mr Sideway.

Ketch And so will I. I'll play all the parts that have dignity and gravity.

Sideway I'll hold auditions tomorrow.

Dabby Tomorrow.

Duckling Tomorrow.

Mary Tomorrow.

Liz Tomorrow.

A silence. (Un ange passe.)

Mary Where are my shoes?

Ralph comes in.

Ralph Arscott, remember to address the soldiers when you talk of recruiting. Look at them: you are speaking to them. And don't forget, all of you, to leave a space for people to laugh.

Arscott I'll kill anyone who laughs at me.

Ralph They're not laughing at you, they're laughing at Farquhar's lines. You must expect them to laugh.

Arscott That's all right, but if I see Major Ross or any other officer laughing at me, I'll kill them.

Mary No more violence. By the way, Arscott, when you carry me off the stage as Jack Wilful, could you be a little more gentle? I don't think he'd be so rough with a young gentleman.

Ralph Where's Caesar?

Ketch I saw him walking towards the beach earlier. I thought he was practising his lines.

Arscott Caesar!

He goes out.

Wisehammer (*to Liz*) When I say 'Do you love fishing, Madam?', do you say something then? –

Ralph (*goes over to Duckling*) I am so sorry, Duckling. Harry was my friend.

Duckling I loved him. But now he'll never know that. I thought that if he knew he would become cruel.

Ralph Are you certain you don't want Dabby to take your part?

Duckling No! I will do it. I want to do it.

Pause.

He liked to hear me say my lines.

Ralph He will be watching from somewhere. (*He goes to Mary.*) How beautiful you look.

Mary I dreamt I had a necklace of pearls, and three children.

Ralph If we have a boy we will call him Harry.

Mary And if we have a girl?

Ralph She will be called Betsey Alicia.

*Arscott comes in with Caesar who is drunk and
dishevelled.*

Arscott Lying on the beach, dead drunk.

Caesar (*to Ralph, pleading*) I can't. All these people. My
ancestors are angry, they do not want me to be laughed at
by all those people.

Ralph You wanted to be in this play and you will be in
this play– .

Ketch I'm nervous too, but I've overcome it. You have to
be brave to be an actor.

Caesar My ancestors will kill me.

He swoons. Arscott hits him.

Arscott You're going to ruin my first scene.

Caesar Please, Lieutenant, save me.

Ralph Caesar, if I were back home, I wouldn't be in this
play either. My ancestors wouldn't be very pleased to see
me here – But our ancestors are thousands of miles
away.

Caesar I cannot be a disgrace to Madagascar.

Arscott You will be more of a disgrace if you don't come
out with me on that stage. NOW.

Mary Think of us as your family.

Sideway (*to Ralph*) What do you think of this bow?

Ralph Caesar, I am your Lieutenant and I command you
to go on that stage. If you don't, you will be tried and
hanged for treason.

Ketch And I'll tie the rope in such a way you'll dangle
there for hours full of piss and shit.

Ralph What will your ancestors think of that, Caesar?

Caesar cries but pulls himself together.

Ketch (*to Liz*) I couldn't have hanged you.

Liz No?

Ralph Dabby, have you got your chickens?

Dabby My chickens? Yes. Here.

Ralph Are you all right?

Dabby Yes. (*Pause.*) I was dreaming.

Ralph Of your future success?

Dabby Yes. Of my future success.

Ralph And so is everyone here, I hope. Now, Arscott.

Arscott Yes, Sir!

Ralph Calm.

Arscott I have been used to danger, Sir.

Sideway Here.

Liz What's that?

Sideway Salt. For good luck.

Ralph Where did you get that from?

Sideway I have been saving it from my rations. I have saved enough for each of us to have some.

They all take a little salt.

Wisehammer Lieutenant?

Ralph Yes, Wisehammer.

Wisehammer There's – There's –

Mary There's his prologue.

Ralph The prologue. I forgot.

Pause.

Let me hear it again.

Wisehammer
From distant climes o'er wide-spread seas we come,
Though not with much éclat or beat of drum,
True patriots all; for be it understood,
We left our country for our country's good;
No private views disgraced our generous zeal,
What urg'd our travels was our country's weal,
And none will doubt but that our emigration
Has prov'd most useful to the British nation.

Silence.

Ralph When Major Ross hears that, he'll have an
apoplectic fit.

Mary I think it's very good.

Dabby So do I. And true.

Sideway It's very good, Wisehammer, it's very well
written, but it's too – too political. It will be considered
provocative.

Wisehammer You don't want me to say it.

Ralph Not tonight. We have many people against us.

Wisehammer I could tone it down. I could omit 'We left
our country for our country's good.'

Dabby That's the best line.

Ralph It would be wrong to cut it.

Wisehammer I worked so hard on it.

Liz It rhymes.

Sideway We'll use it in the Sideway Theatre.

Ralph You will get much praise as Brazen, Wisehammer.

Wisehammer It isn't the same as writing.

Ralph The theatre is like a small republic, it requires private sacrifices for the good of the whole. That is something you should agree with, Wisehammer.

Pause.

And now, my actors, I want to say what a pleasure it has been to work with you. You are on your own tonight and you must do your utmost to provide the large audience out there with a pleasurable, intelligible and memorable evening.

Liz We will do our best, Mr Clark.

Mary I love this!

Ralph Arscott.

Arscott (*to Caesar*) You walk three steps ahead of me. If you stumble once, you know what will happen to you later? Move!

Ralph You're on.

Arscott is about to go on, then remembers.

Arscott Halberd! Halberd!

He is handed his halberd and goes up stage and off, preceded by Caesar beating the drum. Backstage, the remaining actors listen with trepidation to Kite's first speech.

'If any gentlemen soldiers, or others, have a mind to serve Her Majesty, and pull down the French King; if any prentices have severe masters, any children have undutiful parents; if any servants have too little wages or any husband too much wife; let them repair to the noble Sergeant Kite, at the Sign of the Raven, in this good town of Shrewsbury, and they shall receive present relief and entertainment' . . .

And to the triumphant music of Beethoven's Fifth Symphony and the sound of applause and laughter from the First Fleet audience, the first Australian performance of The Recruiting Officer *begins.*

THE LOVE OF THE NIGHTINGALE

For Kate

Listen. This is the noise of myth. It makes the same sound
as shadow. Can you hear it?

Eavan Boland, 'The Journey'

Now, by myself, I am nothing; yea, full oft
I have regarded woman's fortunes thus,
That we are nothing; who in our fathers' house
Live, I suppose, the happiest, while young,
Of all mankind; for ever pleasantly
Does Folly nurture all. Then, when we come
To full discretion and maturity,
We are thrust out and marketed abroad,
Far from our parents and ancestral gods,
Some to strange husbands, some to barbarous,
One to a rude, one to a wrangling home;
And these, after the yoking of a night;
We are bound to like, and deem it well with us.

> Much
I envy thee thy life: and most of all,
That thou hast never had experience
Of a strange land.

Two fragments from Sophocles' lost play, *Tereus*
Translated by Sir George Young

Characters

Male Chorus (1)
First Soldier
Second Soldier
Procne
Philomele
King Pandion
Queen
Tereus
Hero
Iris
June
Echo
Helen
Aphrodite
Phaedra
Nurse
Female Chorus
Hippolytus
Theseus
Male Chorus (2)
Captain
Niobe
Servant
Itys
Sailors, Bacchae, Acrobats *(non-speaking)*

The Love of the Nightingale was first performed by the Royal Shakespeare Company at The Other Place, Stratford-upon-Avon on 28 October 1988. The cast was as follows:

Male Chorus David Acton, Stephen Gordon, Richard Haddon Haines, Patrick Miller, Edward Rawle-Hicks
First Soldier Patrick Miller
Second Soldier David Acton
Procne Marie Mullen
Philomele Katy Behean
King Pandion Richard Haddon Haines
Queen Joan Blackham
Tereus Peter Lennon

Female Chorus
Hero Cate Hamer
Iris Claudette Williams
June Joan Blackham
Echo Joanna Roth
Helen Jill Spurrier

Actors in Hippolytus play
Aphrodite Claudette Williams
Phaedra Cate Hamer
Nurse Jill Spurrier
Female Chorus Joanna Roth
Hippolytus Edward Rawle-Hicks
Theseus David Acton
Male Chorus Stephen Gordon

Captain Tony Armatrading
Niobe Jenni George
Servant Joanna Roth
Itys Nicholas Besley/Alexander Knott

Directed by Garry Hynes
Lighting by Geraint Pughe
Music by Ilona Sekacz

Note on the Chorus
The Chorus never speak together, except the one time it is
specifically indicated in the text.

SCENE ONE

Athens, the **Male Chorus.**

Male Chorus War.

   Two **Soldiers** *come on, with swords and shields.*

First Soldier You cur!

Second Soldier You cat's whisker.

First Soldier You flea's foot.

Second Soldier You particle.

   Pause.

You son of a bitch.

First Soldier You son of a lame hyena.

Second Soldier You son of a bleeding whore.

First Soldier You son of a woman!

   Pause.

I'll slice your drooping genitalia.

Second Soldier I'll pierce your windy asshole.

First Soldier I'll drink from your skull.

   Pause.

Coward!

Second Soldier Braggard.

First Soldier You Worm.

Second Soldier You – man.

   They fight.

Male Chorus And now, death.

The First Soldier kills the Second Soldier.

Second Soldier Murderer!

First Soldier Corpse!

Male Chorus We begin here because no life ever has been untouched by war.

Male Chorus Everyone loves to discuss war.

Male Chorus And yet its outcome, death, is shrouded in silence.

Male Chorus Wars make death acceptable. The gods are less cruel if it is man's fault.

Male Chorus Perhaps, but this is not our story. War is the inevitable background, the ruins in the distance establishing place and perspective.

Male Chorus Athens is at war, but at the palace of the Athenian King Pandion, two sisters discuss life's charms and the attractions of men.

SCENE TWO

Procne, Philomele.

Procne Don't say that, Philomele.

Philomele It's the truth: he's so handsome I want to wrap my legs around him.

Procne That's not how it's done.

Philomele How can I know if no one will tell me? Look at the sweat shining down his body. My feet will curl around the muscles of his back. How is it done, Procne, tell me, please? If you don't tell me, I'll ask Niobe and she'll tell me all wrong.

Procne I'll tell you if you tell me something.

Philomele I'll tell you everything I know, sweet sister. (*Pause.*) I don't know anything.

Procne You know yourself.

Philomele Oh, yes, I feel such things, Procne, such things. Tigers, rivers, serpents, here, in my stomach, a little below. I'll tell you how the serpent uncurls inside me if you tell me how it's done.

Procne That's not what I meant. Philomele, I'm going to marry soon.

Philomele I envy you, sister, you'll know everything then. What are they like? Men?

Procne Look: they fight.

Philomele What are they like: naked?

Procne Spongy.

Philomele What?

Procne I haven't seen one yet, but that's what they told me to prepare me. They have sponges.

Philomele Where?

Procne Here. Getting bigger and smaller and moving up and down. I didn't listen very carefully, I'll know soon enough. Philomele, when I am married, will you want to come and visit me?

Philomele Yes, sister, yes. I'll visit you every day and you'll let me watch.

Procne Philomele! Can't you think of anything else?

Philomele Not today. Tomorrow I'll think about wisdom. It must be so beautiful. Warm ripples of light.

Procne I think most of it you can do on your own. The sponge, I think it detaches.

Philomele I wouldn't want to do it on my own. I want to run my hands down bronzed skin. Ah, I can feel the tiger again.

Procne If I went far away, would you still want to come and visit me?

Philomele I will cross any sea to visit you and your handsome husband, sister. (*Pause.*) When I'm old enough, I won't stop doing it, whatever it is. Life must be so beautiful when you're older. It's beautiful now. Sometimes I'm so happy.

Procne Quiet, Philomele! Never say you're happy. It wakes up the gods and then they look at you and that is never a good thing. Take it back, now.

Philomele You taught me not to lie, sister.

Procne I wish I didn't have to leave home. I worry about you.

Philomele Life is sweet, my sister, and I love everything in it. The feeling. Athens. You. And that brave young warrior fighting to protect us. Oh!

Procne Philomele? Ah. He's dead.

Philomele Crumpled. Procne, was it my fault? Should I have held my tongue?

Procne Athens is at war, men must die.

Philomele I'm frightened. I don't want to leave this room, ever.

Procne You must try to become more moderate. Measure in all things, remember, it's what the philosophers recommend.

Philomele Will the philosophers start speaking again after the war? Procne, can we go and listen to them?

Procne I won't be here.

Philomele Procne, don't go.

Procne It's our parents' will. They know best.

  Pause.

You will come to me if I ask for you, you will?

Philomele Yes.

Procne I want you to promise. Remember you must never break a promise.

Philomele I promise. I will want to. I promise again.

Procne That makes me happy. Ah.

SCENE THREE

The palace of King Pandion. **King Pandion,** *the* **Queen,** **Tereus,** *Procne, Philomele, the Male Chorus.*

Male Chorus Athens won the war with the help of an ally from the north.

Male Chorus The leader of the liberators was called Tereus.

King Pandion No liberated country is ungrateful. That is a rule. You will take what you want from our country. It will be given with gratitude. We are ready.

Tereus I came not out of greed but in the cause of justice,

King Pandion. But I have come to love this country and its inhabitants.

Queen (*to King Pandion*) He wants to stay! I knew it!

    Pause.

King Pandion Of course if you wish to stay in Athens that is your right. We can only remind you this is a small city. But you must stay if you wish.

Tereus No. I must go back north. There has been trouble while I've conducted this war. What I want is to bring some of your country to mine, its manners, its ease, its civilized discourse.

Queen (*to King Pandion*) I knew it: he wants Procne.

King Pandion I can send you some of our tutors. The philosophers, I'm afraid, are rather independent.

Tereus I have always believed that culture was kept by the women.

King Pandion Ours are not encouraged to go abroad.

Tereus But they have a reputation for wisdom. Is that false?

Queen Be careful, he's crafty.

King Pandion It is true. Our women are the best.

Tereus So.

Queen I knew it.

    Pause.

King Pandion She's yours, Tereus. Procne –

Procne But, Father –

King Pandion Your husband.

Procne Mother –

Queen What can I say?

King Pandion I am only sad you will live so far away.

Philomele Can I go with her?

Queen Quiet, child.

Tereus (*to Procne*) I will love and respect you.

Male Chorus It didn't happen that quickly. It took months and much indirect discourse. But that is the gist of it. The end was known from the beginning.

Male Chorus After an elaborate wedding in which King Pandion solemnly gave his daughter to the hero, Tereus, the two left for Thrace. There was relief in Athens. His army had become expensive, rude, rowdy.

Male Chorus Had always been, but we see things differently in peace. That is why peace is so painful.

Male Chorus Nothing to blur the waters. We look down to the bottom.

Male Chorus And on a clear day, we see our own reflections.

Male Chorus In due course, Procne had a child, a boy called Itys. Five years passed.

SCENE FOUR

Procne and her companions, the **Female Chorus: Hero, Echo, Iris, June, Helen.**

Procne Where have all the words gone?

Hero She sits alone, hour after hour, turns her head away and laments.

Iris We don't know how to act, we don't know what to say.

Hero She turns from us in grief.

June Boredom.

Echo Homesick.

Hero It is difficult to come to a strange land.

Helen You will always be a guest there, never call it your own, never rest in the kindness of history.

Echo Your story intermingled with events, no. You will be outside.

Iris And if it is the land of your husband can you even say you have chosen it?

June She is not one of us.

Hero A shared childhood makes friends between women.

Echo The places we walked together, our first smells.

Helen But an unhappy woman can do harm. She has already dampened our play.

June Mocked the occupation of our hours, scorned.

Iris What shall we do?

Helen I fear the future.

Procne Where have the words gone?

Echo Gone, Procne, the words?

Procne There were so many. Everything that was had a word and every word was something. None of these meanings half in the shade, unclear.

Iris We speak the same language, Procne.

Procne The words are the same, but point to different

things. We aspire to clarity in sound, you like the silences in between.

Hero We offered to initiate you.

Procne Barbarian practices. I am an Athenian: I know the truth is found by logic and happiness lies in the truth.

Hero Truth is full of darkness.

Procne No, truth is good and beautiful. See . . . (*Pause.*) I must have someone to talk to.

June We've tried. See . . .

Hero She turns away.

Procne How we talked. Our words played, caressed each other, our words were tossed lightly, a challenge to catch. Where is she now? Who shares those games with her? Or is she silent too?

Echo Silent, Procne, who?

Procne My sister. (*Pause.*) My friend. I want to talk to her. I want her here.

Hero You have a family, Procne, a husband, a child.

Procne I cannot talk to my husband. I have nothing to say to my son. I want her here. She must come here.

Helen It's a long way and a dangerous one for a young girl.

Helen Let her be, Procne.

Procne I want my sister here.

Helen She could come to harm.

Procne Tereus could bring her, she'll be safe with him.

Echo Tereus.

Helen Dangers on the sea, he won't want you to risk them.

Procne He can go alone. I'll wait here and look after the country.

Echo Tereus.

Hero Will your sister want to come to a strange land?

Procne She will want what I want.

Helen Don't ask her to come, Procne.

Procne Why not?

Hero This is no country for a strange young girl.

Procne She will be with me.

Hero She won't listen.

Helen I am worried. It is not something I can say. There are no words for forebodings.

Hero We are only brushed by possibilities.

Echo A beating of wings.

June Best to say nothing. Procne? May we go now?

Procne To your rituals?

June Yes, it's time.

Procne Very well, go.

They go.

This silence . . . this silence . . .

SCENE FIVE

The theatre in Athens. King Pandion, Tereus, **Hippolytus, Theseus.**

King Pandion Procne has always been so sensible. Why,

suddenly, does she ask for her sister?

Tereus She didn't explain. She insisted I come to you and I did what she asked.

King Pandion I understand, Tereus, but such a long journey . . . Procne's not ill?

Tereus She was well when I left. She has her child, companions.

King Pandion Philomele is still very young. And yet, I allowed Procne to go so far away . . . What do you think, Tereus?

Tereus You're her father.

King Pandion And you.

Tereus I only meant Procne would accept any decision you made. It is a long journey.

   Aphrodite *enters*.

Aphrodite I am Aphrodite, goddess of love, resplendent and mighty, revered on earth, courted in heaven, all pay tribute to my fearful power.

King Pandion Do you know this play, Tereus?

Tereus No.

King Pandion I find plays help me think. You catch a phrase, recognize a character. Perhaps this play will help us come to a decision.

Aphrodite I honour those who kneel before me, but that proud heart which dares defy me, that haughty heart I bring low.

Tereus That's sound.

King Pandion Do you have good theatre in Thrace?

Tereus We prefer sport.

King Pandion Then you are like Hippolytus.

Tereus Who?

King Pandion Listen.

Aphrodite Hippolytus turns his head away. Hippolytus prefers the hard chase to the soft bed, wild game to foreplay, but chaste Hippolytus shall be crushed this very day.

Aphrodite exits, The Queen and Philomele enter.

Philomele We're late! I've missed Aphrodite.

King Pandion She only told us it was going to end badly, but we already know that. It's a tragedy.

Enter **Phaedra.**

Queen There's Phaedra. (*to Tereus*) Phaedra is married to Theseus, the King of Athens. Hippolytus is Theseus' son by his previous mistress, the Amazon Queen, who's now dead, and so Phaedra's stepson. Phaedra has three children of her own.

Phaedra Hold me, hold me, hold up my head. The strength of my limbs is melting away.

Philomele How beautiful to love like that! The strength of my limbs is melting away. Is that what you feel for Procne, Tereus?

Queen Philomele! (*to Tereus*) Phaedra's fallen in love with Hippolytus.

Tereus Her own stepson! That's wrong.

King Pandion That's what makes it a tragedy. When you love the right person it's a comedy.

Phaedra Oh, pity me, pity me, what have I done? What will become of me? I have strayed from the path of good sense.

Tereus Why should we pity her? These plays condone vice.

King Pandion Perhaps they only show us the uncomfortable folds of the human heart.

Phaedra I am mad, struck down by the malice of the implacable god.

Philomcle You see, Tereus, love is a god and you cannot control him.

Queen Here's the nurse. She always gives advice.

The **Nurse** *enters.*

Nurse So: you love. You are not the first nor the last. You want to kill yourself? Must all who love die? No, Phaedra, the god has stricken you, how dare you rebel? Be bold, and love. That is God's will.

Tereus Terrible advice.

Philomele No, Tereus, you must obey the gods. Are you blasphemous up there in Thrace?

King Pandion Philomele, you are talking to a king.

Tereus And to a brother, let her speak, Pandion.

Nurse I have a remedy. Trust me.

King Pandion Procne has asked for you. She wants you to go back with Tereus to Thrace.

Philomele To Thrace? To Procne? Oh, yes.

King Pandion You want to leave your parents? Athens?

Philomele I promised Procne I would go if she ever asked for me.

King Pandion You were a child.

Tereus We have no theatre or even philosophers in Thrace, Philomele.

Philomele I have to keep my word.

Tereus Why?

Philomele Because that is honourable, Tereus.

Queen Listen to the chorus. The playwright always speaks through the chorus.

Female Chorus Love, stealing with grace into the heart you wish to destroy, love, turning us blind with the bitter poison of desire, love, come not my way. And when you whirl through the streets, wild steps to unchained rhythms, love, I pray you, brush not against me, love, I beg you, pass me by.

Tereus Ah!

Philomele I would never say that, would you, brother Tereus? I want to feel everything there is to feel. Don't you?

Tereus No!

King Pandion Tereus, what's the matter?

Tereus Nothing. The heat.

Phaedra Oh, I am destroyed for ever.

Philomele Poor Phaedra.

Tereus You pity her, Philomele?

Queen Hippolytus has just heard in what way Phaedra loves him. He's furious.

Hippolytus Woman, counterfeit coin, why did the gods put you in the world? If we must have sons, let us buy them in the temples and bypass the concourse of these noxious women. I hate you women, hate, hate and hate you.

Philomele This is horrible. It's not Phaedra's fault she loves him.

Tereus She could keep silent about it.

Philomele When you love you want to imprison the one you love in your words, in your tenderness.

Tereus How do you know all this, Philomele?

Philomele Sometimes I feel the whole world beating inside me.

Tereus Philomele . . .

Phaedra screams offstage, then staggers on.

Queen Phaedra's killed herself and there's Theseus just back from his travels.

Theseus My wife! What have I said or done to drive you to this horrible death? She calls me to her, she can still speak. What prayers, what orders, what entreaties do you leave your grieving husband? Oh, my poor love, speak! (*He listens.*) Hippolytus! Has dared to rape my wife!

Tereus Phaedra has lied! That's vile.

Philomele Why destroy what you love? It's the god.

Theseus Father Poseidon, great and ancient sea-god, you once allotted me three wishes. With one of these, I pray you now, kill my son.

Queen That happens offstage. A giant wave comes out of the sea and crashes Hippolytus' chariot against the rocks. Here's the male chorus.

Male Chorus Sometimes I believe in a kind power, wise

and all-knowing but when I see the acts of men and their destinies, my hopes grow dim. Fortune twists and turns and life is endless wandering.

King Pandion The play's coming to an end, and I still haven't reached a decision. Queen . . .

Male Chorus What I want from life is to be ordinary.

Philomele How boring.

Queen Hippolytus has come back to Athens to die. He's wounded. The head.

Female Chorus Poor Hippolytus, I weep at your pitiful fate. And I rage against the gods who sent you far away, out of your father's lands to meet with such disaster from the sea-god's wave.

King Pandion That's the phrase. Philomele, you must not leave your father's lands. You'll stay here.

Philomele But, Father, I'm not Hippolytus. You haven't cursed me. And Tereus isn't Phaedra, look.

She laughs.

Tereus I have expert sailors, I don't think we'll crash against the rocks.

King Pandion It's such a long journey.

Tereus We'll travel swiftly. Procne is so impatient to see her sister. We must go soon, or she'll fall ill with worry.

King Pandion When?

Tereus Tomorrow.

Hippolytus Weep for me, weep for me, destroyed, mangled, trampled underfoot by man and god both unjust, weep, weep for my death.

Philomele Ah.

Tereus You're crying, Philomele.

Philomele I felt, I felt – the beating of wings . . .

King Pandion You do not have to go.

Philomele It's the play, I am so sorry for them all. I have to go. My promise . . .

King Pandion (*to Queen*) It's only a visit, Philomele will come back to us.

Queen Where is she going?

King Pandion To Thrace! Weren't you listening?

Male and Female Chorus (*together*) These sorrows have fallen upon us unforeseen.

Male Chorus Fate is irresistible.

Female Chorus And there is no escape.

King Pandion And now we must applaud the actors.

SCENE SIX

A small ship, sailing north. The Male Chorus, Philomele, Tereus, the **Captain**.

Male Chorus The journey north:

Row gently out of Piraeus on a starlit night, Sail around Cape Sounion with a good wind, over to Kea for water and provisions. Kea to Andros, a quiet sea. Up the coast of Euboea to the Sporades: Skiathos, Paparethos, Gioura, Pathoura. Skirt the three-fingered promontory of the mainland: Kassandra, Sithounia and Athos of the wild men and into the Thracian sea. The dawns, so loved by the poets.

Male Chorus Rosy fingered, female.

Male Chorus The dawns get colder and colder as we sail north.

Pause.

Male Chorus Philomele wonders at the beauty of the sea.

Male Chorus Tereus wonders at Philomele's beauty.

Male Chorus We say nothing. And when the order comes.

Male Chorus Such an order.

Male Chorus Six Athenian soldiers have been sent to accompany Philomele. They stand on the deck, watching. On a dark night, they disappear.

Pause.

Male Chorus In the cold dawns, Tereus burns.

Male Chorus Does Philomele know? Ought we to tell her? We are only here to observe, journalists of an antique world, putting horror into words, unable to stop the events we will soon record.

Male Chorus And so we reach the lonely port of Imeros. It is dark, there is no welcome.

Male Chorus We are not expected.

Male Chorus No moon in the sky.

Male Chorus This is unpropitious.

Male Chorus But that we already knew. Could we have done something? And now?

Male Chorus We choose to be accurate, and we record:

SCENE SEVEN

The Captain, Philomele, Niobe.

Philomele Where are we now, Captain?

Captain Far north of Athens, Miss.

Philomele I know that, Captain. How far are we from Thrace?

Captain A few days, perhaps more. It depends.

Philomele On you?

Captain No. On the sea.

Philomele Isn't that a fire over there?

Captain Yes.

Philomele That means we're not far from the coast, doesn't it?

Captain Yes, it does.

Philomele Look how high the fire is. It must be a mountain, Captain.

Captain Yes, it is.

Philomele What is it called, Captain, what is it like? I would like to know about all these lands. You must tell me.

Captain That would be Mount Athos, Miss

Philomele Why don't we anchor there, Captain, and climb the mountain?

Captain You wouldn't want to go there, Miss.

Philomele Why not, is it ugly?

Captain No, but wild men live there, very wild. They kill all women, even female animals are not allowed on that mountain.

Philomele Why not?

Captain They worship male gods. They believe all harm in the world comes from women.

Philomele Why do they believe that? (*Pause.*) You don't agree with them, do you, Captain?

Captain I don't know, Miss.

Philomele If you don't disagree you agree with them Captain, that's logic.

Captain Women are beautiful.

Philomele But surely you believe that beauty is truth and goodness as well?

Captain That I don't know. I would have to think about it.

Philomele I'll prove it to you now, I once heard a philosopher do it. I will begin by asking you a lot of questions. You answer yes or no. But you must pay attention. Are you ready?

Captain I think so.

Philomele And when I've proved all this, Captain, you will have to renounce the beliefs of those wild men.

Captain I might.

Philomele You have to promise.

Tereus enters.

Tereus Why are the sails up, Captain?

Captain We have a good wind, Tereus.

Tereus Take them down.

Captain We could be becalmed further north and then my men will have to row. They're tired, Tereus.

Tereus We're sailing too fast, it's frightening Philomele.

Philomele I love to feel the wind, Tereus.

Tereus Why aren't you asleep?

Philomele It's such a beautiful night. I was watching the fires on Athos.

Tereus Athos? Yes, the hooded men.

Philomele The Captain was telling me about them.

Tereus Lower the sails, Captain.

Captain But Tereus –

Tereus This isn't a battle, we have time.

Exit the Captain.

Niobe I'll take Philomele down with me, my lord.

Tereus Not yet.

Pause.

Come and talk to me, Philomele.

Niobe Entertain his lordship, Philomele.

Silence.

Tereus Well. You were talking easily enough when I came above.

Philomele Tell me about my sister, Tereus.

Tereus I've already told you.

Philomele Tell me more. How does she occupy her time?

Tereus I don't know. She has women with her.

Philomele What do they talk about?

Tereus What women talk about. I didn't ask you to grill me, Philomele. Talk to me. Talk to me about the night.

Philomele The night?

Pause.

Tereus The night. Something! What were you saying to the Captain?

Philomele I was asking him questions, Tereus.

Silence. The **Sailors** *sing a song, softly.*

Philomele How well they sing.

Pause.

Tereus Do you want to be married, Philomele?

Niobe Oh, yes, my lord. Every young girl wants to be married. Don't you, Philomele?

Philomele Niobe, go to bed, please.

Niobe No, I can't, I mustn't. I will stay here. I must.

Philomele Why?

Niobe It wouldn't be right . . . A young girl. A man.

Philomele I am with my brother, Niobe.

Tereus You can go, Niobe.

Niobe Yes, yes. Well . . . I will go and talk to the sailors. Although what they will say to an old woman . . . no one wants to talk to an old woman. But so it is . . . I'm not far, I'm not far. The Queen said I was not to go far . . .

Pause.

Tereus You're beautiful.

Philomele Procne always said I was. But the Athenians admired her because of her dignity. Has she kept that in all her years?

Tereus In the moonlight, your skin seems transparent.

Philomele We used to put water out in the full moon and wash our faces in it. We thought it would give us the skin of a goddess. I still do it in memory of my sister. Does she still let out that rhythmical laugh when she thinks you're being foolish? Always on one note, then stopped abruptly. Does she laugh with her women?

Tereus I don't know . . .

Philomele Does she laugh at you?

Tereus Philomele.

Philomele Yes, brother.

Tereus What sort of man do you want to marry? A king?

Philomele Why not? A great king. Or a prince. Or a noble captain.

Tereus Not necessarily from Athens?

Philomele No. As long as he is wise.

Tereus Wise?

Philomele But then, all kings are wise, aren't they? They have to be or they wouldn't be kings.

Tereus You are born a king. Nothing can change that.

Philomele But you still have to deserve it, don't you?

Tereus Would you marry a king from the north? Like your sister? Would you do as your sister in all things?

Philomele What do you mean? Oh, look, they're making fun of Niobe. Niobe! Here!

Niobe They say I would be beautiful if I were young and if I were beautiful then I would be young. No one is kind to an old woman, but I don't mind, I've seen the world. You made his lordship laugh, Philomele, I heard it, that's good. All is well when power smiles, that I know.

Tereus Philomele wants to marry a king from the north.

Niobe Why yes, a man as great and brave as you.

Philomele I am happy for my sister and that is enough for me.

Niobe Sisters, sisters . . .

Tereus If Procne were . . .

Niobe I had sisters . . .

Philomele Procne.

Tereus To become ill . . .

Philomele What are you saying, Tereus? Wasn't she well when you left? Why didn't you tell me? Why are we going so slowly? Tell the Captain to go faster.

Tereus I didn't say that, but if . . .

Niobe Yes, I had many sisters.

Tereus Things happen.

Niobe Too many . . .

Philomele My love will protect her, and yours too, Tereus.

Tereus Yes . . . But should . . .

Niobe They died.

Philomele Niobe!

Niobe I only want to help. I know the world. Old women do. But I'll be quiet now, very quiet.

Philomele Sister. We will be so happy.

Tereus Philomele . . .

SCENE EIGHT

The Male Chorus.

Male Chorus What is a myth? The oblique image of an unwanted truth, reverberating through time.

Male Chorus And yet, the first, the Greek meaning of myth, is simply what is delivered by word of mouth, a myth is speech, public speech.

Male Chorus And myth also means the matter itself, the content of the speech.

Male Chorus We might ask, has the content become increasingly unacceptable and therefore the speech more indirect? How has the meaning of myth been transformed from public speech to an unlikely story? It also meant counsel, command. Now it is a remote tale.

Male Chorus Let that be, there is no content without its myth. Fathers and sons, rebellion, collaboration, the state, every fold and twist of passion, we have uttered them all. This one, you will say, watching Philomele watching Tereus watching Philomele, must be about men and women, yes, you think, a myth for our times, we understand.

Male Chorus You will be beside the myth. If you think of anything, think of countries, silence, but we cannot rephrase it for you. If we could, why would we trouble to show you the myth?

We row Philomele north. Does she notice the widening cracks in that fragile edifice, happiness? And what about Procne, the cause perhaps, in any case the motor of a myth that leaves her mostly absent?

SCENE NINE

Procne and the Female Chorus

Hero Sometimes I feel I know things but I cannot prove that I know them or that what I know is true and when I doubt my knowledge it disintegrates into a senseless jumble of possibilities, a puzzle that will not be reassembled, the spider web in which I lie, immobile, and truth paralysed.

Helen Let me put it another way: I have trouble expressing myself. The world I see and the words I have do not match.

June I am the ugly duckling of fact, so most of the time I try to keep out of the way.

Echo Quiet. I shouldn't be here at all.

Iris But sometimes it's too much and I must speak. Procne.

Procne What are you women muttering about this time? Something gloomy, no doubt.

Iris Procne, we sense danger.

Procne You always sense something, and when I ask you what, you say you don't know, it hasn't happened yet, but it will, or it might. Well, what is it now? What danger? This place is safe. No marauding bands outside, no earthquake, what? What?

Hero I say danger, she thinks of earthquakes. Doesn't know the first meaning of danger is the power of a lord or master.

316

Helen That one is always in someone's danger.

Echo In their power, at their mercy.

June All service is danger and all marriage too.

Iris Procne, listen to me.

Procne What now?

Hero The sky was so dark this morning . . .

Procne It'll rain. It always rains . . .

Iris Again.

Hero I was not talking metcorologically. Images require sympathy.

Echo Another way of listening.

Iris Procne.

Procne Yes, yes, yes.

Hero Your sister is on the sea.

Procne She's been on the sea for a month. Have you just found that out?

Helen But the sea, the sea . . .

Hero And Tereus is a young man.

Echo Tereus.

Procne He'll move that much more quickly. Tell me something I don't know.

Hero When it's too late, it's easy to find the words.

Iris Procne.

Procne Leave me alone.

Iris If you went down to the seaport. Met them there.

Echo A welcome . . .

Procne I promised Tereus I would stay here and look after his country. I will wait for him here.

Iris Procne.

Procne Enough of your nonsense. Be silent.

Helen Silent.

Echo Silent.

SCENE TEN

The Male Chorus, First Soldier, Second Soldier, Tereus.

Male Chorus We camp on a desolate beach. Days pass.

First Soldier Why are we still here?

Second Soldier Tereus has his reasons.

First Soldier I want to go home.

Second Soldier We can't until we have the order.

First Soldier It's no more than four days' walk to the palace. Why are we still here?

Second Soldier I told you: because we haven't been ordered to move.

First Soldier Why not?

Second Soldier You ask too many questions.

Male Chorus Questions. The child's instinct suppressed in the adult.

Male Chorus For the sake of order, peace.

Male Chorus But at what price?

Male Chorus I wouldn't want to live in a world that's always shifting. Questions are like earthquakes. If you're lucky, it's just a rumble.

First Soldier Why don't we ask Tereus if we can go home? I want to see my girl.

Second Soldier He wants to see his wife.

First Soldier How do you know?

Second Soldier He would, wouldn't he?

First Soldier Then why are we here?

Second Soldier Ask him.

First Soldier Why don't you?

Male Chorus More days pass. We all wait.

First Soldier Why don't we talk to him together? Respectful, friendly.

Second Soldier And say what?

First Soldier Ask him if he's had any news of home. Tell him how nice it is. And spring's coming.

Second Soldier I'd leave out the bit about spring.

First Soldier Why?

Second Soldier Ready?

Pause.

Not today. He's worried.

First Soldier What about me?

Second Soldier You're not a king. His worry is bigger than yours.

First Soldier Why?

Second Soldier It's more interesting.

Male Chorus Days.

Male Chorus Days.

Second Soldier Tereus?

Tereus Yes.

Second Soldier He wants to speak to you.

Tereus Speak.

First Soldier Speak.

Second Soldier Euh.

  Pause. Tereus turns away.

First Soldier Why are we here?

Second Soldier What are we waiting for?

First Soldier Why aren't we going home?

Second Soldier Why haven't any messengers been sent to tell everyone we're safe?

First Soldier We want to go home.

Second Soldier We've had enough.

  Pause.

Tereus I have my reasons.

Male Chorus An old phrase, but it buys time. More days.

First Soldier What reasons?

Second Soldier Yes, what reasons?

Tereus You must trust me.

  Pause.

Am I not your leader?

Second Soldier Yes, Tereus, but –

Tereus My knowledge is greater than yours, that is my duty, just as yours is to trust me. Think: when you fight wars with me, you see only part of the battle, the few enemies you kill, or your own wounds. Sometimes this seems terrible to you, I know, but later you see the victory and the glory of your country. That glory, fame, I have seen all along.

Second Soldier Yes, Tereus, but –

First Soldier Where's the enemy?

Tereus I have information.

Male Chorus More days.

Second Soldier Why do we have to wait so long?

First Soldier For what?

Second Soldier It's this waiting makes me afraid. I'd rather something happened, anything.

Tereus I know this is difficult for you. (*Pause.*) It's difficult for me. (*Pause.*) You're experienced soldiers, responsible citizens, I trust you not to risk the safety and honour of your country because you don't understand yet. Trust me and you'll understand all in time.

Male Chorus In time . . .

Male Chorus What hasn't been said and done in the name of the future? A future always in someone else's hands. We waited, without the pain of responsibility for that promised time, the good times. We asked no more questions and at night, we slept soundly, and did not see:

SCENE ELEVEN

Philomele, Niobe, Tereus.

Tereus Philomele.

Philomele (*to Niobe*) Why does he follow me everywhere? Even Procne left me alone sometimes.

Niobe Don't make him angry!

Tereus Philomele.

Philomele It's spring. Look at these flowers, Niobe, we have them in the woods near Athens. I'll bring some to Procne.

Tereus Philomele.

Philomele And here is some wild thyme, and that is xorta. Procne loves its bitter taste.

Tereus Philomele.

Philomele What is this plant, Niobe? Smell it. It's salty, I've never seen it before. Procne will know.

Tereus Philomele!

Philomele Quiet brother, you're disturbing the butterflies. Procne would not like that.

Tereus Procne. Procne. Procne is dead.

Silence.

There is a mountain not far from the palace. She climbed it with her women to see if she could catch sight of the sea. On a clear day you can look at the sea from there. She climbed to the top, but there was a tall rock and she said she would climb that as well to see us, to welcome the ship. The women begged her not to, no one would follow

322

her. The rock is slippery and on the other side drops straight into the river below. She climbed, climbed higher to welcome her sister and stood there, waving, safe, the women thought. But then she seemed to grow dizzy, she cried out and suddenly fell, down the rock, down the cliff, into the river swollen now because of the winter rains. They are still looking for her body, it was carried with the torrent. Perhaps better not to find it.

Niobe Yes, better. Never look at a battered body, it is worse than the death that came to it.

Tereus Mourn, Philomele, mourn with me. She was my wife.

Philomele Procne.

Niobe Procne.

Philomele begins to cry and scream. Tereus takes her in his arms.

Tereus Sister, beloved sister. My sister.

Philomele Procne. No!
I want to see her body!

Chorus Nor did we see, still sleeping:

SCENE TWELVE

Philomele, the Captain, Niobe

Philomele How long have we been in this place forsaken by the gods, Captain?

Captain Almost a full month, Philomele.

Philomele Why?

Pause.

I can't mourn my sister here. Let me at least remember her where she lived all those years. Why do we wait and wait, for what?

Captain There may be trouble. Tereus keeps these things to himself.

Philomele And you, Captain, where will you go?

Captain I'm waiting for orders.

Philomele South?

Captain Perhaps.

Philomele You won't say, you've been asked not to say, why?

Captain You ask too many questions, Philomele.

Philomele And you ask none, why?

Pause.

Do you love the sea?

Captain Sometimes.

Philomele I used to watch you at night, standing on your deck, an immense solitude around you. You seemed a king of elements, ordering the wind.

Captain No, you guess the wind, you order the sails. The winds have names, they're godlike, man obeys.

Philomele I never understood obedience, Captain philosophical.

Captain You're a woman.

Philomele Does that make me lawless? Do you have a wife?

Captain No, no.

Philomele Why not?

Niobe (*muttering*) Girl without shame. After a captain when she could have a king.

Philomele Take me with you.

Captain Take you. Where?

Philomele On the sea. South . . . Wherever . . .

Captain You're laughing at me, Philomele. Tereus . . .

Philomele Frightens me. Since Procne's accident. Perhaps before. His eyes wander, have you noticed? In Athens the philosophers used to talk about wandering eyes. I forget exactly what they said, but it was not good. Yes, the eyes are the windows of the soul – Tereus has a nervous soul.

Captain You shouldn't speak like that. Not to me. My job is to obey him.

Philomele Again! What about your obedience to the elements? And desire, isn't that a god too?

Captain Philomele . . .

Philomele You touched my hand on the ship once, by mistake, and once I fell against you, a wave, you blushed, I saw it, fear, desire, they're the same, I'm not a child. Touch my hand again: prove you feel nothing.

She holds out her hand. The Captain hesitates and touches it.

So – I was right. Take me with you.

Captain We will ask Tereus.

Philomele We will ask the gods within us. Love . . .

Captain . . . your power . . .

Philomele Not mine . . . Between us, above us.

She takes his hand and puts it on her breast. Tereus enters.

Tereus Traitor! Traitor! Traitor!

He kills the Captain.

A young girl, defenceless.
I'll cut off your genitals.
Go to the underworld with your shame around your neck.

Pause.

Be more careful, Philomele.

Male Chorus (*carrying the body off*) We saw nothing.

SCENE THIRTEEN

Moonlight. The beach. Philomele.

Philomele Catch the moonlight with your hands. Tread the moonlight with your toes, phosphorescence, phosphorescence, come to me, come to me, tell me the secrets of the wine-dark sea.

Pause.

I'm so lonely.

Pause.

Procne, come to me.

Pause. She waits.

Procne, Procne, sister. Help me.
Catch the lather of the moonlight. Spirits, talk to me.
Oh, you gods, help me.

Tereus enters. Philomele senses this.

(*softly*) Phosphorescence, phosphorescence, tell me the secrets of the wine-dark sea . . .

Tereus (*softly*) Philomele, what are you doing?

Philomele Catching the lather of the sea. Moonlight, moonlight.

Tereus I only wish you well . . .

Philomele Let me bury my sister.

Tereus I told you, we never found the body.

Philomele Take me to the gorge, I will find it.

Tereus Nothing left now, weeks –

Philomele I will find the bones.

Tereus Washed by the river.

Philomele Let me stand in the river.

Tereus It's dangerous.

Philomele I don't want to stay here.

Tereus You have everything you want, you loved the spot when we first came.

Philomele Then . . .
Tereus, I want to see my sister's home, I want to speak to the women who were with her. I want to know the last words she said, please, please take me there. Why are we here? What is the point of talking if you won't answer that question?

Silence. Philomele turns away.

Moonlight, moonlight . . .

Tereus Philomele, listen to me.

Philomele Light the shells, light the stones, light the dust of old men's bones . . .

Tereus Philomele!

Philomele Catch the lather of the sea . . .

Tereus Do you remember that day in the theatre in Athens? The play?

Philomele Evansescence, evanescence . . .

Tereus Philomele, I am telling you.

Pause.

I love you.

Philomele I love you too, brother Tereus, you are my sister's husband.

Tereus No, no. The play. I am Phaedra. (*Pause.*) I love you. That way.

Silence.

Philomele It is against the law.

Tereus My wife is dead.

Philomele It is still against the law.

Tereus The power of the god is above the law. It began then, in the theatre, the chorus told me. I saw the god and I loved you.

Philomele Tereus.

Pause.

I do not love you.
I do not want you.
I want to go back to Athens.

Tereus Who can resist the gods? Those are your words.

Philomele. They convinced me, your words.

Philomele Oh, my careless tongue. Procne always said – my wandering tongue. But, Tereus, it was the theatre, it was hot, come back to Athens with me. My parents – Tereus, please, let me go back to Athens.

Tereus The god is implacable.

Philomele You are a king, you are a widower. This is – frivolous.

Tereus You call this frivolous.

He seizes her.

Philomele Treachery.

Tereus Love me.

Philomele No.

Tereus Then my love will be for both. I will love you and love myself for you. Philomele, I will have you.

Philomele Tereus, wait.

Tereus The god is out.

Philomele Let me mourn.

Tereus Your darkness and your sadness make you all the more beautiful.

Philomele I have to consent.

Tereus It would be better, but no, you do not have to. Does the god ask permission?

Philomele Help. Help me. Someone. Niobe!

Tereus So you are afraid. I know fear well. Fear is consent. You see the god and you accept.

Philomele Niobe!

Tereus I will have you in your fear. Trembling limbs to my fire.

He grabs her and leads her off. Niobe appears.

Niobe So it's happened. I've seen it coming for weeks. I could have warned her, but what's the point? Nowhere to go. It was already as good as done. I know these things. She should have consented. Easier that way. Now it will be all pain. Well I know. We fought Athens. Foolish of a small island but we were proud. The men – dead. All of them. And us. Well – we wished ourselves dead then, but now I know it's better to live. Life is sweet. You bend your head. It's still sweet. You bend it even more. Power is something you can't resist. That I know. My island bowed its head. I came to Athens. Oh dear, oh dear, she shouldn't scream like that. It only makes it worse. Too tense. More brutal. Well I know. She'll accept it in the end. Have to. We do. And then. When she's like me she'll wish it could happen again. I wouldn't mind a soldier. They don't look at me now. All my life I was afraid of them and then one day they stop looking and it's even more frightening. Because what makes you invisible is death coming quietly. Makes you pale, then unseen. First, no one turns, then you're not there. Nobody goes to my island any more. It's dead too. Countries are like women. It's when they're fresh they're wanted. Why did the Athenians want our island? I don't know. We only had a few lemon trees. Now the trees are withered. Nobody looks at them. There. It's finished now. A cool cloth. On her cheeks first. That's where it hurts most. The shame. Then we'll do the rest. I know all about it. It's the lemon trees I miss, not all those dead men. Funny, isn't it? I think of the lemon trees.

SCENE FOURTEEN

The palace of Tereus. Procne and the Female Chorus

Procne If he is dead then I want to see his body and if he is alive then I want to see him. That is logical. Iris, come here. Closer. There.

Pause.

Iris, I have seen you look at me with some kindness. You could be my friend, possibly? What is a friend? A friend tells the truth. Will you be my friend? No, don't turn away, I won't impose the whole burden of this friendship. One gesture, one gift. One question. Will you be my friend to the tune of one question? Ah, you don't say no. Iris, answer me. Is Tereus dead?

Pause.

Iris, please, pity. One yes, one no. Small words and yet can turn the world inside out.

Pause.

I have learned patience. It is the rain.

Pause.

The inexorable weight of a grey sky. I can wait.

Silence.

It's only one word.
    Very well, don't. And when I kill myself, it will be for you to bring news of my death, Iris. You don't believe me? Athenians don't kill themselves. But I can be Thracian too. I have been here long enough. Go now.

Iris No.

Procne He is not dead.

Iris No.

Procne But then, why?

Pause.

Yes, my promise. (*Pause.*) Thank you.
   My sister? No, of course, another question. If there is
one, might there not be two? (*She addresses the women.*)
My husband is not dead. Who will tell me where he is?
Why? You have husbands among his men. Don't you ask
yourselves questions? What sirens have entangled them in
what melodies? Is that it? But no, he is not dead, so he is
not drowned. Turned into a wild beast by the power of a
witch, is that it? You've heard barking in the forest and
recognized your husbands? Don't dare say, the shame of it;
my husband is a dog. All fleas, wagging tail and the
irrational bite, well, is that it?
   Weeks, weeks and no one speaks to me.

Pause.

Even a rumour would do.
Where are your men?
Where is mine?
Where is Tereus?

Tereus and the Male Chorus enter.

Tereus Here.

Pause.

A delay.

Procne (*very still*) A delay.

Pause.

There's blood on your hands.

Tereus A wild beast. Or a god in disguise. Unnameable.

Procne My sister?

Tereus (*after a brief pause*) Not here.

Procne No. (*Pause.*) Drowned?

Pause.

Tereus But I am here.

Procne Yes.

She opens her arms. The Male Chorus comes forward, hiding Tereus and Procne.

Male Chorus Home at last.

Male Chorus We said nothing.

Male Chorus It was better that way.

SCENE FIFTEEN

Philomele, Niobe. Philomele is being washed by Niobe, her legs spread out around a basin. Her head is down.

Niobe There. Nothing left. It's a weak liquid, it drops out quickly. Not like resin.

Philomele I can still smell it. Wash me.

Niobe It's your own smell, there's nothing left.

Philomele It's the smell of violence. Wash me.

Niobe It's the smell of fear.

Philomele Wash me.

Niobe Some women get to like the smell. I never did. Too much like fishing boats. I like the smell of pines.

Philomele I want to die. Wash me.

Niobe You will, when it's time. In the meantime, get him to provide for you. They don't like us much afterwards, you know. Now he might still feel something. We must eat. Smile. Beg.

Philomele Beg? Was it my fault?

Niobe I don't ask questions. Get some coins if you can.

Philomele Goddesses, where were you?

Niobe Stop worrying about the gods and think of us. Don't make him angry. He might still be interested. That would be excellent.

Philomele You. You are worse than him.

She pours the dirty water over Niobe.

Filth. Here. Drink his excretions.

Niobe Don't be so mighty, Philomele. You're nothing now. Another victim. Grovel. Like the rest of us.

Philomele No.

Niobe Be careful. Worse things can happen. Keep low. Believe me. I know. Keep silent.

Philomele Never.

Niobe Here's the King. Hold back your tongue, Philomele.

Tereus enters.

Tereus Now I wish you didn't exist.

Pause.

Philomele When will you explain, Tereus?

Tereus Explain?

Philomele Why? The cause? I want to understand.

Tereus I don't know what to do with you . . .

Philomele Me . . .

Pause.

I was the cause, wasn't I? Was I? I said something. What did I do?

Pause.

Something in my walk? If I had sung a different song? My hair up, my hair down? It was the beach. I ought not to have been there. I ought not to have been anywhere. I ought not to have been . . . at all . . . then there would be no cause. Is that it? Answer.

Tereus What?

Philomele My body bleeding, my spirit ripped open, and I am the cause? No, this cannot be right, why would I cause my own pain? That isn't reasonable. What was it then, tell me, Tereus, if I was not the cause?

Pause.

You must know, it was your act, you must know, tell me, why, say.

Pause.

It was your act. It was you. I caused nothing.

Short pause.

And Procne is not dead. I can smell her on you.

Pause.

You. You lied. And you.
What did you tell your wife, my sister, Procne, what did you tell her? Did you tell her you violated her sister, the sister she gave into your trust? Did you tell her what a

coward you are and that you could not, cannot bear to look at me? Did you tell her that despite my fear, your violence, when I saw you in your nakedness I couldn't help laughing because you were so shrivelled, so ridiculous and it is not the way it is on the statues? Did you tell her you cut me because you yourself had no strength? Did you tell her I pitied her for having in her bed a man who could screech such quick and ugly pleasure, a man of jelly beneath his hard skin, did you tell her that?

Pause.

And once I envied her happiness with her northern hero. The leader of men. Take the sword out of your hand, you fold into a cloth. Have they ever looked at you, your soldiers, your subjects?

Tereus That's enough.

Philomele There's nothing inside you. You're only full when you're filled with violence. And they obey you? Look up to you? Have the men and women of Thrace seen you naked? Shall I tell them? Yes, I will talk.

Tereus Quiet, woman.

Philomele You call this man your king, men and women of Thrace, this scarecrow dribbling embarrassed lust, that is what I will say to them, you revere him, but have you looked at him? No? You're too awed, he wears his cloak of might and virility with such ease you won't look beneath. When he murdered a virtuous captain because a woman could love that captain, that was bravery, you say. And if, women of Thrace, he wants to force himself on you, trying to stretch his puny manhood to your intimacies, you call that high spirits? And you soldiers, you'll follow into a battle a man who lies, a man of tiny spirit and shrivelled courage? Wouldn't you prefer someone with truth and goodness, self-control and reason? Let my sister rule in his place.

Tereus I said that was enough.

Philomele No, I will say more. They will all know what you are.

Tereus I warn you.

Philomele Men and women of Thrace, come and listen to the truth about this man –

Tereus I will keep you quiet.

Philomele Never, as long as I have the words to expose you. The truth, men and women of Thrace, the truth –

Tereus cuts out Philomele's tongue.

SCENE SIXTEEN

Philomele crouched in a pool of blood. Niobe.

Niobe Now truly I pity Philomele. She has lost her words, all of them. Now she is silent. For good. Of course, he could have killed her, that is the usual way of keeping people silent. But that might have made others talk. The silence of the dead can turn into a wild chorus. But the one alive who cannot speak, that one has truly lost all power. There. I don't know what she wants. I don't know what she feels. Perhaps she likes being silent. No responsibility.

Philomele seizes her, tries to express something.

I don't know what she wants. She can no longer command me. What good is a servant without orders? I will go. I don't know what she wants.

Tereus enters. Philomele stands still. Silence.

Tereus You should have kept quiet.

Pause.

I did what I had to.

Pause.

You threatened the order of my rule.

Pause.

How could I allow rebellion? I had to keep you quiet. I am not sorry. Except for your pain. But it was you or me.

Long pause.

You are more beautiful now in your silence. I could love you. You should have allowed the god to have his way. You should have kept quiet. I was the stronger. And my desire. Niobe, you will look after her. This is to ease the pain. (*He gives Niobe money, then goes to Philomele.*) Why weren't you more careful? Let me kiss those bruised lips. You are mine. My sweet, my songless, my caged bird.

He kisses her. She is still.

SCENE SEVENTEEN

Tereus' palace. Procne, Itys, *Tereus.*

Procne I wouldn't want to be young again. Time flows so gently as you get older. It used to feel broken by rocks. Five years since my sister died. Tomorrow. I will light a candle towards the sea, as I do every year. But the pain flickers now, almost out. Will you come with me this time, Tereus?

Tereus No.

Procne I used to be angry that you would not mourn my sister. Why should you mourn her? You hardly knew her. Your aunt, Itys. You would have liked her. She was full of laughter.

Itys I have uncles. They're strong.

Procne She could speak with the philosophers. She was bold and quick.

Itys What's a philosopher?

Procne A man who loves wisdom.

Itys What is wisdom?

Procne It brings peace.

Itys I don't like peace. I like war.

Procne Why?

Itys So I can be brave. I want to be a great captain. Lead thousands into battle. Like Mars.

Procne Mars is a god.

Itys What is a god?

Procne Like us. But doesn't die.

Itys Why can't I be a god?

Procne You have to be born one.

Tereus But you'll be a king, Itys, that's almost as good.

Procne A wise king, like your father.

Itys (*turning round with his spear in hand*) I'll fight this way. I'll fight that way. I'll fight this way. I'll fight this way.

   He runs out.

Procne I am happy, as there was to be only one, that we have a son.

   Pause.

Aren't you?

Tereus Yes.

Procne You're quiet.

Pause.

Over the years you have become quiet. I used to be afraid of you, did you know? But we shall grow old in peace. I wish more people came to visit this country. Then we could show our hospitality. No one comes here. Why?

Silence.

And if a god came to visit, he would find us sitting here, content, and perhaps turn us into two trees as a reward, like Baucis and Philemon. Would you like that?

Tereus Not yet.

Procne Ha. I love to see you smile.

Pause.

And tomorrow is the feast of Bacchus. I will go out this time. I will go out with the women of this country. You see how I become Thracian.

Pause.

You're going? Of course, you must. The evening is soft, look, stars too. We do not have many evenings together. I was frightened of your evenings when we were first married. That is why I sent you to Athens for my sister. I am a woman now. I can take pleasure in my husband.

She approaches Tereus, but he puts her away from him and leaves. When he is gone, she holds the bottom of her stomach.

Desire. Now. So late.
Oh, you gods, you are cruel.
Or, perhaps, only drunk.

She begins to dress as a Bacchae as does the Female Chorus. Music.

SCENE EIGHTEEN

Music. The stage fills with **Bacchae**. *Niobe enters leading Philomele, who carries two huge dolls. Behind her, the* **Servant** *carries a third doll.*

Niobe No place safe from the Bacchae. They run the city and the woods, flit along the beach, no crevasse free from the light of their torches. Miles and miles of a drunken chain. These people are savages. Look at their women. You never see them and when you do, breasts hanging out, flutes to their mouths. In my village, they'd be stoned. Out of the way, you, out of the way.

Servant We could move faster without those big dolls, Niobe.

Niobe She wouldn't go without them. Years she's been sewing, making them, painting faces. Look. Childlike pastime for her, what can I say? It's kept her still. And she's quiet anyway. Tereus said, get her out, quickly into the city. She'll be lost there. Another madwoman, no one will notice. Could have cut off her tongue in frenzied singing to the gods. Strange things happen on these nights, I have heard.

Servant Very strange, Niobe. But she was better in the hut.

Niobe No. It gives her a little outing. She's only seen us and the King for five years.

Servant He doesn't come much any more.

Niobe No. They all dream of silence, but then it bores them.

Servant Who is she, Niobe?

Niobe No one. No name. Nothing. A king's fancy. No more.

Servant I feel pity for her. I don't know why.

Niobe Look, some acrobats. The idiot will like it. Look. Look. See the acrobats. Now that's like my village. Except I believe they're women. Shame on them. But still, no harm in watching.

She thrusts Philomele to the front of a circle, watching. A crowd gathers around. The **Acrobats** *perform. Finish. As they melt back into the crowd, the empty space remains and Philomele throws the dolls into the circle. Niobe grabs one of them and tries to grab Philomele, but she is behind the second doll. Since the dolls are huge, the struggle seems to be between the two dolls. One is male, one is female and the male one has a king's crown.*

Niobe A mad girl, a mad girl. Help me.

But the crowd applauds, makes a wider circle and waits in silence. The rape scene is re-enacted in a gross and comic way, partly because of Niobe's resistance and attempt to catch Philomele. Philomele does most of the work with both dolls. The crowd laughs. Philomele then stages a very brutal illustration of the cutting of the female doll's tongue. Blood cloth on the floor. The crowd is very silent. Niobe still. Then the Servant comes inside the circle, holding a third doll, a queen. At that moment, Procne also appears in the front of the crowd's circle. She has been watching. The Procne doll weeps. The two female dolls embrace. Procne approaches Philomele, looks at her and takes her away. The dolls are picked up by the crowd and they move off. A bare stage for a second. Then Procne and Philomele appear,

*Procne holding on to Philomele, almost dragging her.
Then she lets go. Philomele stands still. Procne circles
her, touches her. Sound of music very distant. Then a
long silence. The sisters look at each other.*

Procne How can I know that was the truth?

Pause.

You were always wild. How do I know you didn't take
him to your bed?

You could have told him lies about me, cut your own
tongue in shame. How can I know?

You won't nod, you won't shake your head. I have
never seen him violent. He would not do this.

He had to keep you back from his soldiers. Desire
always burnt in you. Did you play with his sailors? Did
you shame us all? Why should I believe you?

She shakes Philomele.

Do something, make me know you showed the truth.

Pause.

There's no shame in your eyes. Why should I believe you?
And perhaps you're not Philomele. A resemblance. A
mockery in this horrible drunken feast. How can I know?

Silence.

But if it is true. My sister.
Open your mouth.

Philomele opens her mouth, slowly.

To do this. He would do this.

Pause.

Justice. Philomele, the justice we learned as children, do
you remember? Where is it? Come, come with me.

The Bacchae give wine to Procne and Philomele.

Do this.

Philomele drinks.

Drink. Oh, we will revel. You, drunken god, help us. Help us.

They dance off with the Bacchae.

SCENE NINETEEN

Two Soldiers.

First Soldier It's almost dawn. Let's go.

Second Soldier He said to stay by the palace until the sun was up.

First Soldier What is he afraid of? An invasion of Amazons? They're all in there.

Second Soldier Our enemies know this is a strange night.

First Soldier I never liked this festival. All these drunken women. My girl's in there. And she'll never tell what happens. I tell her about the war. Well. Most of it. Let's go.

Second Soldier We can't.

First Soldier There's no law on these nights.

Second Soldier Do you want to look in?

First Soldier They'd kill us.

Second Soldier That window, there. We could see through the shutters.

First Soldier It's supposed to be a mystery. A woman's mystery. That's what my girl says. Give me a break.

Second Soldier You could sit on my shoulders. Make sure your girl's behaving.

First Soldier It's all women in there.

Second Soldier It's all men in a war.

First Soldier You mean, she – they – no.

Second Soldier Have a look.

First Soldier If she – I'll strangle her. So that's what mystery is. Let me see.

The First Soldier climbs on to the Second Soldier's shoulder.

Second Soldier Can you see?

First Soldier Steady.

Second Soldier I'm holding your legs. Can you see?

First Soldier Yeah.

Second Soldier Well?

First Soldier It's just a lot of women.

Second Soldier We know that, stupid. What are they doing?

First Soldier Drinking.

Second Soldier And?

First Soldier Oh.

Second Soldier What?

First Soldier Oh, you gods.

Second Soldier Well? What are they doing? Exactly? What?

First Soldier (*Jumping down, laughing.*) Nothing.

He does a dance with the Second Soldier.

Dancing. Lots of wine. They've swords and lances.

Itys has appeared.

What are you doing here?

Itys I saw you.

First Soldier No men, no boys on the street. Go home.

Itys I saw you looking.

Second Soldier That's Itys. Tereus' son. Why aren't you asleep?

Itys I saw you. I'm going to tell my father when he gets back.

First Soldier Nothing wrong with looking.

Itys Mother, said no one's to see.
I'll tell her, she'll tell father. He'll be angry.

Second Soldier Don't you want to see?

Itys It's not allowed.

Second Soldier Aren't you a prince? A king's son? You let women tell you what is and is not allowed?

Itys You shouldn't have looked.

First Soldier It's just women.

Second Soldier Why don't you see for yourself? A king has to be informed.

First Soldier You can sit on my shoulders.

Second Soldier Do you know how to sit on somebody's shoulders? Are you strong enough?

Itys Of course I know.

Second Soldier You sure? It's difficult.

First Soldier We'll hold you.

Second Soldier No, we won't. You have to climb all by yourself. Like a man. Can you do it?

Itys I'll show you.

Itys climbs on the shoulders of the Second Soldier.

Second Soldier Good. You'll make a soldier yet. You're too small to reach the window, aren't you?

Itys No, I'm not.

Second Soldier I think you are.

Itys stretches himself to the window and looks. Pause.

Itys Oh.

First Soldier Still dancing, the women?

Itys They drink more than my father.

First Soldier But only once a year.

Itys There's Mother.

First Soldier What is she doing?

Itys Why should I tell you?

Second Soldier Quite right, boy. What about the other women?

Itys There's one I've never seen before. She looks like a slave. That's my sword. That slave girl. A slave, a girl slave holding my sword. Let me down.

Second Soldier Where are you going?

Itys To stop them.

First Soldier No.

Second Soldier Wait.

Itys runs off.

First Soldier Let's go.

Second Soldier Let me look. (*He climbs.*) He's there. They've stopped. They're looking at him. It's all right. Procne is holding him. Shows him to the slave girl. He looks up. They've all gone still. He laughs. Oh! (*The Second Soldier drops down.*)

First Soldier What happened?

Second Soldier I'm drunk. I didn't see anything. It didn't happen. The god has touched me with madness. For looking. I'm seeing things. I didn't see anything. Nothing. Nothing. Nothing. Let's go. I didn't see anything. There's Tereus. I don't know anything. I wasn't here.

They run off.

SCENE TWENTY

The Female Chorus. Procne. Philomele.

Hero Without the words to demand.

Echo Or ask. Plead. Beg for.

June Without the words to accuse.

Helen Without even the words to forgive.

Echo The words that help to forget.

Hero What else was there?

Iris There are some questions that have no answers. We might ask you now: why does the Vulture eat Prometheus' liver? He brought men intelligence.

Echo Why did God want them stupid?

Iris We can ask: why did Medea kill her children?

June Why do countries make war?

Helen Why are races exterminated?

Hero Why do white people cut off the words of blacks?

Iris Why do people disappear? The ultimate silence.

Echo Not even death recorded.

Helen Why are little girls raped and murdered in the car parks of dark cities?

Iris What makes the torturer smile?

Hero We can ask. Words will grope and probably not find. But if you silence the question.

Iris Imprison the mind that asks.

Echo Cut out its tongue.

Hero You will have this.

June We show you a myth.

Echo Image. Echo.

Helen A child is the future.

Hero This is what the soldiers did not see.

Itys comes running in.

Itys That's my sword. Give me my sword.

Procne Itys.

Itys Give me my sword, slave, or I'll kick you. Kill you all. Cut off your heads. Pick out your eyes.

Itys goes for Philomele. Procne holds him. Philomele still

*has the sword. Philomele brings the sword down on his
neck. The Female Chorus close in front. Tereus enters.*

Tereus It's daylight at last. The revels are over. Time to go
home.

Silence. No one moves.

We're whitewashing the streets. All that wine. Poured like
blood. It's time for you to go home.

No one moves.

Stupefied? You should hold your wine better. You've had
your revels. Go on. Stagger home. Procne, tell your
women to go home.

*Philomele is revealed. Hands bloodied. There is a
silence.*

Tereus I had wanted to say.

Procne Say what, Tereus?

Tereus If I could explain.

Procne You have a tongue.

Tereus Beyond words.

Procne What?

Tereus When I ride my horse into battle, I see where I am
going. But close your eyes for an instant and the world
whirls round. That is what happened. The world whirled
round.

Pause.

Procne What kept you silent? Shame?

Tereus No.

Procne What?

Tereus I can't say. There are no rules.

Procne I obeyed all the rules: the rule of parents, the rule of marriage, the rules of my loneliness, you. And now you say. This.

Long pause.

Tereus I have no other words.

Procne I will help you find them.

The body of Itys is revealed.

If you bend over the stream and search for your reflection, Tereus, this is what it looks like.

Tereus Itys. You.

Procne I did nothing. As usual. Let the violence sweep around me.

Tereus She –

Procne No. You, Tereus. You bloodied the future. For all of us. We don't want it.

Tereus Your own child!

Procne Ours. There are no more rules. There is nothing. The world is bleak. The past a mockery, the future dead. And now I want to die.

Tereus I loved her. When I silenced her, it was for love. She didn't want my love. She could only mock, and soon rebel, she was dangerous.

I loved my country. I loved my child. You – this.

Procne You wanted something and you took it. That is not love. Look at yourself. That is not love.

Tereus How could I know what love was? Who was there to tell me?

Procne Did you ask?

Tereus Monsters. Fiends. I will kill you both.

Tereus takes the sword of Itys. The Female Chorus comes forward.

Hero Tereus pursued the two sisters, but he never reached them. The myth has a strange end.

Echo No end.

Iris Philomele becomes a nightingale.

June Procne a swallow.

Helen And Tereus a hoopoe.

Hero You might ask, why does the myth end that way?

Iris Such a transformation.

Echo Metamorphosis.

The birds come on.

SCENE TWENTY-ONE

Itys and the birds.

Philomele (*the Nightingale*) And now, ask me some more questions.

Itys I wish you'd sing again.

Philomele You have to ask me a question first.

Pause.

Itys Do you like being a nightingale?

Philomele I like the nights and my voice in the night. I like the spring. Otherwise, no, not much, I never liked birds, but we were all so angry the bloodshed would have gone on for ever. So it was better to become a nightingale. You see the world differently.

Itys Do you like being a nightingale more than being Philomele?

Philomele Before or after I was silenced?

Itys I don't know. Both.

Philomele I always felt a shadow hanging over me. I asked too many questions.

Itys You want me to ask questions.

Philomele Yes.

Itys Will you sing some more?

Philomele Later.

Itys Why doesn't Procne sing?

Philomele Because she was turned into a swallow and swallows don't sing.

Itys Why not?

Philomele Different job.

Itys Oh.

   Pause.

I like it when you sing.

Philomele Do you understand why it was wrong of Tereus to cut out my tongue?

Itys It hurt.

Philomele Yes, but why was it wrong?

Itys (*bored*) I don't know. Why was it wrong?

353

Philomele It was wrong because –

Itys What does wrong mean?

Philomele It is what isn't right.

Itys What is right?

The Nightingale sings.

Didn't you want me to ask questions?

Fade.

THREE BIRDS ALIGHTING ON A FIELD

For Max

Characters

Auctioneer
Biddy Andreas
Alex Brendel
Jeremy Bertrand
Julia Roberts
Nicola
Yorgos Andreas (Yoyo)
Lady Lelouche
David
Marianne Ryle
Stephen Ryle
Fiona Campbell
Sir Philip Howard
Gwen Ryle
Jean
Constantin
Mr Boreman
Mrs Boreman
Mr Mercer
Ahmet
Russet
Russian Priest
Yoyo's Mother
Katerina

Time: End of the eighties
Place: London

Three Birds Alighting on a Field was first performed at the Royal Court Theatre, London, on 5 September 1991. The cast was as follows:

Auctioneer Allan Corduner
Biddy Harriet Walter
Alex Patti Love
Jeremy Robin Soans
Julia Shirin Taylor
Nicola Adie Allen
Yoyo David Bamber
Lady Lelouche Mossie Smith
David Allan Corduner
Marianne Patti Love
Stephen Clive Russell
Fiona Mossie Smith
Sir Philip Robins Soans
Gwen Adie Allen
Odysseus Robin Soans
Neoptolemus Harriet Walter
Jean Adie Allen
Constantin Allan Corduner
Mr Boreman David Bamber
Mrs Boreman Shirin Taylor
Mr Mercer Clive Russell
Ahmet Allan Corduner
Philoctetes Clive Russell
Russett Mossie Smith
Priest Robin Soans
Yoyo's Mother Shirin Taylor

Catherine Adie Allen

Directed by Max Stafford-Clark
Designed by Sally Jacobs
Lighting by Rick Fisher
Sound by Bryan Brown
Costume Supervisor Jennifer Cook
Stage Manager Neil O'Malley
Deputy Stage Manager Katie Bligh
Voice Coach Julia Wilson Dixon

Painting in Scene Nineteen by William Tillyer, courtesy of the Bernard Jacobson Gallery.

Act One

SCENE ONE. AUCTION

*The stage. A well-dressed man standing on a podium
shows a large, white canvas to the audience.*

Auctioneer Lot 208, a painting by Theodore Quick,
entitled *No Illusion*. As you can see: totally flat,
authentically white – (*He looks at the audience and speaks
very fast.*) I shall start this at eighty thousand pounds,
eighty thousand, any advance? (*He looks.*) Ninety
thousand. One hundred thousand at the back. One
hundred and twenty thousand, lady at the front. One
hundred and fifty thousand. Any more? One hundred and
seventy thousand, two hundred thousand, two hundred
and twenty thousand between the doors, two hundred and
fifty thousand, two hundred and seventy thousand, all
over the place now. Three hundred thousand at the back.
Three hundred and twenty thousand: lady's bid. Now, at
the very back, three hundred and fifty thousand, any
more? Three hundred and seventy thousand between the
doors. Madam? Four hundred, four twenty, four fifty, four
seventy, five hundred at the back, at the very back, yes,
five hundred and twenty thousand. Five-fifty, lady on my
left. Five hundred and seventy thousand on the telephone,
six hundred thousand all over the place again. Six hundred
and twenty thousand, six hundred and fifty, six hundred
and seventy, seven hundred, seven-twenty, seven-fifty at
the back. Seven-seventy on the telephone again. It's against
you all in the room at seven-seventy, seven hundred and
seventy thousand. Eight hundred thousand, eight hundred
and twenty, a new bidder, and now at the back, almost in
the street, eight hundred and fifty thousand, are you still

in, madam? Eight hundred and seventy thousand, nine hundred thousand at the back, nine hundred and twenty thousand, lady on my left, nine hundred and fifty thousand on the telephone. Going on? No. Any more? At the side, in the aisle, nine hundred and seventy, last chance at nine hundred and seventy thousand, are you going on, madam? One million on the telephone. (*A gasp.*) One million one hundred thousand at the side, any more? One million two hundred thousand, selling at one million two hundred thousand, all done at one million two hundred thousand pounds, one million two hundred thousand pounds: it's yours, madam. (*With barely a pause, he goes on.*) Lot 209. An illuminated billboard by Laura Hellish – which you can see at the back, between the doors. We can't turn on its lights but they are pink and they say: 'ART IS SEXY, ART IS MONEY, ART IS MONEY-SEXY, ART IS MONEY-SEXY-SOCIAL-CLIMBING-FANTASTIC,' which I believe is a quote from the director of a great national museum across the water. Thirty thousand starts this, gentleman at the back. Thank you.

SCENE TWO. PORTRAIT OF BIDDY IN PROFILE

Biddy I didn't at first understand what was happening. For someone like me, who was used to being tolerated, it came as a surprise. You see, before, everything I said was passed over. Well, smiled at, but the conversation would continue elsewhere. I was like the final touches of a well-decorated house. It gives pleasure, but you don't notice it. The sound of my voice was what mattered, it made people feel secure: England still had women who went to good schools and looked after large homes in the country, horses, dogs, children, that sort of thing, that was my voice. Tony – that's my first husband – said he found my conversation comforting background noise when he read

362

the papers. But then, silences began to greet everything I said. Heavy silences. I thought there was something wrong. Then I noticed they were waiting for more words, and these words had suddenly taken on a tremendous importance. But I was still saying the same things. You know, about shopping at Harrod's and trains being slow, and good avocados being hard to come by, and cleaning ladies even harder. And then, I understood. You see, I had become tremendously rich. Not myself, but my husband, my second husband. And when you're that rich, nothing you do is trivial. If I took an hour telling a group of people how I had looked for and not found a good pair of gardening gloves, if I went into every detail of the weeks I had spent on this search, the phone bills I had run up, the catalogues I had returned, they were absolutely riveted. Riveted. Because it seemed everything I did, now that I was tremendously rich because of my second husband, mattered. Mattered tremendously. I hadn't expected this, because you see, my husband is foreign, Greek actually, and I found that not – well, not quite properly English, you know, to be married to a Greek – After all, Biddy *Andreas?*, I could imagine my headmistress – we had a Greek girl at Benenden, we all turned down invitations to her island – and Yoyo – that's my husband, George, Yorgos, actually – he didn't even go to school here – but he was so rich and I became used to it – him and me: being important.

SCENE THREE. BARE KNUCKLE

The gallery. **Alex Brendel,** *American, 35 and dressed in labelled power clothes is storming around.* **Jeremy Bertrand** *stands still, watching her with fatigue.* **Julia Roberts,** *an elegant Asian woman, mediates.* **Nicola** *is at the desk.*

Alex Nobody wants this stuff any more.

Jeremy These are some of the best works –

Alex My ass. White, flat, zipped, unzipped, everybody's bored with it, bored, And this! Nobody ever took this seriously.

Jeremy You're talking about the most interesting living –

Alex Yesterday's news, Jeremy. Tomorrow, fallout. You couldn't even unload this on an arms dealer.

Julia We've unloaded worse.

Alex Yesterday.

Julia We have three museums interested . . .

Alex Anybody signed a cheque?

Jeremy This isn't a shop.

Alex Yeah, that's the problem. You shoulda got rid of this stuff a long time ago.

Jeremy I worked very hard to get some of these. I don't understand why suddenly no one seems to –

Alex It's going bad. I mean, it's burning, it's burning so fast your gallery's catching fire.

Julia We have a Japanese . . .

Alex They want flowers. I don't see any flowers.

Jeremy Number six. (*Alex looks at number six on the wall.*)

Alex Yeah? It's like the others. Nothing.

Julia The title: *Where There Are No Flowers*. The Japanese wants that one.

Alex The cheque?

Jeremy Really, Alex, he's bought from us before. It's a corporation.

Alex Do you know what's happening in Japan right now?

Jeremy I consider myself generally well-informed. I read *The Times*, I watch the nine o'clock news.

Julia We're rather wrapped up in a by-election, Alex.

Alex Japan's going down the tubes. I have it from *Le Monde*.

Jeremy Alex, *Le Monde*. French . . . only they could call their national newspaper *The World*.

Alex It's time to look at the facts, Jeremy.

Jeremy I didn't know there were facts in art. Dates perhaps . . .

Alex OK, you want dates, I'll give you two dates: December 3. December 12. If Liz Taylor can't sell a Van Gogh and a dead Warhol can't sell himself, something's wrong.

Jeremy I know something's wrong, Alex.

Alex This is next for the bonfire, that's all. This stuff is New York. And this is neo-New York. New York is finished. Mary Boone is in trouble. Castelli's showing Old Masters. Basically, New York is closing down. My company was too late to save New York, but we can save England. Do you want to save England or don't you? Well, if you want to save England, forget about the Japanese. They're looking bad.

Jeremy I thought they were invisible, that was their charm.

Alex I could've given them some advice, but they didn't ask me. Now what you've gotta do is get rid of New York. Dump America.

Jeremy I remember the American shows at the Tate, we were dazzled. The scale, the daring. Rothko's colours.

Alex They're looking old. You wanna look old?

Jeremy The confidence, the freedom. The English *avant-garde* were painting lavatories.

Alex Where are those bathroom paintings?

Jeremy Across the street. I don't think they're doing too well with them.

Alex OK. Forget the bathrooms. This is England, right?

Jeremy I think so. Well, it was.

Alex What do you think of when you think of England?

Jeremy Soft voices. Accents, the sort of accents people used to have – or acquire.

Alex No, I mean, when you think of your childhood.

Julia Jeremy grew up in Egypt, Alex.

Alex Oh, I'm sorry. I mean, am I supposed to be sorry? Does it mean something? In code, you know, in English.

Jeremy No, no, Alex, it means I grew up in Egypt. Julia grew up in England.

Alex And what do you remember?

Julia Accents, yes, that's right.

Alex Maybe you two should be running BBC Radio Three and not an art gallery.

Jeremy No, my brother's doing that: they're in even more trouble than we are. But go on, Alex, what is it you want to say? You can be American about it, we won't mind.

Alex I'm saying: England.

Julia You mean we ought to go national rather than international?

Alex You start that way, then you make it international.

Jeremy That's not so easy.

Alex That's what I'm here for. England: tea and English muffins.

Jeremy I think you mean crumpets.

Julia Stubbs fetched some very good prices last month.

Alex Cricket. Na. Forget the cricket. Croquet.

Jeremy What am I supposed to do, frame illustrations from *Alice in Wonderland*?

Alex English gardens. The countryside. Yeah, Samuel Palmer, Constable.

Jeremy I'm having trouble with my overheads, I can't go around buying a lot of Constables. I couldn't even afford the drawings.

Alex I'm not saying Constable, I'm saying England, but as it looks now.

Jeremy It doesn't look like anything now. It's mostly motorways.

Alex Come on, I walk around London. People have gardens. Big gardens. We don't have gardens in America, we have lawns. Or else you own a mountain. You need something to do with gardens. Landscapes.

Julia The sculptors . . .

Jeremy No, please. I can't have heaps of coal in here. It'll give me asthma. Chalk circles – no.

Alex Well, Jeremy, you'll have to go out there and find

some English landscapes. Trees, a dark piece of water, a windmill, but new, now.

Jeremy Our painters aren't taught to draw any more. They wouldn't risk themselves on a tree. It's very difficult to do a tree, Alex.

Alex It's very simple. Either close down like number eleven and fourteen or find a man who can paint trees.

Julia What about a woman?

Alex I think you want to attract the couples market. It's growing. Couples go in together, she's got the eye, he's got the money. They meet the painter, have him around to dinner. Now if it's a woman and she's young, the wife'll be jealous and if she's old he'll be put off. Stick with a man. Make him big. He can drink, but I can't have him smoke, OK? Put the woman in a group show. The school of new English landscape, no, the English garden school, you'll think of something. Better, invite Morris, he'll think of something. I don't think he understands art, but he sure has a way with words.

Jeremy Morris knows we don't love him.

Alex If he wanted to be loved, he wouldn't have become a critic. OK, now, the spring is good, we'll put a lot of tulips, no, we'll be really English and have one daffodil in a glass, somewhere obvious, it'll look real subtle. Get this guy to do some really big paintings and some jewels, for this wall here. I can see it.

Jeremy I don't think this painter exists.

Alex Well, make him. Send somebody to life class, I don't know.

Julia Let me think. He has to be alive?

Alex Yeah. For the moment. To give interviews.

Julia Stephen Ryle. He's from the North.

Alex The North, that's good. Spirituality. Snow. Yeah. People are getting tired of haystacks and olive trees, parched grass. It looks too much like the greenhouse effect.

Jeremy I think Julia means Manchester, Alex. Stephen will never – he's so angry.

Alex Angry. I like that. That's real sexy. Constable with balls. He's not political, is he? Now I gotta have lunch at Claridge's, can you call me a taxi?

Julia It's down the street.

Alex I know where Claridge's is, Julia, you don't expect me to arrive at Claridge's on foot, do you? I mean, how can I tip the doorman if he doesn't open the door for me?

Alex leaves with Julia. Jeremy, on his own for a moment, looks at his white walls. Julia comes back.

Jeremy Must I pay five hundred pounds an hour to be abused by an ignorant woman?

Julia She worked miracles upstairs. Alex isn't ignorant, she's just American.

Jeremy Julia, you must learn about Americans. There is nothing more elegant than an elegant American. But Alex . . . Her family must have come from Eastern Europe. By the way, I've never tipped the doorman at Claridge's. I've chatted with him when it's been raining.

Julia I'm sure that made him very happy, Jeremy. Shall I get in touch with Stephen?

Jeremy I think I stopped paying him a retainer after I went to see him in the country. He was so rude. And out of touch. Trees. When everybody wanted photomontages of young men in black leather. What made you think of him?

SCENE FOUR. YOYO

The circle bar of an opera house. **Yoyo Andreas** *is making a speech. He is in his mid-forties and speaks with a slight accent.* **Lady Lelouche, David.**

Yoyo . . . Buildings, Pericles told the Athenians, to drive away despondency. And he concluded with these words which will be familiar to all of you: 'Mighty indeed are the marks and monuments of our empire, and future generations will wonder at us as does the present age.' This, my lords, ladies and gentlemen is how the George Andreas Company sees Britain, as it turns to its ambitious project on London's noble, arterial river, so loved and sung by all the poets of Europe. Monuments, however, are not empty shells. Pericles boasted of the Athenian festivals, we boast of the festivals in this august opera house. And just as my company seeks to preserve the excellence of the past, but continue history, so it is sponsoring not one, but two productions: The Andreas Company therefore donates five hundred thousand pounds to the revival of a classical opera and five hundred thousand to the production of a new opera. And now, I have great pleasure in presenting this cheque for one million pounds to our great opera house.

Applause. Lady Lelouche takes the cheque. They kiss. She poses with the cheque.

Lady Lelouche Whenever I look at a businessman I think of marriage. (*Some polite titters.*) I think, that is, of the marriage of business and art. What better partnership than Art – fine, delicate and often wayward – looked after by powerful and hard-headed Business. Yes, let us wish this marriage long and lasting happiness. And now as befits this happy occasion, we will celebrate with the champagne generously provided by Mr Andreas's company. It is excellent, I have tasted it. Several times. (*Applause. Titters.*)

David (*approaching Yoyo*) Very good speech, Yoyo, very good.

Yoyo Thank you, David. You must listen to so many . . .

David Where did you find that quote about monuments? Is it in the dictionary of quotations? I'm always looking for something to open board meetings, I've run out of Shakespeare. You can't say 'nothing will come of nothing' too many times.

Yoyo I remember it from Thucydides. I wanted something from Churchill, but he didn't seem very interested in architecture. Odd for a man with such a sense of history.

David We English aren't city people like you lot, Yoyo. London is where you do your politics and your accounts, and then you go to the country. Of course, I'm all for your flats over the water, but why should I want one when I can go and fish in my own river? Or, in my case, my neighbour's river.

Yoyo You must see the flats, David. They will be – poetic – they will live in the landscape.

David I'll have a look. I suppose they're frightfully expensive?

Yoyo Early buyers will have excellent terms. And friends.

Lady Lelouche approaches.

David Excellent speech, Lady Lelouche.

Lady Lelouche I hope some of these art people got my word of warning, we can't have too much waste and irresponsibility any more. Loved your Pericles, Mr Andreas, suited you very well. Now we must do something for you . . .

Yoyo Thank you, Lady Lelouche, what I would love most would be the Royal Box for the Handel first night. Perhaps you would join my wife and me for dinner, and you too, David.

Lady Lelouche Ah . . . Yes. Well – The Royal Box . . . Mmm. (*She drifts off.*)

David You should have asked me for the Royal Box, Yoyo. I'm off to the club, I'm going to ask for that Thucydides, how do you spell it? I suppose the librarian will know. Any other books with good quotes? I never get a chance to read. I've just agreed to the Tate – at least the art world understands business. So, yes, something Roman . . . you might even become a member, that way you could order the books, save me remembering how to spell them.

Yoyo Ah . . .

David You might enjoy that. Nice club, famous architect, I forget his name.

Yoyo Sir Charles Barry.

David Well done with the million, Yoyo. I hope they don't waste it on something too modern. You can always state a preference for tunes, you know. Don't let them intimidate you with all this artistic independence nonsense. You paid the money, you call the tune.

SCENE FIVE. INTERIORS

Glyndebourne. The gardens. Yoyo and Biddy sit, in full evening dress, shivering with cold and looking apprehensively at the sky. Sounds of voices and the popping of champagne bottles. Biddy lays out an elaborate meal on a tablecloth, champagne glasses, silverware, etc.

Yoyo It was going well. After all, he'd suggested it two months ago and I had been very careful not to seem eager, but I thought I would casually drop it into the conversation and he began to ask me about my interior life. I thought it was one of those English expressions, but I couldn't ask, so I mentioned that film I love, *Interiors*, and finally he came to the point and asked me if I liked walking in the Lake District, but said I probably wrote poetry, most Greeks did, was I keen on hunting? Tell me, Biddy, what does hunting have to do with an interior life?

Biddy Grooming the horses at dawn, the chase, it's thrilling –

Yoyo (*over her*) Isn't that Richard Bede? What is he doing at Glyndebourne? He only owns a restaurant. Then I thought, I have an English wife and surely she must have an interior life. Henry's wife writes biographies, he's always boasting about how he never reads them – That's what David meant, I'm sure – (*Looks around.*) We should have gone to the restaurant, everyone's there.

Biddy Last time you thought only the corporate people went to the restaurant. You wanted a hamper.

Yoyo And Jamie complains about all the concerts Caroline drags him to – and how difficult it is to talk to contemporary composers and so, darling, I'm waiting.

Biddy For what, Yoyo?

Yoyo An interest.

Biddy I'm interested in making you comfortable. Happy. (*Yoyo is cold.*) And in the house.

Yoyo Why doesn't it look more English?

Biddy It did, Yoyo, before you asked me to throw out my grandmother's things.

Yoyo All that chipped china and knives that didn't cut.

Biddy Yes, well.

Yoyo And those sofas.

Biddy I know they were hideous, but that's English: ugly pieces of furniture one inherits from one's grandmother.

Yoyo Biddy, this hamper, didn't you used to have that for the cat?

Biddy Yes . . .

Yoyo Biddy, surely we can afford to buy a new one.

Biddy Why? I'm rather attached to it. Mummy used to use an old knitting basket for Aldeburgh.

Yoyo Aldeburgh – Should we be going to Aldeburgh? What happened to the furniture you had when you were married to Tony?

Biddy Oh, Yoyo, I couldn't ask for that. Not after that frightful girl . . . no.

Yoyo I will not wait another year for the Progress. David could forget. I've just given the opera house all that money, and I'm in the press. Biddy, I don't care what it is, and how much it costs, if you want to write something, we'll publish it ourselves.

374

Biddy I hate writing letters, Yoyo. We could have horses, but you don't like the country that much.

Yoyo It has to be better than that, better than all their wives.

Biddy Are you sure they're that interested in what their wives do?

Yoyo Why else do they talk about them?

Biddy To make conversation . . . like the weather.

Yoyo I think you're allowing yourself to be out of touch, Biddy.

Biddy I'm sorry . . .

Yoyo There's Lady Soames. She's seen us. No, she's looking the other way. We've chosen the wrong part of the garden, no one's even walking this way.

Lady Lelouche and David have come on.

Ah, there's Lady Lelouche and David. Now do be interesting with her, she's everywhere.

Biddy Daddy loathes her.

Yoyo Biddy! Lady Lelouche, do come and join us.

Lady Lelouche Grass looks wet. It'll rain for Wimbledon. I had something urgent to say to you, Mr Andreas, what was it, something about Royal, Royal – Garden Party? No. We've lost our guest, tall, went to look at a flower, you haven't seen him? Christopher.

Yoyo You know my wife?

Lady Lelouche Mm. I remember now. Yes, the Royal Box. Impossible for the Handel, one of the directors wants it, but you can have it for the new thing, next season, what is it called, David?

David Can't remember, but you'll like it, Yoyo. It's about medieval England, kind of Camelot for intellectuals, I think.

Yoyo Thank you, and you'll join us for dinner?

Lady Lelouche Alas, we have some Texans that week.

David I never go to the modern stuff, Yoyo, if I can help it. I've spotted Christopher, Lady Lelouche, he's about to fall into a rose. Christopher!

David and Lady Lelouche go off.

Yoyo Biddy, you didn't say a word. Why aren't we invited to the Royal Garden Party?

Biddy They're so dreadful, even Daddy hates them.

Yoyo Couldn't he have given us his invitation?

Biddy Darling, it doesn't work like that. I don't know how it works, but not like that . . .

Yoyo Now listen, David invited me to lunch at the Progress next week. He will introduce me to one of the older members. Then everything could go through quite smoothly. I want you to come.

Biddy Are you sure?

Yoyo And when you come, I want you to bring it up in the conversation.

Biddy What, Yoyo?

Yoyo You're being deliberately obtuse. Your interior life. And it had better be very interesting. I can't afford a wife who does nothing, Biddy. (*A frozen silence.*) We haven't talked to anybody. If we could get season tickets, we could invite people. Can't your father help?

Biddy The waiting list is fifteen years. He can't change that.

Yoyo Your father can't seem to do anything for us.

Biddy He did try with White's. Apparently the ones who are most against any change in the thing about the schools are all those Russian princes who, strictly speaking, shouldn't be there anyway. They certainly didn't go to school here, but they were irresistible at the time and one expected them to go back. But Daddy did say they were dying off, and if you could wait a few years, he'd try again.

Yoyo With another eight years on the waiting list? No, it'll have to be the Progress. I won't be happy until I sit in one of those large armchairs talking about Thackeray and smoking a pipe.

Biddy But Yoyo, you don't smoke.

Yoyo Biddy, don't let me down. It's over to you.

SCENE SIX. WOMEN TALKING (*when women talk the conversation is always about men*)

Julia, Biddy.

Julia He actually threatened you?

Biddy He didn't wave the divorce papers in front of my face, but he – well, I remember it from Tony: he implied I was no longer suitable. In Tony's case it's because he had this girl half his age and he felt foolish, but Yoyo means it. I'm not helping his ambitions. Julia, help me, I can't go through it again.

Julia Through what?

Biddy Everything: Another divorce, and then living alone, shopping for pre-cooked meals for one at Marks and Spencers.

Julia I cook for myself every night. I have fish, a delicious salad. I listen to music. I have a great time.

Biddy And then the pub. That was in the country, but I would sit there alone and the publican's wife would come and talk to me because she felt so sorry for me. And when the children came home for the weekend, when they weren't spending them at Tony's, I couldn't remember how to talk because I hadn't opened my mouth all week except to ask for two apples.

Julia We had a good time in London.

Biddy You'd put on your sari and go and visit your aunts for the weekend, and I was afraid to go out in the street, I felt everybody knew: rejected woman. The silence, Julia. I know Yoyo doesn't talk much and then he wants to spend all his evenings at this club if only he can get in, but at least he's there. The plumber knows he's there, the dustbin men, even if I have to deal with all that on my own, he's there, in the background. Julia, how can I become more interesting?

Julia Come and work in the gallery.

Biddy You don't understand . . .

Julia I do. You're married to a creepy foreign social climber.

Biddy Julia! *You* can't –

Julia Why not? Because I have foreign skin! I remember Yoyo. Mind you, that's a miracle because you behaved like all married women and immediately dropped your women friends, but never mind. I remember him and I know the type. My father wanted to be an English gentleman too. He wanted to be an Englishman so badly he ended up an empty shell, cashmere suits, his daughter at a convent school, an English wife who recoiled from his dark skin.

Once we were in a taxi and the man was playing Indian music and my father's head started swaying, then his whole body. It was the first time ever I saw him alive, almost smiling and then he shut the glass between us and the driver. I have no heritage, I'm nothing. In India I'm a foreigner and in England, I'm an exotic. And the worst is that I've inherited his pretensions. I want to be a gentleman too, detached, elegant, with a cashmere mind, but maybe I'm confused, maybe I really want to be a Buddhist, except I'm too angry to be a Buddhist. Too ambitious.

Biddy I remember your rages in the flat. You were so funny. Sometimes it was because you'd been out with an Englishman and sometimes because you'd been out with an Indian.

Julia You were very sweet. Trying to understand racial confusion. Might as well have asked you to study quantum physics. I thought we had a good time, going to the cinema, to dinner, remember the holiday we had in Venice? I taught you to appreciate Giorgione.

Biddy I loved being in Venice with you, Julia, but –

Julia It's not your identity. Your identity has to come from a man. Otherwise it's worthless. That's sick. Mind you, my identity comes from my boss and I've just realized how stupid he is. I'm the Julia who works for Jeremy. Well. Not for much longer. I know what Yoyo needs. He needs to become a collector, it's the passport to society in America and it's beginning to work here.

Biddy A collector . . . You mean Picasso? Isn't that expensive, even for us?

Julia The Picassos of tomorrow, you fool. I happen to know who they are.

Biddy Oh. Who are they?

Julia It's not that simple. I'll have to guide you.

    Marianne Ryle *approaches.*

Just the person I wanted. Marianne! What a beautiful hat.

Marianne I thought it might change my life. It didn't and now I can't pay for it.

Julia Why don't you send the bill to Stephen?

Marianne Ha! He doesn't even open his own bills.

Julia How is he these days? This is Biddy, also having some husband problems.

Marianne I hope your husband is rich. Mine's a pauper. He shouldn't have been.

Julia Is he still doing landscapes?

Marianne Can you believe it? He's been studying all those war painters, you know, the ones who were sent out on their bicycles by Kenneth Clark to record England before the Germans invaded, and he's doing these comments, he calls them, on their work. And then some of his own, abstract. Who the hell is interested in the English landscape? I told him what people wanted now were grim depictions of urban blight or else just white, you know, everybody still likes white. Or even black, people respect black, it looks serious, like the Germans. Or you can do a little bit of everything, show you're confused. I do know something about art. He won't listen. I hate him. He hasn't recovered from the sixties. I bet he's still a socialist, secretly.

Julia I would like to go and talk to him. Biddy is a collector, she might come with me.

Marianne Actually his stuff isn't that bad. It's his

personality. These days it's not enough to have talent. (*to Biddy*) Do you buy from Jeremy?

Biddy I'm just starting.

Marianne Jeremy's very good. But it's really because of Julia.

Julia Do you have Stephen's number?

Marianne He'll kill me if he knows I've given it to anyone. (*She writes the number and hands it to Julia.*) I've just put myself down for the Tate lectures. (*to Biddy*) I'll probably see you there. I had a fit last time when they said they were booked up. After all, my husband, well, my ex-husband, sold them some paintings. Of course no one remembers and they're rotting somewhere in their vaults. Everybody's at those lectures. I want to find a really nice pen to take notes with. Black, with some red, no, white and black. Get my husband to show you his early work. It was brilliant. Door handles. We had John Lennon at our show.

She drifts off.

Julia We were talking about art . . .

Biddy Yes, Yoyo . . . Yoyo has to get into the Progress Club.

SCENE SEVEN. UNTITLED

The gallery. Biddy, Julia and Jeremy stare intently at a painting. Nicola reads a magazine.

Jeremy Possibly his best. (*All concentrate.*) It's extremely rare for something like this to come on the market. It's only because of the divorce. I heard she was in tears when he decided to sell it.

Biddy Who?

Jeremy (*surprised*) Charles, of course. Jane.

Biddy What was it, euh – Jane liked about it?

Jeremy That there's nothing there.

Biddy I see . . .

Jeremy Julia spoke to her.

Julia She would be on the street and there was all this noise, cars, litter, mess, then she would come home and look at this. Columns and columns have been written about this painting. It's about America. I've got some of the articles at home, I'll let you read them.

Jeremy But really, one need only look. (*Biddy looks.*) This is irrelevant, but you might like to know his prices have gone up by four hundred per cent in two years.

Biddy My husband says the art market is rather depressed at the moment.

Jeremy Good things never lose their value, Mrs Andreas, it's the second rate that's not selling. And I'm very pleased about that.

Biddy Have many people expressed an interest in this?

Jeremy People don't call us, we call them. I'm very careful whom I associate with this gallery. I have two or three people I might offer it to, but I'd prefer it stayed in England. Will you open your collection to the public, Mrs Andreas?

Biddy Ah? Well, not immediately, I mean – I'll have to see . . .

Jeremy I understand: a great collection is very personal. This is a difficult work, what we call a slow work. A great painting always is.

Biddy I find it, euh, very interesting, the, euh, emptiness, but, mm, could I take it home and try it, with the house . . .

Jeremy Alas, this isn't a carpet from Liberty's, Mrs Andreas, the insurance . . .

Biddy walks towards and back from the painting.

Biddy I like it, I'm very interested, I just wondered, well, my husband tends to like things that are very English.

Jeremy Why don't you bring him along? Did you tell me he was Greek? He'd like its Apollonian quality.

Biddy He's busy, he's left it to me, but, well, he'll want something English. You see, my husband . . . loves Jane Austen . . . so . . .

Jeremy I'm afraid only one English painter has reached international stature and you wouldn't like him, Mrs Andreas, believe me.

Biddy Do you mean Francis Bacon?

Julia Biddy!

Biddy I only know about him because I found two tickets to a show by him in Tony's pocket one day. (*to Jeremy*) I knew my first husband was having an affair because he was doing all these strange things like going to health farms and concerts and so I went to the Francis Bacon to find out more about her.

Julia What did you find out?

Biddy Nothing, but . . . something about myself. Those men isolated – in their circles, so uncomfortable and smudged, well, I felt like that. It was so sad, but I left the exhibition feeling, I don't know, recognized, better. Do you have any of his paintings?

Jeremy No. And he's hardly new, Mrs Andreas.

Biddy No, of course, well . . . I'm sorry . . .

Jeremy Please . . . shall Nicola call you a taxi?

Biddy No, I'll walk, I need the fresh – I mean, I need some exercise –

Jeremy Come to our next private view, Mrs Andreas.

Biddy Oh, yes, I'd love to – thank you.

Jeremy It's a group show, but I may have one painting there . . . I believe I've discovered, well, rediscovered an unusual English painter, I'll let you in on his name. (*Pause.*)

Biddy Stephen Ryle?

Jeremy Who told you about him? Have you read something? He's mine! What I mean is that he shows exclusively with this gallery.

Julia I told Mrs Andreas about Stephen, Jeremy.

Julia leads Biddy out. A silence as Jeremy stares at the painting.

Jeremy (*explodes*) I can't sell it! (*to Nicola*) Do you like it? (*Nicola nods. Then she shakes her head.*) I read yesterday about an Italian clerk who had saved great Italian paintings from the Nazis. He knew exactly which ones to save, well, it wasn't difficult, he saved the Raphaels, the Leonardos, in fact, he tried to save everything there was. If we had an invasion here, what would I save? Would I save this painting? Would I save it because it is worth half a million, or was, yesterday, or would I save it because I was convinced humanity would be the poorer without it? *Would* humanity be the poorer without it?

Nicola and Jeremy look at the painting.

SCENE EIGHT. THE ARTIST'S MODEL

Stephen Ryle's *studio in the country. Stephen, a big man of 50, is lying on the bench, very still. He is naked under a toga-like sheet, which covers odd parts of his body, and he wears a crown of leaves on his head. Standing not far from him is* **Fiona Campbell,** *a woman of 30. She is sketching quickly, looking mostly at his back, which is bare, and his profile. A moment.*

Stephen You won't get the curve of my back if you're so tentative.

Fiona Don't move. (*She keeps working.*)

Stephen You're scratching that paper, not making love to it.

Fiona I said, don't move.

Stephen Assurance and speed. This is nature, it's a moment. You can fiddle all you want in the comfort of your studio.

Fiona You've gained weight.

Stephen Will it be my back or a generalized back? Do it again.

Fiona No, Stephen, you can correct it later – if it needs it.

Stephen All those years teaching you detail.

Fiona I remember when I couldn't do a floor. You were so horrible. Paint the object, you shouted, then the shadow. The shadow will make the floor.

Stephen Well, now you can do floors. But can you do my back? Come and touch it. Make love to my back.

Fiona You moved your head.

Stephen Bring me your breasts . . .

Fiona Stephen.

Stephen I used to be able to draw them in two seconds. With my eyes closed. The breasts of a frontierswoman. Your awful father must have had a wonderful mother with wonderful American breasts, covered wagon breasts, the breasts of the Wild West.

Fiona She was from Boston.

Stephen Mayflower breasts. Come here.

Fiona I think we'll go to America after the show and look up some relatives.

Stephen I have an erection. Can you draw that?

Fiona If you can hold it long enough. You didn't even notice I said we. Stephen: I've met someone. I'm getting married.

Stephen What happened to that woman?

Fiona That was just power. She modelled for me, I decided to seduce her. I'd like to be faithful: a new experience. I've treated men like restaurants. You were my favourite, but I liked to try the food in the others. I'd like some stability. I know that sounds Victorian.

Stephen No, worse: new age. You're having your first show in a glitzy gallery. Isn't that enough? You don't want babies as well, do you?

Fiona Why not? You did.

Stephen It's not the same. Fiona, you won't paint. I know it. I'll have wasted my time.

Fiona I'm not Marianne. I'll never stop painting. You can't talk.

Stephen I keep working.

Fiona And don't show it. You rail against the marketplace like some effete modern composer.

Stephen The marketplace dumped me ten years ago.

Fiona Please come to my show.

Stephen I don't go to London. Is he an aromatherapist?

Fiona Who?

Stephen A medium? A social worker? No, even you wouldn't fuck a social worker. But of course, you're getting married, you don't have to fuck him.

Fiona Shut up. I warned Jeremy you'd be there. I'm your prize pupil.

Stephen I had a letter from Jeremy the other day. How was I? He still had the door handles on his sitting room wall, wouldn't sell it. Was I doing anything new? Could he see it?

Fiona Aren't you?

Stephen I showed him some work five years ago, my best. What does it mean, he said. I told him it wasn't a piece of conceptual art, it didn't need a book to go with it. What could I tell my clients, he said, why should they buy a landscape in 1985? Couldn't I do some more door handles? He could charge anything for those now. Then he asked me if I'd ever thought of making paintings that looked upside down, he said it could be a breakthrough for me. I threw him out. I told him he should be selling cars.

Fiona Don't move. Maybe he's coming round.

Stephen Fuck him.

Fiona You can't hide your landscapes for ever.

Stephen I see them.

Fiona You taught us art was public.

Stephen The world has changed. The public doesn't deserve art.

Fiona Maybe it's changing again. I can make it change. You can. I will make it change. Everyone will be there. Please don't be rude and drunk.

Stephen I'm not your husband, Fiona, I get drunk when I please. Does he like your work?

Fiona He's not that visual. He has other qualities.

Stephen Like what? He's kind to animals?

Fiona I'm finished.

Stephen gets up, stiffly, messily draping the cloth around him.

Stephen I'm sure you've made it too elaborate. You always do. (*He goes to the painting and looks carefully. A silence.*) You've made me look old.

Fiona I drew what I saw. You taught me not to flatter. I sketched you the way Velasquez would.

Stephen You don't love my skin. When Degas drew his old tired washerwomen, their skin was still sensual.

Fiona That's not what it's about.

Stephen It's a nude, isn't it? What's it called?

Fiona Philoctetes. He was a great Greek warrior who sailed for Troy. But he was bitten by a snake and the wound wouldn't heal, causing him inexorable anguish. It also festered, so that he began to stink. His friends couldn't stand his smell any more, so Odysseus tricked him to an island where he was abandoned, with only a cave for shelter and berries for food. And his festering sore. Ten years on, the Greeks were told in a prophecy they could only win the war if Philoctetes returned to Troy.

Stephen What happened?

Fiona It's a long story.

SCENE NINE. POOR LAYMAN I, FOR SACRED RITES UNFIT . . .

The Progress Club. Yoyo and Biddy stand, waiting, awkward. David approaches Yoyo and Biddy.

David George. Good. Philip's still struggling with the roof committee, we have more leaks every time it rains and we're running out of buckets. You've brought your wife, how charming. We're very progressive here, Mrs Andreas, we actually have a women's division, about four I think, my favourite is a charming old bird with a patch. We like to continue our liberal traditions. Will you join us for lunch?

Yoyo Yes . . .

Biddy No . . . I don't think . . .

Sir Philip Howard, *an ancient and distinguished member, comes in.*

David And there's Philip. Philip, Mr Andreas and his wife. Mrs Andreas: Sir Philip Howard, who single-handedly is trying to stem the tide of decay sweeping over us – oh, dear, I believe I'm mixing my metaphors, are you literary, Mrs Andreas?

Biddy This is a beautiful room.

Sir Philip Isn't it? And it changes remarkably with the light.

David Yes, we take it for granted, don't we, we're such Philistines.

Yoyo My wife is very interested in the arts.

David How charming. Charming. The arts. What would we do without the arts? Pity they're so expensive.

Biddy (*to Sir Philip*) I've heard my uncle talk about this hall . . .

Sir Philip I don't want to bore you with a guided tour, Mrs Andreas, but if you look, you will notice the friezes above the columns and the heavily faceted glass. It was completed in 1841 by Sir Charles Barry and is widely considered his masterpiece.

David Philip, I never knew all that, but why do we have so many leaks? Isn't it funny, George, Philip says this is the most beautiful building in London, but we're a ragbag of a club and we can't repair the roof.

Sir Philip Don't say that, David, or Mr Andreas will defect to White's. (*All laugh.*)

Yoyo My wife's father is a member of White's.

Biddy He says he only goes there for the puddings. It reminds him of school.

Sir Philip Ah, yes. Treacle tart with custard. Bread and butter pudding.

David Do you know, the other day I had a bread and butter pudding made with brown bread, and I, who never complain, lost control of myself. The French chef came out and told me it was healthier. Mind your *onions*, I said, I remembered that bit of French from school, and leave bread and butter pudding to the English. Speaking of which, we'd better get into the dining room before the old codgers take the best tables. Are you joining us, Mrs Andreas?

Yoyo nods.

Biddy No, I'm afraid I have things to do . . .

Sir Philip Quite right. My wife won't set foot in this place, says it reminds her of our son's gymnasium. She goes to Fortnum's and has a frightfully good time.

Yoyo Biddy . . .

Biddy I must go and look at a painting. The exhibition closes tomorrow . . .

Yoyo My wife is very interested in contemporary art. We're starting a collection.

David How charming. All that modern, blank stuff that everyone likes so much? Is it still blank, no, I read somewhere it's upside down now, German and upside down.

Biddy The painting I'm looking at is English. It's full of colour.

Sir Philip English? Do we paint? I know we write. And we garden. I didn't know we painted. We used to . . .

Biddy Yes, we have a great tradition of landscape painting and it seems to be reviving. Of course, it's different –

Sir Philip We used to do so many things. We used to know how to repair roofs, make windows . . . I called a builder to my house the other day about some windows. He tried to convince me to replace my leaded windows with aluminium ones. More practical, he said. I do try to keep in touch, Mrs Andreas, I go to the odd private view. It all looks like aluminium windows.

Biddy You would like this, Sir Philip, it has that care.

David I hate anything abstract. Reminds me of algebra.

Biddy It's a language that can be learned. But these paintings are landscapes. And you recognize England in them. Of course, there's a lot of controversy, some people say this is parochial, one ought to like – the upside down paintings. I disagree. But please excuse me, you see why I must look at these paintings again. I'll let you enjoy your lunch in peace. (*She goes.*)

David Charming.

Sir Philip They're so clever – women, these days. So – convinced, I understand why one might want to get away occasionally. Now Mr Andreas, perhaps you can give me some advice. I'm on the politics committee –

David Philip, I thought you were going on to the dining committee –

Sir Philip That would have been much more interesting, David, but I'm afraid they insisted they need me on this politics thing. It seems the club wants to shed some of its insularity, have better communication with Europe, particularly countries we've never thought of before, Spain, Greece, Turkey . . .

Yoyo I would be loath to call Turkey a European country, Sir Philip.

Sir Philip Ah? You must. Tell me about it.

David Why do we have to worry about Europe, Philip, what's wrong with England?

Sir Philip That's what the Europeans will tell us.

David What do they know? They're European.

Sir Philip Now, you were saying Turkey is not . . .

David You can't ask him, Philip, he's one of us now.

Sir Philip Yes, but who are we?

SCENE TEN. THE ARTIST AND HIS FAMILY

Stephen's garden. **Gwen Ryle**, *18, is weeding, vaguely. Stephen is cutting grass.*

Gwen What I've thought is first I'd fly to New York and spend a few weeks, and then I'd go up to New England and watch their leaves, what's it called, the Fall, then I'd go to Canada and meet Robert and we'd take that train that goes across the mountains and – is this a weed? Well, I'm pulling it out anyway – then we'd go to Alaska –

Stephen How are you going to live?

Gwen I thought you'd pay for some of it, and then I'd work, waitress or look after children in Canada, they have children there, don't they? (*Pause.*) Can you pay for some of it? I'm going to be a very limited person if I don't see the world.

Stephen There are lots of things to see in England.

Gwen Oh, Daddy, Devon, the Lake District, B–O–R–I–N–G. Sheep. Then Australia, I want to study the aborigines, New Zealand, Antarctica –

Stephen There are lots of sheep in New Zealand.

Gwen Yeah, but they're not the same, they'll look different, I'm sure, they'll be more – well, they won't be English sheep. And then I could find a world cruise and work as a chambermaid back to England. Or maybe I'll stay in Australia, will you miss me? Or maybe I could stop in Morocco and take a camel across the desert like in *The Sheltering Sky* –

Stephen As in –

Gwen As in. Daddy, you're such a pedant. I'm going to need a camera to record all those travels, I thought if I had one now, I could practise so I learned to take brilliant pictures, *as in* Lord Snowdon. I saw some really good second-hand cameras in a shop and I could even take a course . . .

Stephen How much?

Gwen You could come and help me choose, Daddy, that would be fun. About two hundred. Maybe more for a good one. Will you come?

Stephen Not to London.

Gwen Why not? Why won't you ever come to London?

Stephen It's my Troy.

Gwen Troy? What's a Troy?

Stephen It's a place where the Greeks and the Trojans fought. What did they teach you in that expensive school of yours, Gwen? And by the way, when are you going to retake? You must go to university.

Gwen Daddy . . . maybe I don't really want to study, maybe I'm stupid, I don't know . . .

Stephen You would have done better in a comprehensive instead of what's really no more than a finishing school.

Gwen Daddy . . . don't start. I might become a great photographer. Will you buy me the camera? Oops, here comes Mummy, I suppose you two are going to have an argument, I'm going to sunbathe. (*She goes.*)

Marianne comes in. A short silence.

Marianne What are you planting now?

Stephen An avenue of horse chestnuts.

Marianne How long do they take to grow?

Stephen Fifty years.

Marianne What's the point? (*A pause.*) I need some money.

Stephen You know I don't have it.

Marianne What happened to that illustration work?

Stephen I did three books, *A Guide to Breeding Gloucester Canaries, Castle's List of Grasshoppers of the World*, I've blocked out the third, and when the editor rang me to tell me the crest of the canaries should look more like woks and less like frying pans, I swore I'd never do another one. *Japanese Carp*, yes, that was the other one. I'm a painter.

Marianne I have a friend who wants a portrait done of her and her husband.

Stephen No.

Marianne You're completely irresponsible. You have children, a wife.

Stephen Ex-wife.

Marianne You're still responsible for me. (*Pause.*) I wish I'd never married you.

Stephen You didn't think so at the time.

Marianne That's cheap. You seemed so promising in those days. That show of yours, I knew you'd be impossible, but I didn't mind, I thought I'd be helping a great artist. I should've kept on painting myself. I gave it up to help you. All I wanted was to be an artist's wife. What a joke.

Stephen I never stopped being an artist.

Marianne I'm not so sure.

Stephen (*dangerous*) What do you mean?

Marianne This going back to nature stuff. It was all right in the sixties, but to do it in the eighties? It's perverse. I don't think a real artist is perverse, I think a real artist reflects the times.

Stephen What times?

Marianne You could learn something in London. You stick yourself up in the country like some sour hermit, nobody lives in the country any more, you should see other people's work. You might learn something. I don't know why I even bother. The trouble with you is you don't know how to listen, and you have no values.

Stephen And you do? You call money a value?

Marianne It's a hell of a lot better than trees, isn't it? I could've married Richard. He's a millionaire by now. He hasn't compromised, he's just been a little more polite than you and more in touch. Well. I've always backed the wrong horse. I had feminist friends in those days, they told me I was crazy to get married at all, they were right. Now they've got great careers and I'm just stuck here doing nothing, in a tiny London flat and it's all your bloody fault.

Stephen I never recommended London.

Marianne Oh, shut up, you know what I mean. And the girls. Gwen has to beg you for a secondhand camera. It's pathetic. Camille doesn't even bother any more, I don't blame her. And you don't even care.

Stephen Look, Marianne, I paid for those awful public schools you sent the girls to, and now I want to work. I happen to believe in what I'm doing.

Marianne Yes, well –

Stephen I'm not interested in art taken from the art magazines, I'm interested in this, these shapes, this energy around us, these trees growing . . . why don't you look? Try to feel something? Forget about money for five minutes.

Marianne I have bills to pay, Stephen. I don't throw them in the fire the way you did when those bailiffs came around and you stopped teaching. It's all very well for you to look at me with contempt and treat me like a nag, but I don't have a studio to escape to, I devoted my life to you, and now I have nothing to show for it. Nothing. Nothing. Nothing.

Stephen You have two very good-looking and spoiled daughters.

Marianne They're growing up. They're getting competitive. I bore them.

Stephen What happened to the counselling job? I sent you money so you could train.

Marianne It was a dead end. The salary was pathetic. I gave such great parties when you were starting out. I thought I could do something in that line, for young artists, but they get famous so quickly these days and they're mostly twenty-five-year-old girls anyway. I'm not needed. I have no worth.

Stephen I'm sorry.

Marianne That's not good enough. I made all the wrong choices . . . I hear your mistress is in Jeremy's new show.

And getting married. Serves you right. By the way, Jeremy's asked after you. Look, if he asks to see something of yours don't be your usual rude self. Richard's been talking about nature, and he's always sensed the fashion, that's why he's so rich. I have a feeling you may be given a second chance. (*Pause.*) I should've got married again. But successful men want blonde bimbos. And I couldn't marry another failure. Where's Gwen?

Gwen I'm here, I've been listening. I'm remembering it all in case I become a writer. I'm never getting married. I'm going to support myself with photography, but Daddy, you'll have to buy me a camera.

SCENE ELEVEN. PRIVATE VIEW

Jeremy's gallery. A tray of wine and minute bits of food. Jeremy and Julia are waiting nervously.

Jeremy I forgot the daffodil.

Julia I thought of something better and ordered wild flowers. They're coming from Ireland, they'll be here later.

Jeremy Can I afford wild flowers?

Julia No. Worry about Fiona. Her fiancé couldn't come tonight because he leads a trauma group every Tuesday. Read in this that his work is more important than anything she does.

Jeremy Doesn't Fiona qualify for trauma therapy? It's her first show.

Julia Fiona's furious and she's drinking. I'll look after her, but you'll have to help me get rid of that fiancé.

Jeremy Women are so unattractive when they drink.

Perhaps everyone's right, they don't have what it takes to be successful artists.

Fiona approaches and overhears.

Fiona I heard that, Jeremy. That's a shitty thing to say.

Julia It's a slightly old-fashioned concept, that's all, Fiona, we'll change it.

Fiona I have what it takes.

Marianne comes in.

Marianne I seem to be early. Or is no one coming? Where are your artists?

Jeremy Germany, New York . . . You know Fiona.

Marianne (*looking around*) Bit of a ragbag, Jeremy. I can't tell whether you're going for the international or the English. Or are you trying both out? Fiona's are good.

Fiona Do you know my future husband said he was worried it might be celebrating cruelty to animals. Because I put a fucking Greek myth on a canvas. What's he going to fucking do, censor Greek myths to save the Green Party? Where's Stephen?

Marianne He won't set foot in these places, you know that.

Fiona He said he'd come.

Jeremy Did he? Marianne, you must talk to him.

Marianne Fiona can do it better than me. (*to Fiona*) I'm sorry you've split up. It's the only thing that made him still attractive to me, the fact that you loved him. He must have some value, I thought, if you were so besotted.

Fiona I hate men, but I really hate women.

Julia Don't: We have to stick together. I want this to be a great evening for you.

Fiona Here come some rich people, I can smell it. (*to Jeremy*) Tell them about how buying art makes being rich all right.

Marianne I see Stephen didn't only teach you how to paint, but how to be unpleasant, as well.

Fiona No, Marianne: I can be as two-faced as you.

Yoyo and Biddy have come in. They look around, politely.

Biddy You could buy the whole show. Right now.

Yoyo No, that would seem foreign, brash.

Biddy I don't think so. How are you feeling?

Yoyo Better. I still have some pain. I don't understand these.

Biddy You don't need to. That one's good, by a woman. She's over there. Do you want to talk to her?

Yoyo What do I say.

Biddy Platitudes.

Yoyo Biddy, are you sure this sort of stuff would impress Sir Philip?

Biddy This is so exciting. She paints Greek myths.

Yoyo But darling, you know I loathe Greek myths, they're so violent. And she looks violent, male, is she, euh, a lesbian?

Biddy Yoyo, these are artists, it doesn't matter. (*They go to Fiona.*) Talk to her. Yoyo.

Fiona Hello. I'm the artist.

Yoyo How do you do? A pleasure to meet you.

Biddy My husband's very interested in your Greek myths.

Julia joins.

Fiona These two are part of a series called *Solitude*. Most Greek myths are about solitude, I think.

Yoyo Oh? Yes. (*A pause.*) Yes.

Julia Have a look at the sunsets, Mr Andreas, you will like those. Sunsets over the Thames.

Yoyo That interests me very much. I have a project on the Thames. It's a beautiful river, isn't it? I don't understand why people still resist living there.

Jean, *an androgynous person, walks in, looks around critically. Jeremy joins her.*

Jean What's going on?

Jeremy Hello, Jean.

Jean What's the theme?

Jeremy Mmm.

Jean You've got some international art, you've even got a couple of paintings of Baselitz. A few Beuys drawings. And then you've got some romantic English new stuff, whatever you call it, and what's this?

Jeremy That's also landscape. English.

Jean What's this with the English, Jeremy? Since when are their parochial doodles important?

Jeremy It's the newest of the new.

Jean Says who? Morris? Who did you get to write your catalogue? Yeah, I thought so.

Stephen comes in and looks at the paintings.

Jeremy My God, there's Stephen, I can't believe it.

Jean Who's he? Ah – Stephen Ryle. Why is he here? Is he important? Didn't Charles de-accession him some time ago? What's he doing?

Jeremy Landscapes.

Jean The English are hopeless. Landscape. That went out fifty years ago. Fiona's sunsets, really. The Greek stuff is better, sort of a cross between Rauschenberg and Clemente. Of course, Clemente's gone off too. There's only Baselitz really, yeah, Baselitz. That's the best.

Jeremy Why?

Jean Because we say so, all of us. I like you, Jeremy, you used to have good stuff. What am I going to write about this?

Julia and Yoyo have joined them.

Julia Call it *At the Crossroads*. Or *Buy British*.

Jean Yes, that's good. It's shoddy, it's parochial, it's old-fashioned, but its British.

Yoyo You should not put down British products, they are very often good. We need to make them better, not give up. And English history is magnificent, and landscape is part of history. So many English things are admirable.

Jean Not the art. You're a collector, I can tell by your suit. You're in the wrong place. You could buy that Baselitz over there, it's art. Otherwise – nothing. Take my word for it, don't buy the sunsets. The only thing cutting edge here is the food: crab and seaweed wonton.

Stephen (*having joined the others*) What do you know about art?

Julia Jean writes for *Élan*.

Stephen What's the rag trade got to do with art?

Jean Everybody reads my magazine. I determine style. I tell people what's important.

Stephen Why don't you just tell them to look.

Jean It's not enough to look with modern art. You have to understand. Good modern art must be difficult. And so it needs us – the interpreters. Art criticism is undervalued in this country, the English are so amateur about everything. In America you'll soon be able to get a degree in it.

Stephen What exactly do you explain, how to match recipes to the paintings?

Jean The fact is, the critic these days is the equal of the artist and without the critic to point out significance and deconstruct it, the artist's work is incomplete. Every artist needs a good critic and if you don't have one, you're nothing.

Stephen I'm going to vomit. You wear black and the most hideous shade of lipstick I've ever seen and you're going to discourse on the significance of colour in contemporary art?

Jean I've written on colour and sensuality, yes.

Stephen You look as sensual as a tube of toothpaste.

Jean And I'm going to lecture to the Patrons of New Art. They want my advice for the Turner prize. I certainly couldn't recommend any of the stuff in here.

Jeremy Jean, you haven't looked carefully yet.

Jean I've seen what I need to: it's English.

Yoyo Why do you hate England so much?

Jean Doesn't everybody? The whole place is falling apart. Look at this gallery, it's lost its nerve.

Julia You mean we're not following international fashion blindly? We're not being American?

Jean There you go. When the English feel insecure they always attack the Americans.

Jeremy I never attack Americans, but I suppose I never feel insecure.

Constantin *has come in and joins the group.*

Constantin Hello, I am Romanian.

Stephen You're the only thing that's wrong with this country, you, your puerile magazines and vapid television programmes.

Jean The English ambition: back to reading by candlelight.

Marianne Stephen, you've ruined your own career, now you're wrecking Fiona's.

Julia (*to Jean*) I've heard of collectors buying paintings they see in a magazine without even looking at the original. I think that's what Stephen's worried about.

Constantin From Romania, I have come to look at the paintings. Are you having a political discussion?

Julia No, it's about art.

Constantin Same thing, how interesting, in my country we have many discussions now and I have come for some art. I want some of your paintings.

Julia We'll give you a price list.

Constantin You don't understand, I am Romanian.

Stephen (*to Jean*) Why don't you unglue your mascara and look at this show? It has two strands. One is original, rich, well-painted, and then you see painters who have been reading the magazines, that one, fashion.

Jean That's the one I like. It's contemporary.

Stephen It's badly painted.

Jean It's difficult. I can write about it.

Stephen It's bad. It's ugly. But you can write about it. Why don't you write about pots and pans and stop smearing art with your lipstick mind?

Jean Domestic utensils have great significance in contemporary consciousness.

Stephen That's my point. Everything looks the same to you. Come on, Fiona, this is a gallery for the blind.

Jean Beauty, you know, that's a rather old-fashioned concept. I suppose you could say Fiona's here are beautiful. So what? And those in the corner, back there. They're by you, I think.

Stephen Wait a minute. Jeremy, who told you you could show my paintings here?

Jeremy It's only three. I own them.

Marianne (*to Stephen*) I sold him the landscapes.

Stephen I don't care. Take them off the wall. Now!

Constantin May I look at these? I am Romanian.

Stephen Yes, you can have them.

Jeremy Stephen, you can't –

Stephen No, Jeremy, you can't. I don't show in this gallery any more. You dropped me.

Jeremy I never dropped you –

Stephen You dropped me from that group show.

Jeremy You weren't in the mainstream – you wanted to do your own thing, as they said in those days. You could paint – it's just what you were painting –

Stephen Didn't fit in with the dictates of *Art Forum*.

Jeremy Stephen, watercolours . . . really, that was perverse. It was the beginning of the eighties, Thatcher, no one wanted to look at watercolours. I couldn't help that, but now . . . well.

Stephen Now I wouldn't show if you got down on your knees and licked my paintbrushes.

Jeremy I paid your mortgage.

Constantin I like these paintings very much, yes.

Jeremy They're very expensive . . .

Constantin Good. I tell them that in Bucharest.

Biddy (*having joined the group*) Actually, I – we – wanted to buy those paintings.

Stephen Who are you?

Biddy A collector. That is, my husband is.

Stephen You look like the type who should be taking lessons in flower arranging.

Biddy (*charmingly*) Yes, I'm very good at that.

Stephen And your husband is buying you an art collection to show off instead of diamonds?

Yoyo Please, this is not polite.

Biddy (*to Yoyo*) It's all right. (*to Stephen*) Well . . . in a way . . . is that wrong?

Stephen Do you know what I hate about the rich? They
can't spot a compliment from an insult. You buy your way
out of criticism of your behaviour and you feel you can
ignore the difference between good and evil – if you even
remember there is a difference.

Biddy I was so looking forward to this evening. I thought
this world would be different, not like my husband's
world, the business world, where you expect to be jostled
and everything to shift. But here . . . I thought art would
have value, I mean, real value. Something eternal,
reassuring, like church when I was little, or school. I know
I was only invited here because I'm very rich, but I felt
honoured, like paying your way into heaven if you're a
Catholic, well, why shouldn't you?

Stephen Art, yes, but this world is more putrid than any
hell. Your husband would be in prison if he imitated the
practices of the art world. Look at Jeremy. He's going to
try to convince you that the inferior work of a young
painter is worth thirty thousand pounds. And he has stuff
he tries to sell for half a million you wouldn't want to pee
on.

Jeremy Stephen!

Stephen You can always tell when Jeremy's putting up the
price of something. He begins to put quotes before the
name, a little pause, a little intake of breath. You don't just
say Schnabel. You say breathe, pause, look mysterious:
Schnabel. And when he does that to someone new, they've
been Schnabelized. Fiona now stands in danger of being
Schnabelized. But in a few years, she could be dumped. A
minor painter could be fashionable and envious, the two
often go together. He will refuse to show with Fiona. At a
foreign show, let's say. And then Fiona will begin to have a
smell. A wound, and –

Biddy And that's what happened to you? The only thing is, he's beginning to put that silence around your name. And I understand why. They're beautiful.

Constantin (*coming up to Jeremy*) I like these and those two over there.

Jeremy You don't understand, it costs a lot of money.

Constantin No, you don't understand. I am Romanian, you give me the paintings. People want to give us food, blankets, but I come here to collect paintings and then I have a gallery. We are very ignorant.

Stephen Take them. A gift to the people of Romania. Fiona will give you hers, as well. Help Romania, Fiona.

Fiona Stephen, I don't want my work to be given to the people of Romania, thank you very much. Don't be such a fucking male bully.

Stephen Show some guts, Fiona.

Fiona I am showing guts, I'm painting and I'm admitting I want to be successful.

Stephen You mean you're selling out?

Fiona No, I'm buying in.

Jean I like that, you have a personality, I'll write about you.

Julia Fiona's work is very original, it takes a while to understand it, have a careful look, Jean.

Jean Yes, I can see it, we have to go back to myth because the world is so fragmented. It's a distillation of modern sensibility.

Fiona The colours are important. We have a genetic memory of colours.

Constantin (*to Fiona*) You are an artist? We like artists. You come visit us in Romania. You are very welcome. When do I pick up the paintings? Now I will go and look at other galleries. We Romanians have very sick souls, bad-nourished, you know, retarded. I think maybe this will help, some painting, this reminds our souls of what we have not known. Our own artists, it is as if their hands have been frozen. Maybe they will see now and remember too. London is beautiful, capitalism is beautiful. You people here, so elegant, so good, you discuss things, I don't understand well, it's too quick, all about art. Beautiful. I hope that fast we learn to be like you.

Stephen (*to Constantin*) Come to my studio, there's more.

Jeremy I'm calling my lawyers.

Marianne I can't stand this. Stephen, why do you always have to make scenes, ruin everything? Why is nothing sacred to you?

Stephen This filthy art world scene isn't sacred to me, Marianne, why is it to you?

Marianne Because I grew up believing in it, I studied it, I loved it, because I believed in your work, because if even art is a joke, what's serious?

Stephen I haven't turned art into a joke, Jeremy has. His interest in art is as convincing as Ceaucescu defending the Save the Children Fund.

Constantin Romania is serious. Romania needs everything. I invite you all to Romania.

Stephen Here's another painting. It's also quite good. It's called *Philoctetes Returns to Troy*. See that, that's me. They'll like it in Romania. I'm the model, so I can give it to you. Now come and look at these. (*He drags Constantin around the room.*) No, you don't want any of these. These are awful and they'll sell for a lot of money.

Constantin I take these too, to show them.

Yoyo Biddy, I think it's time to leave.

Biddy Why, Yoyo?

Yoyo This isn't distinguished . . . And that painter insulted you . . .

Biddy No, you don't understand. He was just being English, defensive. We'll have a great collection. I can feel it.

Julia Stephen, I'm coming to see you.

Jeremy (*to the audience*) I wonder if the Medicis had to put up with these antics. I like my painters. I only want to help them. Most of them are whores. Occasionally you get an angry virgin. I think I prefer the whores. We all have to live. Great art . . . great art happens two or three times a century. But there's a fair amount of beauty around. Why should beauty be cheap? I know people come and buy paintings because they want status, but they get beauty thrown in. That's a good deal, at any price.

Act Two

SCENE ONE. BIDDY REMEMBERS

Biddy I remember the end of 1989 when the walls came
tumbling down. Yoyo was excited because it meant new
markets and he needed them. People walked the streets
with smiles on their faces, but there were chill winds
blowing already. I know when it happened for me. I was
watching the *Channel Four News*, waiting for *Brookside*,
which I like because it's so exotic, and I was about to pour
myself a drink during the *Comment*, but suddenly I heard
this man talk about Nostradamus and I listened. I listened
because one of the girls at Benenden had gone a little mad
over Nostradamus during the last year. She was a little
strange anyway, I mean, her parents were odd, journalists,
or Canadians or something, but she began to talk about
the horrors of the future and she became depressed about
this thing, the future. Eventually the headmistress
confiscated her Nostradamus and told her to worry about
herself not history, that was for others, men maybe. The
future, the general future, was not a problem for Benenden
girls. So when I saw this man talking about Nostradamus I
listened and he said terrible things were predicted for the
nineties and a chill came through me because everything
was going so well and we were so rich, Yoyo and me – and
now Eastern Europe was going to get rich as well so we
wouldn't even have to feel guilty or nervous about
communism, and I was angry at this man for saying things
would go badly. But maybe I had already noticed that
actually things weren't going so well for Yoyo and he was
looking worried and ill and muttering about confidence
and that was partly why I had to do something showy like
become a collector of modern art. It was just a chill that

night, a draught coming under a door, but now I think
about it a lot.

SCENE TWO. THE HERMITAGE

Biddy, Stephen. Stephen cleaning brushes.

Biddy I hope you don't mind . . . (*Stephen doesn't
answer.*) You don't answer the phone . . . Julia gave me
the address. They all know you in the village. It's beautiful
here. I thought . . . I thought it would be wilder, inside, I
mean, outside it is. I could hear the sea. Here it's very neat.
Cosy. When do you stop working?

Stephen I don't.

Biddy Don't you need the right light?

Stephen I can work by electric light. I know what colours
look like.

Biddy Ah – I see . . . You do remember me? Are you
surprised I came?

Stephen Not really . . . (*A silence.*)

Biddy Do you mind? I suppose you think I'm a silly
society lady who doesn't understand anything about art
and I've come to amuse myself. (*A pause.*) Perhaps you're
right, my husband is very ill at the moment . . . I am trying
to understand art, I've been rather bitten I think, it's odd,
and I do like your work. It makes me feel at home . . . at
peace . . .

Stephen It's not for sale.

Biddy Are you really giving it all to Romania?

Stephen If Jeremy's sent you, you can go straight back –

Biddy No . . . I swear. Why are you so angry?

Stephen Why aren't you?

Biddy I have nothing to be angry about. I'm married. I'm rich. I have a lovely big garden. I know, you're thinking what about others, the ones who've bought their council houses and now can't pay for them, the refugees . . . I can't be angry about that. I'm sorry, about the famines in Africa, the homeless, all that, but it's not my fault. It's nobody's fault, really, is it? (*Stephen shrugs.*) Is it? I've made you even angrier. Now that we know that communism doesn't work, we know there have to be famines, don't we? Do you believe in God?

Stephen You don't mean that question.

Biddy I wish I did, because then the famines would be God's will and that's all right. Now it just seems the luck of the draw. You see, I do think about these things, good and evil, although I admit I don't think about them well. I wasn't trained to.

Stephen Nobody knows how to think about them any more . . .

Biddy I actually want to be good. Women's magazines, they tell you how to be thin, charming, cook well, even how to have a brilliant career, but not how to be good. (*A pause.*) Nobody talks about being good. I think once or twice I've seen the question raised in a political article Yoyo reads, but I can't see the connection. Yoyo supports the Tories, but he doesn't think they're good.

Stephen Maybe he's supporting the wrong party.

Biddy The Labour Party is so snobbish, they wouldn't want his money. The good. I don't even know what the word means. I'm sorry, I'm talking about myself. It's funny about artists, you want to confess to them. It's because I saw something in those paintings at Jeremy's that I was looking for all the time. I can't explain. Do you? Think about the word 'good'?

Stephen Look at a Titian. A Velasquez. A Turner. Maybe it's not the good, but it's wonder, and that's a start.

Biddy Isn't there anybody modern? Besides you.

Stephen You'll have to find that for yourself. And then you can buy cheap and sell at great prices. Moral questions have been out of fashion for ten years, maybe they'll come back into vogue. For six months . . . or until our society discovers it's too bankrupt to afford morals.

Biddy Why do you despise everybody? How can you paint if you're so full of hate?

Stephen I'm not full of hate, I'm disappointed . . . Twenty years ago I knew exactly what was right for the world, what art, what politics. I'm not sure about anything any more. Sometimes I'm not even sure that painting trees isn't a sign of exhaustion rather than renewal. As for my politics . . . a rubbed-out canvas in a corner somewhere.

Biddy Your landscapes, they're not exactly landscapes . . .

Stephen It's my contribution to history. I paint what is vanishing. As it vanishes. Sometimes I paint the memory of something that was there long ago. A shape. We drool over the aborigines because they hold their land sacred. But we must have all done that once. Even the English. Particularly the English. Islands are mysterious . . . our land is so watery, that is its beauty, you don't understand a word I'm saying.

Biddy Not yet, but I will, Stephen . . . I promise . . . (*A silence. They look at each other.*) Sometimes I feel I have two pairs of eyelids. The first pair are like everyone else's, but behind them, there's a kind of clingfilm, and if I could open those too, I would see the world differently. Maybe the way you do.

Stephen You wouldn't want that.

Biddy I would like this blur removed. It's not really a blur, it's a flatness. Nothing is more in focus than anything else. You're an artist. That's what you do, isn't it? Perspective?

Stephen I'm a modern artist, my world is as fragmented as yours. I'm in pieces.

Biddy You never paint figures? People?

Stephen Is that what you want? Is that what you came for?

Biddy What do you mean? Oh, no, please, I wouldn't dream . . . dare, no, I'm not vain, I mean, Yoyo always says he wants to have our portraits done, I think he imagines a kind of Gainsborough, a lot of green land, me in a hat, but no . . .

Stephen goes towards her.

Stephen I wouldn't paint your portrait. I would find your Significant Form.

Biddy What's that?

Stephen I don't know yet. (*He moves her head gently towards him.*)

SCENE THREE. VALUE ADDED

The Gallery. **Mr Boreman, Mrs Boreman,** *Jeremy. And Nicola, at the desk.*

Mr Boreman The first Mrs Boreman and I met him at your private view. I think he was on drugs. He mumbled a lot and he was very rude to my then-wife. Still, I was very sorry to hear of his death. His stuff was rocketing through the roof, but I thought, no, I'll wait.

Jeremy Mm, waiting, yes . . .

Mr Boreman But I don't like it. Fact is I never did. Too much . . . yellow. It was my ex-wife, I don't think she looked at it much, she liked the idea of it, because he was black, from the slums, she was one of those guilty liberals.

Jeremy Mmm.

Mr Boreman Anyhow, you convinced us.

Jeremy I? . . .

Mr Boreman I remember your very words. Savage. Noble. The genetic imprint of the jungle.

Jeremy I said that?

Mr Boreman I should have known then, I took a trip to the jungle when I was in Brazil. I hated it. Too, too . . . green.

Jeremy Mmm. Green.

Mr Boreman Anyway, the new Mrs Boreman doesn't like it, do you dear?

Mrs Boreman I hate it.

Jeremy Ah, yes, I see, that happens. Redecoration. You can always put it in another room.

Mr Boreman My wife says it reminds her of graffiti.

Jeremy I think that's what it is supposed to do. The genius of the people.

Mr Boreman Yes, but Mrs Boreman is from the people herself.

Mrs Boreman I'm from the working class.

Jeremy Ah, I thought you were American.

Mrs Boreman I am American and I'm from the working class. My father worked in a factory. I grew up on the wrong side of the tracks in a small town that had a college. I was bright, so I got a scholarship to the college. I don't need graffiti on my walls. I like Constable. Gainsborough.

Jeremy Not many of those about.

Mr Boreman Do you have anything like that? But contemporary.

Jeremy Yes. I might.

Mr Boreman I'd like to make an exchange.

Jeremy An exchange? Ah. I'm afraid that's not possible.

Mr Boreman I paid two hundred and fifty thousand dollars for it. Have you got something for three hundred thousand, four hundred thousand?

Jeremy Yes. But we don't exchange . . . We aren't Marks and Spencers.

Mrs Boreman Why don't you just take it back and give us the money.

Mr Boreman Dear, let me . . . but that's an idea.

Jeremy Buy it back? I'm – well, cash flow, as you people say . . . These artists, I'm supporting so many of them, they're so lazy . . .

Mr Boreman Sell it for me then.

Jeremy I don't know what I could get . . . People are cautious these days . . .

Mr Boreman This stuff is supposed to go up and up. That's what you told me.

Jeremy No . . . I'd never say anything – so practical.

Mr Boreman I heard that said here. That's why I bought it.

Jeremy That must have been my assistant, Michael. I had to get rid of him. Some of my assistants had the souls of city people. Now Nicola would never say anything like that.

Nicola shakes her head.

Mrs Boreman What exactly would you have said, Nicola?

Jeremy She would have said you must only buy a painting because you love it, wouldn't you, Nicola?

Nicola nods.

Mrs Boreman It's hard to know what you love when all these people are telling you what you're supposed to love. I used to love that girl in the cornfield by Andrew Wyeth, you know, *Christina's World*, the print of it. Then I heard I was supposed to love the abstract expressionists. I got to love Rothko and after ten years of trying I even love Jasper Johns.

Mr Boreman I've looked into Jasper Johns. Eight million.

Jeremy And there's a queue.

Mrs Boreman But this guy, even if he cost forty million, I wouldn't love him. I hate this painting.

Jeremy Odd about this painter. He had everything going for him: young, black, new, there wasn't much else that year, he even died young, very good of him, in a business sense, but . . .

Mr Boreman But?

Jeremy It's so difficult . . . His paintings should be selling for three-quarters of a million by now. But they're not. Why? Sometimes you make a mistake. The value of the stock goes down, I suppose it's loss of confidence. We may have sold his paintings to the wrong people. I mean, he's not in the most famous collections. Some of the people who bought his paintings are now in prison. All those stock market scandals. It's not good. People change. And then some critics laid into him. Mmm. We're all slaves to fashion.

Mrs Boreman I thought we were talking about art.

Mr Boreman And we're also talking two hundred and fifty thousand dollars here. Are you saying you sold me shoddy goods?

Jeremy No, the canvas hasn't disintegrated. It isn't like Schnabel's plates all falling off. And his stuff is still worth millions, even without the plates.

Mrs Boreman We're not asking for plates, we want some art.

Jeremy There's my dosser. I've told him always to make sure no one's here. I'm usually closed at this time. (*Rushing out.*) Vincent, I told you –

A silence. Nicola looks up. Smiles.

Nicola Art is very mysterious.

Mrs Boreman Nicola, when Mr Bertrand sold my husband that painting, what was it really worth?

Nicola It was worth what you paid for it.

Mrs Boreman You mean because that's what we were prepared to pay for it.

Nicola No – well, yaah.

Mrs Boreman And what is it worth now?

Nicola What somebody else might be prepared to pay for it.

Mr Boreman And what's that?

Nicola That could be nothing.

Jeremy comes back on.

Jeremy The Strand's full, so the homeless are moving up Cork Street. I have a deal with him: I don't let anyone else occupy the doorway, but he leaves as soon as the gallery opens in the morning and doesn't come until I've left. Vincent . . . he's rather nice. Young. I wouldn't want one of those fat bagladies. He seems to like the art. Twenty years ago he might have got a grant and gone to art school or a polytechnic. I think we valued potential more in those days. It's like our poor artist here. He wasn't much of a painter, but he might have become one, or a media star, like Warhol, it's just as good, so we all valued his potential. But potential itself lost value. What can I do? I'm just an ordinary art dealer. I'm terribly sorry, Mr and Mrs Boreman, but Vincent needs his doorway. (*He pushes them out, gently, with the painting.*)

SCENE FOUR. WORTHY CAUSES

The grounds of Kenwood House on Hampstead Heath. Lady Lelouche and Constantin are sitting, waiting.

Lady Lelouche They're late. The only person who really matters is Biddy Andreas, Constantin, but I invited the others to make it less obvious.

Constantin What a beautiful house, there, very beautiful.

Lady Lelouche Yes, all my dissidents love Kenwood, it's so graceful. I see them. The concert will begin in twenty minutes, so you have a little time to put your proposals.

Constantin A concert yes, I love outdoor concert, The Sex Pistols, The Beatles, too.

Biddy, Marianne and Julia have come on. Constantin kisses the ladies' hands.

Biddy Sibelius' Violin Concerto, how lovely, Lady Lelouche.

Lady Lelouche There's a piece by Bartók, same general area as Constantin, I thought he might enjoy it.

Marianne Were you in prison for long?

Constantin Yes, all of Romania is a prison.

Marianne Were you tortured?

Constantin I suffer very much. My poor country . . .

Lady Lelouche That's what Constantin wants to talk to us about. He is very concerned about the monasteries in his country. Constantin?

Constantin begins to talk very fast.

Constantin These monasteries they are beautiful because they are painted. On the outside. They are small, all covered outside like embroidered vestments.

Lady Lelouche My mother used to go dance the carnival in Bucharest, but she went to the monasteries. She loved them. Very handsome monks.

Constantin Ceaucescu wanted to destroy them.

Lady Lelouche We did something about that, slapped a UNESCO order or something.

Constantin Now they are in bad neglect, and the vandalism and also very bad pollution.

Lady Lelouche You people really must do something about your pollution, we're all frightfully concerned about the Danube.

Constantin There are five monasteries and they are famous for colour. The most famous, Voronetz, has blue, a blue that goes dark in the rain. The colour is a secret, they do not know how to ever get it back. This church, painted in the sixteenth century has – we call it the *Sistine Chapel of the East* – it has a *Last Judgment*. Another, *Humor*, has all the episodes of the Akathistos, you know the Akathistos, an Orthodox long prayer before Holy Week. So the painting is also a story: every square like a chapter.

Biddy My husband is Orthodox but he never went to church until he became ill.

Julia It sounds interesting: early narrative art.

Constantin The monasteries are small villages. You eat well there, and artists go and rest.

Marianne Who painted all this?

Constantin That is the beauty, no name, they were monks. They were protected by Stephen the Great, you know Stephen the Great, our national hero? And every time he won a battle against the Turks, he built another church.

Biddy Yoyo will like that.

Lady Lelouche You have something very interesting there, Constantin, and the next step would be for you to give a lecture . . .

Marianne I could help you write it, I'm good at that. I love the idea of anonymous art, after all the egomaniac painters in the West.

Lady Lelouche (*ignoring her and over her*) I think it would interest your husband, Mrs Andreas, it's a worthy cause and I could make it a very public one.

Biddy I'm happy to give a little money, we're slightly overstretched . . .

Lady Lelouche I hear you've been buying some very new paintings –

Biddy I can't buy what I really want.

Marianne He won't sell?

Biddy shakes her head.

Julia It's because of Jeremy. Without Jeremy we'd be all right.

Lady Lelouche The concert is about to begin. Now Constantin, when I spoke to you in Romania you said you were getting slides. The light is still good enough and I've brought my glass.

Constantin Slides, yes, I show you. (*He takes out two crumpled papers and unfolds them.*)

Lady Lelouche (*very slowly*) No, *slides*.

Constantin Yes, slides: here, beautiful, here is Voronetz.

Lady Lelouche But this is just some pages torn from a book – rather greasy I might say and coffee-stained.

Marianne Slides are colour photographs, which you look through.

Constantin These are very good, taken twenty years ago by French man. Very good book. The only book on our monasteries.

Lady Lelouche I can't raise money for monasteries with two pieces of paper.

Constantin But I talk too, I give good lecture, Marianne help me.

Lady Lelouche People supported the orphans because they saw them on television, it wouldn't have done any good just describing them. There's a lot of competition for people's sympathy, Constantin.

Marianne Why not alert the television news, Lady Lelouche?

Lady Lelouche You might get monasteries on the news if they were in the process of being demolished, but that would defeat the purpose, wouldn't it?

Constantin Well, they come to Romania and see. I show them.

Lady Lelouche My dear man, Romania is very uncomfortable and there's nothing to eat. I simply couldn't invite Friends of the Tate to see some torn out pages of a book. Come back to me when you have slides. I'm sorry to have wasted your time, Mrs Andreas . . .

Biddy Please . . .

Lady Lelouche Constantin, you will have to understand that in the West, we expect people to be – how shall I say – professional. I've always been very impressed by the professionalism of dissidents.

Constantin I am Romanian.

Lady Lelouche Yes, but what exactly does that mean?

Constantin You do not know what it is to lose your soul for twenty-five years. We had Ceaucescu, yes, but we were all little Ceaucescus . . . Now we look around, we know nothing and we are ashamed. I know what a slide is. How can I have slides when I do not have a camera, or film, when we have no scaffolding to get close to the painting and it is crumbling every day?

Marianne This is terrible: we have to help.

Lady Lelouche I'm beginning to sense Romania is one of those hopeless causes.

Marianne I'm very good at hopeless causes, I was married to one. And I take very good pictures. I've been looking for something to do. I've done counselling, yoga, visualization, I've seen mediums, astrologers. My children are growing up, I have twenty, maybe thirty years left. Yes, I'm going to Romania to save the monasteries. Constantin: we'll start a charity today.

Lady Lelouche My dear girl, you have to be extremely rich and well connected to do any good in this world. Charity is a glamorous business and not all art can be made fashionable. Wouldn't you agree, Mrs Andreas?

Biddy nods, non-committal.

Julia I'll come and have a look at the contemporary painters. All that suffering must have produced something, otherwise what was it for?

Constantin We ask ourselves that. Biddy, you come too?

Biddy My husband's ill . . . and I love England at the moment . . .

Biddy looks out. The concert begins.

SCENE FIVE. THE PRICE OF EVERYTHING

Mr Mercer's office: white walls, paintings on the walls, an antique bust. **Mr Mercer** *and Biddy.*

Biddy I thought I'd come first. And then I can convince him that it will be simple and comfortable. (*Mr Mercer nods.*) He couldn't stand a machine. He doesn't like – well, the insides of a body, the mess. He's very clean, very private. Very discreet. (*Mr Mercer nods.*) But if he can just go to sleep and wake up completely well.

A silence. Mr Mercer looks through some notes, as doctors do.

Mr Mercer I have one coming in that would match.

Biddy Oh, that's wonderful.

Mr Mercer Of course, I would have to see your husband.

Biddy Oh, yes. Will it be terribly expensive? You see if I paid for it myself, it would – well, the decision would have been made. I have quite a lot of money at my disposal, I was going to buy a painting, but I can do that later.

Mr Mercer You like art? So do I. I collect antique statuary. And you?

Biddy I'm just starting.

Mr Mercer I have a very good contact if you go for the Med.

Biddy The Med?

Mr Mercer (*points to his bust*) That sort of thing. Cradle of civilization.

Biddy Oh, yes, yes . . . (*A silence.*)

Mr Mercer The kidney itself costs two thousand five hundred pounds.

Biddy Is that all? I mean – well. But, will it be a good – I mean, at that price . . . I'd be willing to pay more, if there's a better one going, you know. (*A pause.*) It is English?

Mr Mercer I'm afraid not, Mrs Andreas. You can only get an English kidney when somebody dies in an accident and then it goes straight to the National Health. There's a long

queue for kidneys and the National Health favours young
people, whereas I suppose you could say private medicine
favours useful members of society like your husband.

Biddy So these . . . euh . . . come from . . .

Mr Mercer Somebody who is quite happy to give a kidney
away, at a price, of course. It may not be such a good idea
to have someone who lives in this country, in case they
change their minds. That would be awkward. Having to
give it back. (*He laughs. A silence.*)

Biddy Where does the – euh – it come from?

Mr Mercer We get them from Turkey. But I assure you
they come from very healthy specimens. I have a long list,
Mrs Andreas, if you would prefer to wait . . . but I can't
guarantee anything, I just happen to have this one coming
in. Today.

Biddy Do you have it here? I mean, euh . . .

Mr Mercer I have the man over here. He can be operated
on in a few days and we will give it straightaway to your
husband, who should then be able to lead a productive life
for years to come.

Biddy This man, he's all right, is he? I mean, he's not a
criminal. I'm sorry, I know so little about medicine, I
suppose it doesn't matter, it's not the brain, is it? It's just
that – Well, yes, fine. I couldn't – euh – meet him? I'd feel
better. (*A pause.*) I'm afraid otherwise I couldn't, I simply
wouldn't be sure . . .

Mr Mercer It's unusual, but I suppose you can, he's in my
waiting room. Now the operation itself is only one
thousand, but seven days in hospital, fifteen hundred
pounds a night for a private room, that will be (*He takes
out his calculator.*) fourteen thousand. You only need
deposit five thousand pounds. Non-returnable if you

427

change your mind as we have to save the room.

Biddy I understand. Of course. (*She takes out her cheque book.*) Who do I make it out to? I mean, do I make out two cheques, one for the euh . . . young man?

Mr Mercer No, we take care of all that.

Biddy It isn't very much for a kidney, is it?

Mr Mercer It's the going rate. There are lots of them about.

> *Biddy hands over the cheque and looks at the ancient bust.*

That comes from Turkey, too. But it's unique. And very expensive. There are two more by the same sculptor and my obsession is to find them. Get them. I dream about it at night. Touch it, Mrs Andreas. (*Biddy touches it.*) You have touched the antique world, the mid-morning of civilization. A sculptor moulded these features more than two thousand years ago, a sculptor who spoke to Plato, who fought Sparta, who knew Alcibiades.

Biddy I see, yes. It's very smooth. Doctor Mercer, I must ask you one thing.

Mr Mercer I don't know who the model was, a young soldier I think.

> **Ahmet,** *a young Turk, comes in. He is baffled and clearly does not understand much or indeed any English.*

Ahmet, this is Mrs Andreas. Your kidney is going to be given to her husband.

> *Ahmet nods, smiles, bows.*

You understand? Your kidney.

Ahmet smiles.

Biddy It's – euh – very kind of you, I mean, well, we're very grateful.

Ahmet No problem. No problem.

Mr Mercer And Mrs Andreas is giving you the money, for your mother. The money.

Biddy Yes, I hope it's – euh, well – I'm very pleased to meet you. (*She stretches out her hand. Ahmet seizes it and kisses it.*) I hope you don't mind the operation. My husband is frightened. (*She mimics fear by shivering as if cold.*)

Ahmet No problem for Ahmet. Yes. No problem.

All smile.

Mr Mercer Good boy.

Ahmet laughs.

Ahmet Yes. Yes.

Biddy He's very sweet. (*to Ahmet*) I hear Turkey is very beautiful. Beautiful. (*She points to her eyes. Ahmet looks in panic at Mr Mercer, shakes his head, and covers his eyes with his hands.*)

Mr Mercer No, Ahmet, only one kidney. (*He ushers him out.*)

Biddy He does understand what he's doing?

Mr Mercer Oh, yes, he's signed the form.

Biddy Doctor Mercer, when you speak to my husband, please don't tell him the – the – euh – the kidney – is Turkish. You see, he is Greek, and you know, the history of the Ottoman domination, well, he takes it personally. He might reject a Turkish organ.

SCENE SIX. BLACK

A small room at Harrod's where shoplifters are questioned. Store detective **Russet** *and* Yoyo.

Russet And now I shall have to ask you a few questions, if you don't mind, sir.

Yoyo I was hot . . .

Russet takes out a form.

No. Please. I can't answer. I was only looking at it in the light . . . no . . . You don't understand. I am a rich man. I have a business.

Russet Are you having trouble with your business, Sir?

Yoyo Yes, of course, like everyone else, too much borrowing. The interest rates. Prince Charles doesn't like my buildings on the river. If the press – they're always after us. Please. It takes years to build up a business, but twenty-four hours can tumble it – you know?

Russet Your name?

Yoyo No . . . Please. Andreas, Mr Andreas. This mustn't – I'm a member of the Progress Club. In my closet I have three coats from Harrod's, one like this one, better, you must believe me.

Russet I do believe you, Sir. Perhaps you can tell me what happened.

Yoyo I tried it on. It didn't even fit very well. My wife usually comes with me – she mustn't –

Russet Are you having difficulties with your wife, Sir?

Yoyo No, we've been married four years. She's lovely, very English, pale . . .

Russet Is there another woman, perhaps, Sir?

Yoyo Only is so far as is usual with men in the city . . . I can't talk to my wife about – hard things, business. This is such a bad year. And she's spending so much money, now, she didn't before, but we're art collectors . . . I have a lot of pain too. Kidneys. I have great faith in English medicine, but it is not as good as it was.

Russet You have a kidney problem, Sir?

Yoyo Just pain . . . it's worry.

Russet So you've been under a lot of pressure.

Yoyo Yes . . . but please, don't write it. I relax at the club, but the conversation is not as interesting as I thought it should be. There are too many thrusters. Young businessmen, they want to talk about money. And the old ones about Europe. I want to talk about England. But the library is beautiful. I could take you to lunch there, of course without your uniform.

Russet (*coldly*) So you say you were trying on the coat. And then?

Yoyo I can't remember.

Russet You put it over your arm. (*Pause.*) And then you walked out of the store.

Yoyo I didn't – think.

Russet I believe you did think, Mr Andreas, I believe you thought you could get away with it.

Yoyo No. I'm a rich man.

Russet I've worked five years in this store and I've observed this about the rich, the very rich I'm talking about, they think they can get away with it, they think they're above the law. You should see the people we get here, titles, princesses, usually women, but more and more men.

Yoyo I haven't been rich all my life. I've worked hard. I don't – I'm not like that.

Russet Then why are you trying to bribe me?

Yoyo Bribe you? No. You mean the Club? No, no, it's so you'll understand I am a gentleman.

Russet I think you need counselling.

Yoyo Sorry? Sometimes I have so much pain, I can't hear.

Russet Harrod's offers most services to its customers, but it hasn't opened a counselling service yet. I can give you the name of a doctor.

Yoyo Please, I have so many doctors, I'm going into hospital. (*Short pause.*) I love England! Please don't write anything down.

Russet Your doctor's name?

Yoyo I can't remember. Murder . . . no, Mercer.

Russet I will need to take your photograph.

Yoyo No! (*He starts crying.*) I'm sorry. It's not very – stiff upper lip –

Russet Listen. I'm going to let you go. I don't know why, but I am. I don't think you're an habitual shoplifter, you're what I call a crisis shoplifter. But I will have to ask you one thing.

Yoyo On my honour.

Russet I shall have to ask you, sir, never, as long as you live, to set foot in Harrod's again.

Yoyo But my wife – we love coming here – the food halls – the fish –

Russet May I ask you, sir, to hand me the coat.

Yoyo hands over the coat he has been clutching.

And the silver letter opener.

SCENE SEVEN. PHILOCTETES RETURNS TO TROY

Stephen's studio. A large canvas. Stephen, Jeremy, Julia, Alex, Fiona. Jeremy stares at the canvas, Alex rummages around.

Jeremy You've been angry for a long time. Ten years ago people wanted Chia, Clemente, subjectivity. Artists who could say like Baselitz that art is asocial. When I look at it now, I have to agree with you, most of it was meaningless. The world wanted something meaningless in its art. Maybe it reflected the emptiness of its own self-absorption. What you were doing didn't speak to anybody. So we did drop you, but now there is a change. We need to redefine ourselves and you seem to touch something. I look at what you're doing and it fills me with longing. You must want to show your work, whatever you say.

Alex This one's great. English.

Stephen Ireland. I painted that of Ireland.

Alex Well, you English own Ireland, don't you? Anyway, you used to. And this one, wow, boy, you could be famous, I mean famous.

Stephen I was famous.

Alex Well, isn't it great to be famous? What's wrong with you English? People in America will die to be famous. Think about it, Stephen, a major exhibition, one-man. It'll be like Jasper Johns and the American flag. Stephen Ryle and the English landscape. Are you afraid, or what?

Jeremy Stephen . . . The world needs you. The art world, I don't know about the other world, I don't know what it is . . .

Julia There are galleries where people don't feel intimidated – they're warm, people are friendly, the paintings are there to be looked at, not always sold to someone rich . . . that's the kind of gallery you need.

Jeremy I'm going to tell the girl at my desk to be more forthcoming in future.

Julia Your gallery's in the wrong place.

Fiona You used to tell us artists needed isolation, but only up to a point.

Julia If you stay cooped up much longer, your work could get mouldy.

Alex Yes, and your roof will rot. The termites will eat your foundations.

Jeremy Alex, we don't have termites in England.

Alex Well, whatever the English equivalent is.

Jeremy Damp. No, actually, it's drought. Rather it's the change from damp to drought.

Alex What?

Jeremy That undermines foundations. It's the extremes. England doesn't like extremes. Well, English houses don't. It's rude . . . We wouldn't have allowed the Alps in this country . . . Wales is bad enough.

Alex Maybe you enjoy being poor. I know people who love being failures. They know where they are, and they hate everything: it's easy.

Fiona If you were teaching us now you'd tell us not to

allow ourselves to suffer from passive anger, despair, but to fight, in whatever way we can. I was looking up all my old notes . . .

Stephen As you close that chapter of your life . . . and move into the corrupting lights of success? And marriage, I forgot . . .

Fiona You have no right to go back on everything you said – it's too easy to rant from the wilderness.

Stephen On one of those days when tens of thousands were told they would never work again, I heard a group of well-known artists asked to discuss what kind of television was needed for the millions of unemployed. Fewer daytime programmes on home decorating perhaps, less foreign cooking, could they suggest something? And not one of those artists answered that the question itself was evil. No, they vied with each other to come up with witty suggestions, afraid of being boring and afraid to admit they'd been asked to collude in papering over a hideous, widening crack. No, they were flattered at being asked their opinion. After all, they were artists, visual, what did they know, and if they became serious they'd never be asked again. Why should I go back to that world? I don't want to play the fool, Fiona, you can give the interviews on the feminist use of colour –

Constantin and Biddy come in.

Biddy I'm sorry . . . Constantin said you'd invited him and he doesn't have a car. I didn't know . . . shall we leave?

Stephen No. Stay. I need your advice.

Biddy Mine? (*Pause.*) They want you back?

Stephen What do you think?

Biddy Aren't you unhappy . . . here . . . ?

Constantin I have come to look at your paintings to take them back to Romania, thank you.

Alex Wait a minute, who are you?

Constantin I am Romanian.

Alex I can see that, but who are you?

Jeremy I love the Americans. I could never have asked that question.

Constantin I have paintings to show to our people in Bucharest.

Alex Where?

Constantin I don't know yet, we arrange that.

Alex When?

Constantin Soon. We get help.

Alex When? In ten years' time when you straighten the country out?

Jeremy What happens to Stephen's paintings in the meantime?

Alex Same thing as the toys which disappear? Warehouses of books which never surface? Food and blankets rotting on the black market?

Julia Alex is right. Can you tell us exactly what you were doing during Ceaucescu's regime?

A pause.

Constantin I was . . . making do . . .

Stephen How?

Constantin But now, I am businessman, like him. And you said I can take these paintings – please.

Julia I don't think Stephen wants to give his paintings to a Romanian version of Jeremy.

Jeremy Corki Street.

Stephen I thought you were serious . . . I wanted to help –

Constantin Yes, I understand. I – We disappoint you. We are not doing things right, we are not pure. The trouble for us is we have to carry your dreams, your ideals, always. You were on the left in your country, no? You believed in socialism, even communism, no? That's what I thought. You are the worse. I don't mind the silly society ladies – I never really expect to get help from them because we Romanians are not chic, I know that. But you – you never came to Romania when we were communist. You preach communism in your country, but you let us make the experiment for you. So we have the destroyed land in co-operatives, the bread tails, but it doesn't matter, because we are your ideal. And when it has completely failed, and we have a revolution, you love us because we are having a revolution and that is exciting to you, even if it is a revolution against what you are preaching for in your country. And again we carry your soul for you. And now you're unhappy because we are not perfect revolutionaries, because we have not wiped out all Securitate people, which is most of Romanians, because we are not completely good. You forgive your own evil because you say it's built into capitalism, but we are not allowed – We have to be moral, perfect martyrs. Now you don't want me to have your paintings because I am not great dissident hero. Where were you when they were beating and killing us? You despise me because I want to live. You socialist? I go walk in the garden now. Biddy, you pick me up when you are ready. And you, Stephen, artist, you blush, not me.

A silence.

Alex Latins, they love to talk. Mind you, better than the English, who don't.

Jeremy There's a man who wears his fifteen minutes of historical significance on his sleeve.

Fiona (*at Stephen*) At least he has one.

Biddy (*looks at the canvas*) You didn't show me this before.

Stephen I may not have been thinking very well in the last ten years, but I have been looking. Working.

Biddy Explain it . . .

Stephen It's not an answer, it's not a solution –

Biddy I know . . .

Stephen At the most, it's a suggestion.

Biddy Please, take us through it . . .

Stephen Go from right to left. It's about landscape. Not a literal landscape: shapes that repeat themselves in nature. Here: a tree, a field. A cloud. The energies of nature are advancing, pressing – You should know it's English because there's so much green. Earth colours too. Move to the left, and these colours, forms are countered by a strict and more conventional geometry. The colours are warmer here, it's a man-made arrangement . . . I've always been fascinated by architecture . . . here is stability – around which our lives and emotions can circulate. It's an affirmation and in an age of cynicism, that requires some courage.

Alex I'm submitting this for that new Constable prize and I'm booking you an interview.

Jeremy Don't overdo it.

Alex I know artists. Somewhere, they've always got a streak of responsibility. Stephen wouldn't be spending ten hours a day on something this big if he was gonna hide it for ever. Or he really would have to blush.

Julia (*to Stephen*) I don't think you should go back to Jeremy. You need a new gallery.

Jeremy What are you talking about?

Julia I'm starting my own gallery. Fiona's coming.

Jeremy You give women a chance and they turn into hungry hounds. Where will you get the backing?

Julia When I get the artists, I'll get the backing. Alex is going to help and my father is rich. I suppose you thought he was a bus conductor.

Jeremy I never thought anything.

Julia Exactly.

Jeremy You can't strike out on your own. Look, why don't we get married? You wouldn't have to, as you know I don't – we could have a partnership like the de Clares. I can't do it on my own, I don't know how to see any more. You should get married. It would make you belong more.

Julia I don't need you for that. (*She leaves, followed by Jeremy.*)

Fiona (*to Stephen*) I see that where arguments fail, the love of a rich woman succeeds –

Stephen It's not that simple . . . and you ditched me.

Fiona That doesn't mean I wanted you to be consoled. (*Pause.*) I never thought you would return.

Stephen Even Philoctetes must have got tired of his island.

Fiona I never told you the end of the story. He went back, the Greeks won the war, destroyed Troy and set sail for Greece. The thing is, there was a big storm at sea and most of them drowned. (*Fiona goes.*)

Alex (*to Stephen*) She's bound to be jealous, you're gonna get all the attention at that gallery. How tall are you? Six foot? Let's make it six foot two. Would you consider wearing a black leather jacket? (*She leaves. Stephen and Biddy remain together.*)

Stephen That's the world you want me to go back to?

Biddy I never asked you.

Stephen But you did.

Biddy Did I? I'm sorry. No. You're right. I did. I wanted it. And I'm not sorry.

SCENE EIGHT. BLACK ON BLACK

An elegant private hospital room. Yoyo in a dressing gown sits in a chair. Next to him sits his **Mother** *– a Greek woman dressed in black – and* **Katerina,** *a woman of 30. A Russian Orthodox* **Priest** *reads the service.*

The Priest Almighty Father, put away from your servant Yorgos the spirit of disease and every malady, wound, fever and seizure. And if he has sins or transgressions, loose, remit and forgive them for the sake of your love towards mankind. (*He sprinkles Yoyo with water.*)

Biddy comes in.

Yoyo (*weakly*) I didn't expect you so soon . . .

Biddy I was at a gallery.

Yoyo This is my mother . . . Mama, my wife.

Mama (*in a heavy Greek accent*) You have a lovely wife and a beautiful mistress. You have done very well, Yorgos.

Biddy stares at Katerina.

This one look English, but the other one is younger.

The Priest continues praying.

My son: he has become such a gentleman.

Katerina (*goes to Biddy*) I thought you knew. I am sorry.

Biddy Please! (*She brushes her away. Katerina kisses Yoyo, then the Priest's hand, and leaves.*)

Yoyo Biddy, please, come close. (*She doesn't.*) I am sorry: Katerina . . . three years, so – I have to tell you: one of the houses has to be sold . . .

Mama 'He who has two wives loses his heart, but he who has two houses loses his head . . .'

Yoyo The Banks . . . There's some good news . . . I've been asked on a committee at the Progress, the roof committee, it's the most prestigious. It's because of the paintings. Thank you. Mama has the letter.

Mama Beautiful letter, beautiful. The ink.

The Priest comes next to Biddy.

The Priest If he dies and you are angry with him, you will feel tormented for the rest of your life.

Biddy He's not going to die. The doctor said the kidney was taking . . . it's a temporary rejection.

The Priest I knew a man once who had left his girlfriend after a furious argument. She was killed suddenly. He spent twenty years trying to find peace. That is what it means to be haunted.

Biddy He has a mistress.

The Priest That was foolish . . .

Biddy I suppose she's more interesting than I am.

The Priest You will be interesting if you forgive him.

Biddy I don't know what forgiveness means.

The Priest It is accepting the weight of another's pain, which, measured against your own, is found greater. Even if you have to cheat at the scales.

Biddy His mother . . . He was never in touch with her.

The Priest She is letting him go in peace.

Mama Yorgi, sing, you have such a beautiful voice. I remember it so well. Sing.

Biddy He never sings.

The Priest I've noticed that people who deny their childhood often lose their voices . . .

Mama Where is your mistress, has she gone? Does she know what a beautiful voice you have, Yorgi?

The Priest At the orthodox funeral service –

Biddy He's not going to die!

The Priest We stand with lit candles. It is to say that this person has brought at least a flicker of light into the world – and that we will keep this light and set out to be continuation of what was good in this person – who then will not have lived in vain.

Yoyo (*to Biddy*) I miss Greece . . . I'll take you there, would you like that? I am not sure England is what I thought it was, and I have made fussy buildings . . . a lie . . . Biddy, do you understand?

Biddy sits next to him.

Biddy Yes . . .

Yoyo Thank you. You'll continue the collection . . .

Biddy Why a Russian priest?

Yoyo They're more . . . well, better class. Émigrés . . .

Mama Sing, Yorgi, sing, I'll sing with you. We'll sing something Greek.

Yoyo and his mother sing.

SCENE NINE. FIONA, SELF-PORTRAIT

Fiona's studio.

Fiona I've always felt sorry for the ugly sisters. In some versions, their mother tells them to cut off part of their foot to get it into the slipper. It works and they go off with the prince until he notices blood. No fine prince wants to see a lot of blood, so he sends them back and eventually gets the diaphanous Cinderella, who will not bleed. Great, but what happens to the sisters with their half-foot? How do they spend the rest of their lives? Are they angry with their mother for telling them to cut off their foot? Or do they just get on with it. I am living alone in a big house with a great big studio. Julia gave me a lot of money to get me to leave Jeremy. It was stupid of her because there isn't much money about and art isn't selling very well. And so I pace about and paint. I work very hard. I am not happy, but I don't think I ever expected that. I wake early every morning. Some days the world is at war, some days that doesn't matter. Sometimes I paint the darkness of it all, sometimes I paint light. Sometimes I paint laughter. I know you, you're waiting for the sentence that is going to click it all into place. I don't have it. This is the nineties. I'm not going to pretend to have it.

SCENE TEN. BIDDY IN THE LANDSCAPE

Stephen's studio. Biddy, draped in a cloth, is posing. Stephen is painting her.

Biddy I like posing. I think of so many things. I remember my last year at Benenden, noticing beautiful things. The Kent spring, the oasts, the tennis teacher. I felt drunk on it all . . . it was like a Constable. And then, then, I stopped looking. That first marriage, now I see it was minimalist, a Lewitt, or possibly a Carl Andre. Then Yoyo. That was a kind of Schnabel, a mess. Because we were always stuffing ourselves, houses, cars, then art. And now it's fashionable to be sober and lead a quiet life, looking for a forgotten meaning, depth. How long will that last?

Stephen Don't move. When England began doubting itself, why did it have to stop loving itself? It keeps gashing its own limbs.

Biddy Are you enjoying being famous again?

Stephen I don't think Julia's gallery is going to last. The art market may be terminally ill.

Biddy It could reject you and die, like Yoyo.

Stephen No one trusts anybody's opinion. I'm waiting to meet someone who feels certain about something, anything. But yes, I'm enjoying not being angry.

Biddy I've been asked to give a lecture on England and the new art. I've become interesting. It's what Yoyo wanted . . . Yoyo. I wonder if someone told him it was a Turkish kidney, or if his body just knew. I'm going to have to charge them a high price for that lecture. All that wealth: vanished. And I won't sell the paintings. I'm lucky to have a flat. He bought it for that mistress of his, you know, but luckily it was in his name and there was no will. Well, there was a piece of paper, but I got rid of that. It wasn't legal anyway. She could have gone to a lawyer and claimed to be a kept mistress – apparently the law is very generous to kept mistresses. She must have been stupid, or maybe she was proud. I didn't even let her know when the funeral was. You can't have two widows wandering around, it looks silly. And grief makes you cruel. I'm sorry now. (*Pause.*) I was always afraid of being alone. And now it's happened, it isn't so bad.

Stephen goes to rearrange some drapery on Biddy. She looks down on herself.

It's rather good, my body . . .

Stephen When I started this painting, there were three birds, and you were a vanishing figure, but you've taken over the canvas. (*He puts his hand on her breast.*)

Biddy When you do that, Stephen, I think: I am happy, in a most ordinary way, happy to be painted among the daffodils. I am happy to be loved today, that's all I want, I don't want more.

Stephen Not daffodils. Foxgloves, fireweed and a wood anemone. And then, only a shape, a colour. (*He goes back to his painting. Biddy looks out. Fade.*)